W9-ATL-307

I T A L Y ' S

B E S T - L O V E D

D R I V I N G

T O U R S

Macmillan ▪ USA

Written by Paul Duncan

Revised second edition 1995, published in this format 1997
First published January 1991
Reprinted December 1997
Second edition of revised format 1999

Edited, designed and produced by AA Publishing.

Published by AA Publishing

Published in the United States by Macmillan Travel
A Simon & Schuster Macmillan Company
1633 Broadway, New York, NY 10019

Macmillan is a registered trademark of Macmillan, Inc.
Frommer's is a registered trademark of Arthur Frommer.
Used under license.

ISBN 0-02-862936-1
ISSN 1520-9997

Cataloging-in-Publication Data is available from the Library of
Congress.

Color separation: Daylight Colour Art, Singapore

Printed and bound by G. Canale & C. s.p.a., Torino, Italy

Opposite: *Vatican guard, Rome*

CONTENTS

ABOUT THIS BOOK

This book is not only a practical touring guide for the independent traveller, but is also invaluable for those who would like to know more about Italy.

It is divided into 5 regions, each containing between 3 and 6 tours which start and finish in major towns and cities which we consider to be the best centres for exploration.

Each tour has details of the most interesting places to visit en route. Panels catering for special interests follow some of the main entries — for those whose interest is in history, wildlife or walking, and those who have children. There are also panels which highlight scenic stretches of road and which give details of local events, crafts and customs.

The simple route directions are accompanied by an easy-to-use tour map at the beginning of each tour, along with a chart showing how far it is from one town to the next in kilometres and miles. This can help you to decide where to take a break and stop overnight, for example. (All distances quoted are approximate.)

Before setting off it is advisable to check with the information centre at the start of the tour for recommendations on where to break your journey and for additional information on what to see and do, and when best to visit.

Banks
Usual banking hours are 8.30am–1.30pm and 3pm (or 3.30pm) to 4pm (or 4.30pm) Monday to Friday. Check locally as times vary in the afternoon from bank to bank. All banks are closed at weekends and on national holidays. On weekdays, evenings and holidays, money can be changed at main railway stations and airports.

Camping and Caravanning
For information on camping and caravanning in Italy see pages 160–5.

Credit Cards
All principal credit cards are accepted by most establishments, but not petrol stations.

Currency
The unit of currency is the lira (plural lire). Notes are issued in denominations of 1,000, 2,000, 5,000, 10,000, 20,000, 50,000 and 100,000 lire. Coins are issued in denominations of 5, 10, 20, 50, 100, 200 and 500 lire. You will find lire is abbreviated to 'L' in shops.

Customs Regulations
Items for personal or professional use may be brought into Italy free of charge, but take receipts for valuable articles to

View over Firenze (Florence)

avoid paying duty on them. Travellers' allowances for Italy are the same as other EU countries. Please check current guidelines.

Electricity
The current is 220 volts AC, 50 cycles, with plugs of the two 'round' pin type. British, Australian or New Zealand appliances normally requiring a slightly higher voltage will work. For visitors from North America with appliances requiring 100/120 volts, and not fitted for dual voltage, a voltage transformer is required.

Emergency Telephone Numbers
Fire, police and ambulance tel: 113.

Entry Regulations
The only document necessary for UK, Irish, Commonwealth and US citizens is a valid passport for any stay that does not exceed three months. For visitors from EU countries, a visitor's card is sufficient.

Health
Health insurance is recommended, but visitors from other EU countries have the right to claim health services available to Italians. This means obtaining, prior to departure, Form E111 or equivalent from the post office. To find a doctor or dentist, consult the Yellow Pages or your hotel.

The high cost of treatment makes insurance essential if you are a non-EU citizen. For medical treatment and medicines, keep all bills and claim the money back later.

Vaccinations are unnecessary unless you are travelling from a known infected area. However, it is advisable to drink bottled water and to wash all fruit and vegetables.

Maps
The spellings of place-names on the maps include accents to help with pronunciation. These do not occur in the text.

Motoring
For information on all aspects of motoring in Italy, including accidents, breakdowns and speed limits, see pages 158–60.

Post Offices
Post offices are usually open 8/8.30am–2pm Monday to Friday (to 12.30pm on Saturday). On the last day of the month offices close at noon. Times do vary, however, from place to place.

Practical Information
The addresses, telephone numbers and opening times of the attractions mentioned in the tours, including the telephone numbers of the Tourist Information Centres, are listed tour by tour on pages 164–75.

Public Holidays
1 January – New Year's Day
6 January – Epiphany
Easter Monday
25 April – Liberation Day (1945)
1 May – Labour Day
2 June – Proclamation of Republic (celebrated on following Saturday)
15 August – Ferragosto (Assumption)
1 November – All Saints
8 December – Immaculate Conception
25–26 December – Christmas

Route Directions
Throughout this book the following abbreviations are used for Italian roads:
A – Autostrada (motorway)
SS – Strada Statale (state road)
dir, ter, bis, q, qu – suffixes to state roads (SS) relating to links and extensions of major roads minor roads – unnumbered roads.

Shops
Shops are generally open Monday to Saturday 8.30am–1.30pm and 3.30pm–7.30pm. Many close Monday mornings, and food shops often close Thursday afternoons.

Telephones
Some phones still take tokens called *gettone* which cost 200 lire each and can be purchased at post offices, tobacconists, some bars or slot machines. It is much easier to use a *carta telefonica* (a pre-paid telephone card) which you buy at the same outlets. They have a value of either 5,000, 10,000 or 15,000 lire and can be used for international calls. Call boxes also take 200 and 500 lire coins which you insert before lifting the receiver. The dialling tone is short and long tones.

To call abroad, first dial 00, then the country code, followed by the city code and the number itself. The prefix for the UK is 0044; for Eire 00353; for the US and Canada 001; and for Australia 00 61. If you wish to make a reverse charge or person-to-person call you will need to go through the operator – dial 15 for European countries or 170 for elsewhere.

Time
Local standard time is one hour ahead of Greenwich Mean Time (GMT). Italian Summer Time (when clocks go forward an hour) is in operation from the last weekend of March to the last weekend of September. The time is one hour ahead of Britain except for a few weeks from late September to late October when the time is the same.

Tourist Offices
The Italian State Tourist Office (ENIT) is represented in the following:
Australia/New Zealand – 61–9 Macquarie Street, Sydney 2000, NSW (tel: 02 9247 8442) or 36 Covant Road, Thorndon, Wellington (tel: 04 736 065).
Canada – 1 Place Ville Marie, Suite 2414, Montreal 113, Quebec H3B 3M9 (tel: 514/866 7667)
UK – 1 Princes Street, London W1R 8AY (tel: 0171 408 1254)
US – 630 Fifth Avenue, Suite 1565, New York 10111 (tel: 212–245 4822).

PIEDMONT, LOMBARDY, EMILIA-ROMAGNA, VENETO

Italy is separated from the rest of the continent by the massive bulk of the Alps. The great range's southernmost peaks and valleys encroach upon Piedmont and Lombardy and on a clear day, from Torino (Turin), Piedmont's capital, and the centre of an arena of mountains, it is possible to look back and admire Mont Blanc. From Torino to Milano (Milan) the landscape descends gently towards the Po, the river that divides Piedmont practically in half. It continues into Lombardy which, with its five magnificent lakes, its rivers and its canals, is endlessly watery and enviably fertile. The Po forms the region's southern border with Emilia-Romagna before it flows out to the Adriatic at the bottom of the Veneto.

Piedmont and Lombardy combined are the cradle of Italy's industry and the source of much of its wealth. It is not by accident that here are the huge Fiat works (Piedmont), some of Europe's best design studios and manufacturers (in Lombardy, especially Milano), the vineyards that produce some of Italy's most excellent wine (eg Barolo from Piedmont) and the vermouth industry (Torino).

The great plain of the River Po, which continues southwards into Emilia-Romagna, was once northern Italy's greatest attraction. Every inch of the plain of Emilia-Romagna, right up to the Apennines in the south, is still under cultivation. So prolific is the area's produce that Bologna, Emilia-Romagna's capital, is known as 'La Grassa', 'The Fat'.

The Veneto is as lush as any of the other regions mentioned. From the flat plain of the Po to the Dolomites of the eastern Alps and the marshy lagoons around Venice, the Veneto is also just as varied. But its reputation has more to do with art and architecture, particularly of the Renaissance. Its hills and southern plain are filled with towns and villages whose past affinities with Venice are acknowledged usually by an ancient stone-carved lion of St Mark — the Venetian symbol — placed conspicuously in the centre of the town.

Milan's French Gothic-style Duomo

The Duke of Savoy presides over Torino's Piazza San Carlo

Torino

Torino is one of the most intellectually active cities in Italy. This, mixed with a dose of Piedmontese sobriety, has provided Italy with marvellous museums, libraries, theatres, exhibitions and a university. Torino's Egyptian Museum is the second most important in the world (after Cairo's), while its Armería Real (Royal Armoury), the Museo dell'Automobile (Motor Museum) and Museo del Cinema are stacked with varied treasures. A baroque-style centre contributes to an almost courtly atmosphere in this elegant and dignified city.

Milano

Milano, capital of Lombardy, is also the economic capital of Italy, and is unquestionably northwest Italy's major art centre. In the Castello Sforzesco (Sforza Castle), the Pinacoteca di Brera (Brera Gallery), the Museo Poldi-Pezzoli and the Pinacoteca Ambrosiana (Ambrosia Gallery), you will find endless works by the 'greats' of the history of Renaissance painting. The Duomo (cathedral) of Milano is the most striking example of northern Italian Gothic architecture that you will see anywhere.

Bologna

Bologna has a well-deserved reputation as Italy's culinary capital: if you like dishes with cream, butter and cheese, or succulent red meat, this is where you will find them at their best. There is a feast of architecture too, as Bologna's medieval and Renaissance centre is still intact. Its old streets are lined with arcades which come into their own when it rains. Museums, galleries, an ancient university, night-clubs and shops are Bologna's other attractions.

Rímini

Rímini has one really important monument, the 15th-century Tempio Malatestiano (Malatesta Temple), with a famous Renaissance façade designed by Leon Battista Alberti for Sigismundo Malatesta. Otherwise, the town is famous for its entertainments of the not so intellectual sort. Sunbathing, night-clubbing and lazy days contribute to Rímini's reputation as one of the Adriatic's most seductive resorts.

Asolo

Not only does the small hill-town of Asolo preserve the memory of famous inhabitants such as Robert Browning and Eleanora Duse, but its ancient centre is full of well-maintained medieval and Renaissance buildings and villas. It has a good monthly antiques market.

Verona

Verona's many treasures include the 14th-century tombs of the Scaligeri, noble medieval palaces, Roman ruins such as the famous Arena (the best preserved amphitheatre in Italy after the Colosseum) and a clutch of medieval and Renaissance churches.

The Foot
of the Mountains

Piedmont is the most western region of Italy. Here you will find some of the country's best known ski resorts. To the east is the great plain of the Po River, beyond which are the hilly and fertile Langhe and Monferrato districts. More or less in the middle is Torino (Turin), the region's capital, with its baroque architecture, a well preserved city centre, Roman remains and an active street life.

3 DAYS • 411KM • 255 MILES

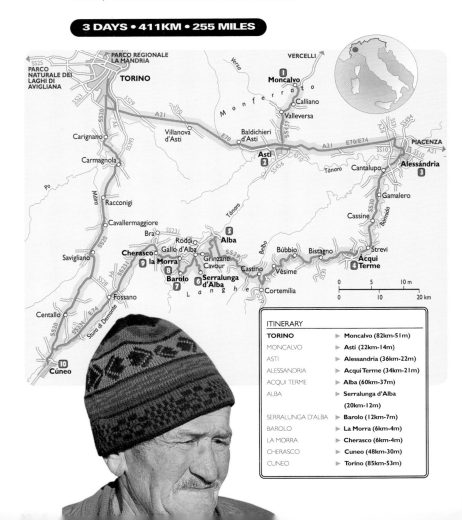

ITINERARY

TORINO	▶ Moncalvo (82km-51m)
MONCALVO	▶ Asti (22km-14m)
ASTI	▶ Alessandria (36km-22m)
ALESSANDRIA	▶ Acqui Terme (34km-21m)
ACQUI TERME	▶ Alba (60km-37m)
ALBA	▶ Serralunga d'Alba (20km-12m)
SERRALUNGA D'ALBA	▶ Barolo (12km-7m)
BAROLO	▶ La Morra (6km-4m)
LA MORRA	▶ Cherasco (6km-4m)
CHERASCO	▶ Cuneo (48km-30m)
CUNEO	▶ Torino (85km-53m)

---

[i] *Via Roma 226, Torino*

▶ *From Torino, take the A21 towards Asti, about 60km (37 miles). Leave the autostrada at the Asti Est exit taking the SS10 towards Asti, then the SS457 going north to Moncalvo, 22km (14 miles).*

0 Moncalvo, Piedmont
Moncalvo is where you will get a real taste of the Piedmontese countryside. Terraced vineyards and tidy, ordered rows of poplar trees climb the slopes on the edge of town. Situated in the middle of the immensely fertile Monferrato district, it is a gastronome's delight – a good place to try the local truffle crop at the annual auction. Moncalvo itself has the pretty Gothic Church of San Francesco, which, along with the remains of an old moated castle, towers over the surrounding countryside. The old centre of town has some 14th-century houses.

▶ *From Moncalvo, retrace the route to Asti.*

2 Asti, Piedmont
Asti is full of places to see and is awash with festivals. Once the city rivalled Milan, and it is well worth spending some time in its old centre. The Gothic Duomo (cathedral) contains fonts made from Romanesque capitals supported on inverted Roman capitals, and 18th-century inlaid choir stalls. Other churches include San Pietro in Consavia with its 10th-century circular baptistery and little adjacent archaeological museum housed in the cloisters. In Piazza San Secondo is the large Gothic Church of San Secondo in which you can see an altarpiece by Ferrari who was much influenced by Leonardo. The Torre San Secondo, a Romanesque tower on a Roman base, is the bell tower for the Church of San Caterina. In fact there are quite a few towers scattered around Asti – the medieval Torre Troiana, and the octagonal Torre dei De Regibus are just two. The town is the scene of a great wine fair at the end of September.

Wild mushrooms, one of Piedmont's gastronomic delights

[i] *Piazza Alfieri 34*

SPECIAL TO...

In Asti, the Palio is held in the Campo del Palio on 18 September. This event dates back to the Middle Ages and consists of a colourful horse race, ridden bareback. The 'offering of the Palio' takes place in May. The events include flag-tossing and the participants wear medieval costume.

▶ *From Asti, return to and take the A21 going east to Alessandria, about 36km (22 miles).*

3 Alessandria, Piedmont
Alessandria is the centre for the manufacture of the *borsalino*, the ubiquitous felt hat – in fact the city has the world's best hat museum, Museo del Capello

The bold red wine Barolo takes
its name from this hilltop town

Borsalino. Not much of old
Alessandria has survived except
in the 18th-century Duomo
(cathedral) and the older
Church of Santa Maria di
Castello. Among the city's
palaces is the Palazzo della
Prefettura, designed by
Benedetto Alfieri. The 18th-
century Cittadella (citadel) is
particularly well preserved.
The countryside all around
Alessandria is as fertile as
anywhere in Piedmont, supporting rice fields, wheat, fruit and
acres of poplar woods which are
used in the making of furniture.

[i] *Via Savona 26*

▶ *From Alessandria, take the
SS30 for about 34km (21
miles) to Acqui Terme.*

4 Acqui Terme, Piedmont
Acqui Terme is noted for its hot
sulphuric springs, in particular
one which bubbles up out of the
ground in a fountain at the

centre of town. The hottest
spring, La Bollente, is housed in
a special pavilion, the Nuove
Terme. The Romans were
aware of its properties but all
that remains from their time
here are four arches of an aqueduct. The Romanesque Duomo
(cathedral) has a very fine 17th-
century loggia (gallery), and a
good entrance portal. Next to
the cathedral are the remains
of the Castello dei Paleologi
(Castle of the Paleologi) in
which there is now an
Archaeological Museum
containing the finds from the
old baths of Acqui – including
mosaics.

▶ *From Acqui Terme, go via
Bistagno, Bubbio and Castino
(west) across country to Alba,
about 60km (37 miles).*

5 Alba, Piedmont
Alba is the capital of the
Langhe district, an area famous
for its vineyards and its white
truffles (*tartufi bianchi*). Set
beside the Tanaro River, Alba
has buildings of terracotta-

coloured brick. The Duomo of
San Lorenzo was rebuilt by

FOR HISTORY BUFFS

The Langhe countryside
around Alba is dotted with
little towns, each one dominated by a castle. They do not
necessarily have any particular
sites of interest, but the towns
themselves are picturesque
and worth visiting if you have
time.
Among the best with interesting and dramatic-looking
castles are Grinzane Cavour,
whose castle was lived in by
the Marquise of Cavour – the
family of the prominent 19th-
century statesman Camillo
Cavour – about 6km (4 miles)
from Alba on the way to
Barolo and Roddi.
Roddi's castle passed through a
variety of noble ownerships,
ending in 1836 with King
Carlo Alberto. Today the
property of the Catholic
Church, it is about 6km (4
miles) from Alba.

Bishop Novelli in 1486 and inside is Barnardino Fossati's chancel with its 35 carved and inlaid wooden stalls. Other churches include Santa Maria Maddalena and the baroque Church of San Giovanni. Inside the latter you can see the *Madonna delle Grazie* by Barnarba da Modena, 1377. The Council Chamber of the Town Hall, the Palazzo Comunale, houses the *Virgin Crowned* by Alba's greatest painter, Macrino (dated 1501). Much of Alba is still medieval – there are narrow arcaded streets and old door-ways. In the old centre is a Saturday market which has been held on the same spot since 1171.

▶ *From Alba, follow the signs pointing to Diano d'Alba, about 8km (5 miles). From there proceed via Gallo d'Alba to Serralunga d'Alba.*

SPECIAL TO...

Alba has another Palio, this time a donkey race. Held in October, it is supposed to parody the Asti Palio, and to keep alive the memory of a horse race staged by the soldiers of Asti around the walls of Alba in 1275, when they were laying siege to the town.

⑥ Serralunga d'Alba,
Piedmont
This picturesque place is domi-nated by a stately castle built between 1340 and 1357 to support the castle at nearby Barolo (see over). These two buildings, as well as other local castles built for the same family, were aligned so as to allow a system of communication using torchlight at night and coloured

drapes during the day. The entire town retains its medieval character. Little houses cluster in circles around the castle and nearly every one has an amazing

FOR CHILDREN

Just to the north of Turin is Parco Regionale La Mandria (La Mandria Regional Park). Part of it is a sanctuary for animals – deer in particular, but there are horses and unusual cattle as well. Also near Turin, just to the west, children might enjoy a visit to the Parco Naturale dei Laghi di Avigliana (Avigliana Lakes Nature Park). Here the specialities are ducks, moorhens, kingfishers and other waterfowl.

A wide selection of fine olive oil and wine for sale

view of the surrounding countryside. San Sebastiano, the parish church, was reconstructed in about 1630, but is far older and still preserves its 14th-century bell tower.

▶ *From Serralunga d'Alba, return in the direction of Gallo d'Alba, turning left before the village to Barolo, about 6km (4 miles) further on.*

7 Barolo, Piedmont
Tiny Barolo is perched on a hill overlooking countryside filled with vineyards. Dominated by a vast castle, the Castello Faletti, it gives its name to one of the most renowned Italian red wines. The castle itself is no longer a private home, but the centre of the Barolo wine production, and housed in it is a museum, a vintage cellar and an *enoteca*, a place for tasting the local wine. The castle is open to the public and has interesting furnished rooms with perhaps the best views in Barolo.

The town is a picturesque place, predominantly terracotta-coloured. You could walk around it in about half an hour. The local parish church is Romanesque and was most probably once the castle chapel – it is filled with the memorials to the Faletti family who once owned the castle.

▶ *From Barolo, travel north to La Morra, about 6km (4 miles).*

8 La Morra, Piedmont
La Morra has two churches, the bigger one dedicated to San Martino, the town's patron saint, and the smaller to San Rocco. However, the principal reason for coming to La Morra is not to look at old monuments, but to indulge in wine-tasting. There are plenty of places in which to do this. Apart from the Enoteca Civica, with its exhibition and sales of Barolo wine produced by local vineyards, there are smaller, private cellars all over this small hilltown. Even the most obscure wines can be

Picturesque La Morra is a popular stop-over for wine lovers. It boasts a wine museum and walks following designated wine routes

found here and the range of prices is huge. Near by is the Museo Ratti (Ratti Wine Museum), housed in the former Abbey of the Annunciation.

▶ *From La Morra, cross the River Tanaro, to Cherasco, about 6km (4 miles) away.*

🟐 Cherasco, Piedmont
Cherasco is famous as the centre of the National Association of Snail Breeders. Not that you will meet any snails within the precincts but the town is the centre of gastronomic events relating to edible snails. The Torre Civico, a 36m (118-foot) high tower, is the most important monument here. It sports a rare clock

(1552) showing the phases of the moon.

Among Cherasco's churches, Sant'Agostino, with its baroque altar, and San Pietro, the oldest church in the town, are the most interesting. In the Palazzo Fracassi you can see treasures dating from when the Holy Shroud was housed in the town in the early 18th century. In fact, in 1706, the Shroud itself

---

SPECIAL TO...

Cherasco holds the National Gathering of Snail Breeders on the second weekend in June, with associated gastronomic events.

---

was kept in the Palazzo Salmatoris. The 14th-century Castello (Castle of the Visconti) still survives in excellent condition.

▶ *It is a short distance to the SS231 which leads directly to Cuneo, about 48km (30 miles).*

🔟 Cuneo, Piedmont
Cuneo is an important market town. The huge market, which swamps the town's centre every Tuesday, filling every corner of the porticoed Piazza Galimberti, is best known for its chestnuts and raw silk. There are porticoed streets all over town, Via Mondovi being the most characteristic. In the centre, too, is the 13th-century Church of San Francesco, which also houses the local museum. Many of the Piedmontese towns have festivals, relating to the consumption of food and drink and Cúneo is no exception.

At the Piedmontese Cheese Exposition held here in November you can taste locally produced cheeses – some of which you will never find anywhere else in Italy.

ℹ️ *Corso Nizza 17*

BACK TO NATURE

Cuneo is practically on the edge of the Parco Naturale dell'Argentera (Argentera Natural Park), a protected mountainous area which is home to various wild alpine animals and birds. Ibex and chamois are among the rare species sometimes seen. Alpine marmots are widespread in the alpine meadows and bird life includes citril finches, alpine accentors, griffon vultures and ptarmigan.

▶ *From Cuneo, take the SS20 back to Torino, about 85km (53 miles).*

Of Alps, Lakes
& Plain

Lombardy is crossed by the huge River Po and studded with great lakes – Maggiore, Garda, Como, Iseo and Lugano. Since the Middle Ages it has been a prosperous commercial region. Milano (Milan) nowadays is the thriving economic capital of Italy but the traces of its cultural past are everywhere.

4 DAYS • 728KM • 452 MILES

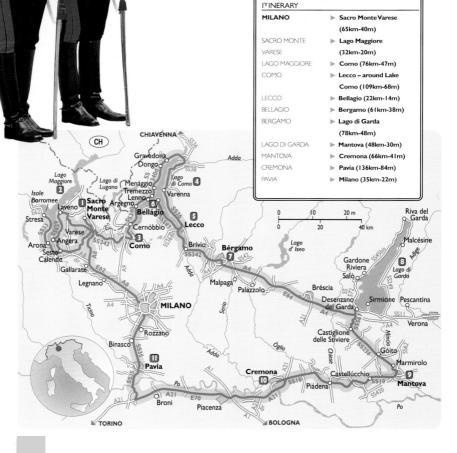

I^TINERARY		
MILANO	►	**Sacro Monte Varese** (65km-40m)
SACRO MONTE VARESE	►	Lago Maggiore (32km-20m)
LAGO MAGGIORE	►	Como (76km-47m)
COMO	►	Lecco – around Lake Como (109km-68m)
LECCO	►	Bellagio (22km-14m)
BELLAGIO	►	Bergamo (61km-38m)
BERGAMO	►	Lago di Garda (78km-48m)
LAGO DI GARDA	►	Mantova (48km-30m)
MANTOVA	►	Cremona (66km-41m)
CREMONA	►	Pavia (136km-84m)
PAVIA	►	Milano (35km-22m)

Map labels: CH, CHIAVENNA, Gravedona, Dongo, Adda, SS38, SS36, Lago Maggiore, Lago di Lugano, Menaggio, Tremezzo, Lenno, Lago di Como **4**, Varenna, Isole Borromee **2**, Laveno, Argegno, **Sacro Monte Varese 1**, **Bellágio**, Stresa, Cernóbbio, **Lecco 5**, Varese, Angera, **Como 3**, Brívio, **Bérgamo 7**, Lago d'Iseo, Riva del Garda, Arona, Sesto Calende, SS342, Malcésine, Gallarate, A8, A9, Malpaga, Palazzolo, Gardone Riviera, Salò, Lago di Garda **8**, Legnano, A4, Bréscia, SS249, Adige, Ticino, Serio, E64, Desenzano del Garda, Sirmione, Pescantina, **MILANO**, Rozzano, Óglio, Castiglione delle Stivíere, Verona, Binasco, Adda, Chiese, Góito, Marmirolo, **Pavia 11**, **Cremona 10**, Castellúcchio, **Mantova 9**, Piádena, Po, A21, E70, Broni, Piacenza, Po, BOLOGNA, TORINO

Scale: 0 — 10 — 20 m / 0 — 20 — 40 km

i *Via Marconi 1, Milano*

▶ *From Milano, take the* **A8**
*going north (via Legnano and
Gallarate) – the latter about
38km (24 miles) – to Varese,
about another 17km (10
miles). About 10km (6 miles)
north of Varese lies Sacro
Monte Varese.*

❶ Sacro Monte Varese,
Lombardia

The 'Sacred Mountain of
Varese', with its narrow passages
and ancient covered alleys, is
only the backdrop for a pilgrimage route more famous nowadays for its art than for its saintly
connections. It is supposed to
have been founded by St
Ambrose in thanks for
Lombardy's deliverance from
the Arian heresy (the doctrine
put forward by the 4th-century
theologian Arius, that Christ is
not one body with God).

From the bottom of the Sacro
Monte to the top, about 800m
(2,625 feet), is a cobbled route
with 14 chapels at intervals
along the Sacred Way, each one
dedicated to the Mystery of the
Rosary. The shrines are the
work of Bernascone and each is
filled with life-size terracotta
figures, by Bussola, acting out
some religious episode. At the
top is the lavishly decorated
Church of Santa Maria del
Monte. The views from the
Sacro Monte are wonderful and,
to restore you after the climb,
you will find cafés and restaurants in the town.

▶ *From Sacro Monte Varese,
go back to Varese, then
continue on the* **SS342** *to
Lago Maggiore, about 22km
(14 miles).*

❷ Lago Maggiore,
Lombardia

Only the eastern shore of Lago
Maggiore (Lake Maggiore) is in
Lombardia. Its western shore is
in Piedmont and its northern
part in Switzerland. It would
take days to drive around the
lake seeing all that there is to
look at. The highlights are the
towns of Angera, Arona, Stresa
and Isole Borromee (the
Borromean islands) in the
middle of the lake opposite
Stresa.

At Angera is the Visconti
castle (open to the public),
which contains well-preserved

Lago (Lake) Maggiore, with its
'Beautiful Isle', Isola Bella

14th- and 15th-century frescos.
At Arona is another castle, this
time ruined. Visit the Church
of Santa Maria with, in the
Borromeo Chapel, an altarpiece
of 1511 by Ferrari.

Stresa is the largest resort on
the lake. Full of Victorian-style
hotels, it is also dotted with old-
fashioned villas and luxurious
gardens running down to the
water's edge. Some gardens are
open, including the Villa
Pallavicino.

But the real gem of
Maggiore is the Borromean
islands. Isola Bella, perhaps the
best known, is a huge private
garden surrounding a palace
(Palazzo Borromeo) – both
open to the public. The
gardens were laid out for Count
Carlo III Borromeo in the 17th
century by Angelo Crivelli. The
elaborate complex includes
white peacocks, grottoes, fountains and statuary. Isola Madre
is another of the islands, famous
for its large botanical garden
which, with its palace, is well
worth a visit. Boats to these
islands leave from Stresa.

▶ *Make for Varese from Stresa,
take the **SS33** to Sesto
Calende at the very foot of
the lake, about 25km (16
miles), then follow the signs
to Varese, about 23km (14
miles). From Varese, take the
SS342 to Como, about 28km
(17 miles).*

❸ Como, Lombardia

Como was the birthplace of the
Roman writer Pliny the Elder.
In fact you will see signs dotted
around Lago di Como (Lake
Como) pointing to the sites of
the various villas the Pliny
family owned here. One of the
most elegant towns on the lake,
Como has, facing the water, a
huge promenade which fills
with people at dusk. There are
busy cafés, palm trees and
parks. The Duomo (cathedral)
dates mainly from the 14th
century. The rose window on
the façade is Gothic in style and
there is excellent carving by the
Rodari brothers of Maroggia,
from about 1500.

Other relics of old Como
include the churches of
Sant'Abbondio, and San
Fedele, which was once the
cathedral, and the Porta Vittoria,
the late 12th-century city gate.
In the Museo Civico (Civic
Museum) you will see objects
dating from the neolithic period
to World War II. See also the
Museo Alessandro Volta, which
houses equipment used by the
man who gave his name to the
electric volt.

⎣ *i* ⎦ *Piazza Cavour 17*

▶ *From Como, drive around the
lake, starting on the **SS340**
up its left-hand side.*

❹ Lago di Como, Lombardia

All around the lake you will see
vast villas and castles overlooking the water. Cernóbbio is a
pretty town about 7km (4½
miles) from Como. Here is the
grand Hotel Villa D'Este, once
the home of the English Queen

Caroline. At Tremezzo is the
Villa Carlotta, once lived in by
Princess Carlotta of Prussia,
who laid out its gardens in the
1850s. You can visit this as well
as the Villa Arconati, just a few
kilometres outside Tremezzo, at
Lenno. The parish church of
Lenno has an ancient crypt that
is well worth a visit. Further on
around the lake are Menaggio
and Gravedona. The latter has
the interesting Church of Santa
Maria del Tiglio which contains
early frescos of St John the
Baptist.

At nearby Dongo, Mussolini
was captured by the partisans in
1945. On the other side of the
lake, at Varenna, visit the Villa
Monastero with its formal
gardens and the Romanesque
Church of San Giorgio. One
really good way to see the lake –
and admire the towns from a
distance – is to take a boat trip
around it. It is possible to take
one that stops at a number of
places, using it like a bus. Begin
at Como.

▶ *Lecco lies at the foot of the eastern arm of Lake Como, from Como itself a direct distance of 29km (18 miles).*

5 Lecco, Lombardia

Lecco is in direct contrast to its illustrious neighbour Como. More industrial than prettier Como, Lecco's claim to fame is that it was the birthplace of Alessandro Manzoni, the great 19th-century Italian novelist. The Villa Manzoni, his former home, is now a museum – you will find it in Via Promessi Sposi, named after the writer's most famous novel which, translated, means 'The Betrothed' (the street is also known as Via Amendola). While you are in town, visit the Duomo, with its 14th-century frescos in the style of Giotto, and the Ponte Azzone Visconti, a medieval bridge over the Adda river. Although much altered (it no

Bellagio – sometimes called the prettiest town in Europe

longer has any towers) and enlarged, it still has much of its early character.

▶ *From Lecco, take the SS583 up the western edge of Lecco's portion of Lake Como, called the Lake of Lecco, to Bellagio.*

6 Bellagio, Lombardia

Bellagio is one of the most beautiful points on Lake Como. Not only is it an interesting old town, but it is splendidly sited on a promontory overlooking the three arms of the lake. There is plenty to do here apart from just sitting in the sun enjoying the view. The 12th-century Church of San Giacomo has good carving in the apse and on its capitals. There is the Villa Serbelloni, with good gardens which can be visited, and the Villa Melzi d'Eril, which is open to the public and contains a collection of sculpture from Egypt. If time is short, the Villa Sebelloni gardens, supposed to

stand on the site of the younger Pliny's villa 'Tragedia', are the more interesting.

▶ *Return to Lecco, then take the SS36 going south for about 15km (9 miles) until it cuts the SS342. Take the latter to Bergamo, about 24km (15 miles).*

FOR HISTORY BUFFS

Near Bergamo, just off the SS573 south of the city, is Malpaga, in whose castle you can see frescos of Bartolomeo Colleoni hosting a banquet in honour of a visit by the King of Denmark in 1474. This is fascinating if you have already seen Colleoni's grandiose tomb in Bergamo.

---

7 Bergamo, Lombardia

Bergamo is divided into the Città Alta and the Città Bassa, the Upper City and the Lower City. The former is the more interesting, as well as being the older. Its best monuments are in the Piazza Vecchia. In it is the Biblioteca Civica (Civic Library), a late 16th-century building modelled on Venice's great library building, designed by Sansovino. Across the square, past Contarini's fountain surrounded by stone lions, is the 12th-century Torre Civica with its 15th-century clock that still tolls the curfew hour (10pm). Behind the 12th-century Palazzo della Ragione are the Duomo and the ornate Colleoni Chapel. You can just see the base of the latter through the pointed arched loggia beneath the Palazzo della Ragione. Built in 1476, the façade of the Colleoni Chapel is a mass of sculptured decoration and coloured marble. Inside is the tomb and a statue of Bartolomeo Colleoni, who controlled Venice's armed forces in the 15th century. The ceiling fresco is by Tiepolo.

The Church of Santa Maria Maggiore, in Piazza Duomo, is a

fine Romanesque building. Also in the Upper City is the Cittadella (citadel), which contains the Natural History Museum, and the Museo Donizetti – this great composer was born in Bérgamo, and you can visit the Teatro Donizetti in

Bergamo's splendid Piazza Vecchia is the town's historic centre

the Lower City. Between the Upper and Lower Cities is the Galleria dell'Accademia Carrara, a first-class collection of art, well worth taking in.

[i] *Via Vittorio Emanuele 20*

▶ *From Bergamo, take the **A4** via Brescia to Lago di Garda, about 78km (48 miles) – at*

Desenzano del Garda at the foot of the lake.

8 **Lago di Garda,** Lombardia The most interesting ports of call around Lago (Lake) di Garda are Salò, Gardone Riviera, Riva del Garda, Malcesine and Sirmione. All are accessible by the steamer, and rather than drive around the

Castello Scaligero, Sirmione, built by the Della Scala family

archaeological finds from the area, housed in the Rocca.

Malcesine, halfway down the eastern edge of the lake, is the proud possessor of the magnificent Castello Scaligero (Scaliger Castle) dramatically situated at the water's edge. But the castle at Sirmione is more remarkable. Also from the 13th century and one of the Scaligeri castles, its battlements and its dramatic situation half in the water make it possibly the most memorable sight on the Lago di Garda.

▶ *From Desenzano del Garda, take the SS567 for 11km (7 miles) to Castiglione delle Stiviere, at which branch on to the SS236 and continue on to Mantova, about 37km (23 miles).*

9 Mantova, Lombardia
Mantova (Mantua) sits on a swampy, marshy bend in the Mincio River. Its claim to fame is that it was the seat of one of the most intellectually active and refined courts of the Italian Renaissance. The Gonzaga family were the rulers and they embellished the town with a remarkable Palazzo Ducale (Ducal Palace) that still contains some of their art collection. The neo-classical rooms have a set of early 16th-century Flemish tapestries and the duke's apartments have a fine collection of classical statuary. Here you will see Rubens' vast portrait of the Gonzaga family. The Camera degli Sposi in the Castel di San Giorgio is world famous for its brilliant frescos by Mantegna, finished in 1472. Apart from a series of portraits of the family, there are others of their favourite dwarfs. In the Casetta dei Nani, the House of the Dwarfs, you can see the miniature rooms where the latter were once thought to have lived. The Palazzo del Té is another Gonzaga palace built by Giulio Romano in 1527 for Federico II Gonzaga's mistress. The Sala dei Giganti, the Room of the Giants, is its masterpiece:

lake, you could leave the car at Desenzano del Garda and go by boat. Salò has a fine Gothic Duomo (cathedral) with a noteworthy Renaissance portal. At Gardone Riviera, most things to visit have something to do with Gabriele d'Annunzio (1863–1938), one of the greatest writers and poets of his generation. His villa, Vittoriale degli Italiani was specially built for him and can be visited. The villa and grounds are filled with an extraordinary array of bits and pieces, like the great ornate organs in the music room, among which the writer chose to live. There is also a museum and a mausoleum in the villa's grounds.

At Riva del Garda, right at the northern tip of the lake, about 95 breathtaking kilometres (60 miles) away from Desenzano del Garda up the western edge of the lake, and actually in the Trentino region, is a 13th-century tower, the Torre Apponale, and a clutter of other ancient edifices of which the Palazzo Pretorio and the 12th-century Rocca (fortress) are the most interesting. The town's Museo Civico (Civic Museum) contains an interesting collection of armour and

---

FOR CHILDREN

At Pescantina, about 12km (7 miles) from Lazise on the bottom eastern edge of Lago Garda, is a zoo and reptilarium, and a dinosaur park – although the dinosaurs are the concrete kind.

---

huge frescoed fighting giants seem to bring down the ceiling. The Basilica of Sant'Andrea, designed by Leon Battista (1472), houses a chalice of Christ's blood, a relic once much venerated by the Gonzaga.

i *Piazza A Mantegna 6*

▶ *Take the SS10 for 66km (41 miles) to Cremona.*

🔟 **Cremona,** Lombardia
You cannot come to Cremona and not visit the Museo Stradivariano (Stradivarian Museum). The modern violin was developed in this city in 1566, and one of the great masters of violin-making here –

Pavia, capital of the Lombard kings for two centuries

though much later – was Antonio Stradivarius. There is also the Museo Civico (Civic Museum) in which much space is devoted to Roman Cremona. Here, too, are works of art from defunct local churches. The Duomo (cathedral) has five wonderful 17th-century Brussels tapestries as well as a series of frescos by local artists. Among the town's most interesting churches is Sant' Agostino with, in the fifth chapel on the south, a *Madonna and Saints* by Perugino, who was once Raphael's teacher.

i *Piazza del Comune 5*

▶ *From Cremona, take the A21 via Piacenza for 33km (20 miles) as far as the Casteggio turning, 82km (51 miles), for the SS35 to Pavia, a further 21km (13 miles).*

1️⃣1️⃣ **Pavia,** Lombardia
Pavia was at one time an important Roman city (*Ticinum*). Not a lot remains from this period, though the Museo Civico (Civic Museum) does contain finds from Roman times and earlier Pavia. On an upper floor you will find the picture gallery with works by, among others,

Bellini and Van der Goes, the latter one of the most important of the Netherlandish Renaissance painters.

But in Pavia, the most noteworthy monument to visit is the Certosa di Pavia, a remarkable and highly decorative Renaissance monastery complex, situated just on the outskirts of town. A tour will take in the vestibule, the Little Cloister, the Great Cloister and the church with Gothic, Renaissance and baroque decoration.

Back in the town once again, Leonardo was partially responsible for the design of the Duomo, begun in 1488, and in addition to the cathedral, there are about six other churches worth seeing in the city.

i *Via Fabio Filzi 2*

▶ *Take the SS35 back to Milano, about 35km (22 miles).*

La Grassa –
the 'Fat' Country

This tour reveals two of the finest Romanesque churches in Italy, well preserved fortified cities, great Renaissance painting and sculpture, grand opera, thermal spas, Parma ham and a sparkling local wine – Lambrusco – which is never at its best outside the region. Bologna is the most cosmopolitan city on the tour. It has a huge, ancient university, its shops mirror those of Milan and it has a wide range of excellent restaurants giving it its nickname 'La Grassa' – 'Bologna the Fat'.

3 DAYS • 378KM • 234 MILES

ITINERARY

BOLOGNA	▶ **Ferrara (53km-33m)**
FERRARA	▶ **Piacenza (185km-115m)**
PIACENZA	▶ **Parma (49km-30m)**
PARMA	▶ **Reggio nell'Emilia**
	(28km-17m)
REGGIO NELL'	▶ **Modena (24m-15km)**
EMILIA	
MODENA	▶ **Bologna (39km-24m)**

La Grassa – the 'Fat' Country

[i] *Galleria d'Accursio, Piazza Maggiore 6, Bologna*

▶ *The autostrada A13 goes north from Bologna until the Ferrara Nord exit.*

0 Ferrara, Emilia-Romagna
The centre of Ferrara is dominated by a vast castle, the Castello Estense. Begun in 1385, it was the backdrop to the splendid court of the Este family, the rulers of Ferrara. It was designed to ward off any potential threat to this little city state, and its moat, drawbridge and military bulwarks are still formidable and do nothing to relieve its prisonlike appearance. A tour round the castle includes the dungeons in which Nicolò III d'Este imprisoned his lovely young wife Parisina Malatesta and her lover before they were beheaded. After these, the various decorated chambers of the castle are a welcome relief. Nicolò III's son Ercole I (1471–1505) was responsible for an addition to the medieval town known as the 'Herculean Addition', making Ferrara the first 'modern' town in Europe. At the heart of the Herculean Addition is the extraordinary Palazzo dei Diamanti whose façade is studded with 12,600 stone 'diamonds', the Este badge.

On the other side of the castle is the Duomo (cathedral). Begun in 1135, it has a lovely sculpted portico, with scenes from the Last Judgement. Inside, look for the painted *Martyrdom of St Lawrence* by Guercino in the south transept. But it is the cathedral museum treasury that contains splendid works, including a marble *Madonna of the Pomegranates* (1408) by Jacopo della Quercia, the greatest Sienese sculptor of the early Renaissance. Back outside in the Piazza Trento e Trieste, which abuts the long flank of the cathedral, you come down to earth at the colourful market. There is also the Museo Archeologico (Archaeological Museum), housed in the Palazzo di Ludovico il Moro, with its collection of vases from the Greek and Etruscan necropolis of nearby Spina. See also the Palazzo Schifanoia with its lovely Renaissance frescos by Cosimo Tura.

[i] *Via Borgoricco 26*

FOR CHILDREN

There are few activities specifically designed for children in this part of Emilia-Romagna; your best bet is to take them to see the displays of puppets and dolls for sale in Ferrara, in the Circus Atelier in Via Mazzini.

▶ *Leave Ferrara on the SS16 going north. After crossing the Po, turn left towards the A13. Cross the motorway and continue west to Ostiglia, 56km (34½ miles). The SS482 continues to Mantova, a further 33km (20 miles). From Mantova, the SS10 continues west for 62km (39 miles) to Cremona immediately before which the autostrada A21 branches southwest for 30km (19 miles) towards Piacenza. Leave the autostrada at the*

Castello Estense, Ferrara, is heavily fortified with moat and drawbridge

Piacenza Est exit and follow the signs into the city.

2 Piacenza, Emilia-Romagna
This is a town that visitors to Emilia-Romagna tend to ignore unwittingly: its treasures and attractions are less obvious and less well known than those of other places. It has an interesting old centre filled with churches including a 12th-century Romanesque Duomo with a bell tower topped by a gilded angel and interior frescos by Guercino, a notable baroque illusionist painter of the 17th century. The cathedral stands at the top of the Via XX Settembre looking down to the Piazza Cavalli, named after its equestrian statues of Alessandro Farnese and his brother Ranuccio. These early 17th-century statues by Francesco Mocchi, a pupil of Giambologna, who was the most famous sculptor in Florence after the death of Michelangelo, are the pride of Piacenza. The 16th-century Palazzo Farnese is a huge unfinished palace of the Farnese family which houses the Museo Civico (Civic Museum) containing works by Botticelli and the school of Botticelli. It also has another very peculiar relic known as *Il Fegato di Piacenza*, 'Piacenza's Liver', an Etruscan bronze sheep's liver marked with the names of local deities.

To the south of the Piazza Cavalli, in a warren of little streets near the cathedral, is an

Frescos from Parma's baptistery – a glimpse of medieval Italy

early 19th-century theatre, an elegant neo-classical building still used during the various seasons of chamber and orchestral music and ballet. It has an eccentric little museum attached to it containing relics from the theatre's past. Near by, the Galleria d'Arte Moderna Ricci Oddi (Ricci Oddi Gallery) contains a collection of modern art, including work by Boldini (1845–1931), a fashionable portrait painter who was the Italian equivalent of Sargent.

[i] *Piazzetta dei Mercanti*

▶ *Leave Piacenza by the SS9 which runs directly to Parma 49km (30 miles).*

3 Parma, Emilia-Romagna
Parma is built on the flat so visiting its monuments is not such a strain on the calf muscles. Bigger than either Piacenza or Ferrara it has much

more to see. If you start in the heart of the city, in the Piazza del Duomo, you will see the two buildings for which Parma is best known – the 11th-century Duomo and the 12th-century baptistery alongside it. The exterior of the cathedral is richly patterned, and the interior contains work of the painter Correggio, who was influenced by Michelangelo. In the cathedral his *Assumption* (1526–30) can be seen in the vault of the dome: notice how the painted 'architecture' and the apparently three-dimensional clouds and angels almost seem a part of the real world.

In the Church of San Giovanni Evangelista, just behind the cathedral, you can see Correggio's *Vision of St John* (1520), also in the dome. While you are here, take a look at the work of Parmigianino, a pupil of Correggio, which can be seen in the first two chapels on the northern side of the interior. In the Camera di San Paolo you can see Correggio's very earliest documented works, painted in about 1518 for the abbess of the now defunct convent of San Paolo. The little Church of SS Placid e Flavia is one other place to see his work and so is the Pinacoteca (National Gallery), housed in the Palazzo della Pilotta. Back in the Piazza del Duomo, the baptistery is well worth a visit. Most of the sculpture, both inside and out, is by Antelami (12th-century) and there are interesting frescos in the vault.

For a complete change of scenery, visit the Teatro Regio, one of Italy's great theatres. The great conductor, Toscanini, who was born in Parma, played in the orchestra here. There is another theatre in Parma, called the Teatro Farnese. Built entirely of wood by Aleotti (a pupil of Palladio) in 1618, it is part of the Palazzo della Pilotta, along with the Museo Archeologico Nazionale (National Museum of Antiquities). In its majestic interior performances took

Piazza Prampolini in Reggio nell'Emilia

place in honour of the ruling family of Parma – the Farnese. Have prosciutto di Parma (Parma ham) as an antipasto for lunch and sprinkle Parmigiano (Parmesan) cheese on your pasta. Both are local favourites.

FOR HISTORY BUFFS

In the province of Parma are two interesting castles that would make a detour from Parma more than rewarding. Northwest of the city, at Fontanellato (take the A1 westwards for 20km/12 miles, as far as the Fidenza-Salsomaggiore Terme exit), is the moated Castello di Sanvitale. It has good frescos by Parmigianino, and is open to the public.
Just to the north of this, at Soragna (only 8km/5 miles), is the furnished and frescoed Palazzo di Soragna. The castle, begun in the 8th century and converted into a palace in the 19th century, contains fine period furniture and art. This is also open to the public.

---

i *Piazza Duomo 5*

▶ *The SS9 leaves Parma going southeast to Reggio nell'Emilia 28km (17 miles).*

❹ **Reggio nell'Emilia,** Emilia-Romagna

This town, almost halfway between Parma and Modena, is another centre of Parmigiano cheese manufacture. Here, so good is the cheese, and so well does it mature, that it goes up in value. People buy huge cakes of it as an investment. Reggio nell'Emilia, sometimes known as Parmigiano-Reggiano, is a thriving, bustling little capital. You would not really need to spend more than a morning here. Like the rest of this part of the region, it is completely flat. Also, like the other towns, it is built of characteristic small red bricks. Perhaps the most interesting – and the oldest – historic relic to be seen here is the mysterious 'Venus of Chiozza', reputedly 12,000 years old. You can see it in the Museo Civico (Civic Museum) along with a great many other ancient pieces.

Reggio was once an important Roman city, *Regium Lepida*, which was cut in two by the great ancient Via Emilia, also built by the Romans. In the public gardens behind the theatre is a Roman family tomb (Monument of the Concordii), dating from AD 50. In the Museo Numismatico (Coin Museum) are the finds from a 5th-century treasure dug up in the locality of the city in the 1950s.

Reggio nell'Emilia's Duomo (cathedral), while as old as any others on the tour, has fewer artistic treasures. However, the Church of the Madonna della Ghiara is full of the work of the Emilian painters, particularly those of the 17th century. All over town are unexpected architectural treasures, such as the courtyard of the baroque Palazzo Sormani-Moretti. Another baroque building is the Palazzo Spalletti-Trivelli. There are also a great many lovely neo-classical buildings from the 19th century, including the Palazzo Corbelli and the municipal theatre whose season of opera, concerts and plays runs from December to March.

i *Piazza Prampolini 5c*

▶ *From Reggio nell'Emilia, the SS9 runs straight to Modena.*

5 Modena, Emilia-Romagna
Modena vies with Parma for status as the most prosperous city in the region, though Modena has a head start over Parma due to the existence of the Maserati and Ferrari car works on its territory. Modena was once an Etruscan colony, then a Roman city, but the earliest apogee of its power was under the 11th-century Canossa Countess Matilda, a powerful ally of the Pope. Until the middle of the 19th century, the Este family, through a variety of judicious marriages, were its rulers. The Duomo, dedicated to San Geminiano, built between 1000 and 1200, was constructed largely from material taken from the old Roman city. The external sculptures are worth examining in some detail, particularly those on the west portal and on the apse. The tomb of the patron saint of the city, San Geminiano, is in the crypt, and a wooden statue of the saint lurks in the shadows of the north aisle.

Just beside the cathedral is the Museo Lapidario del Duomo (Lapidario Museum) which contains finds from the necropolis of the old Roman city. Also close to the cathedral is the medieval Ghirlandina Tower, which contains an eccentric relic in the form of an old wooden bucket which, as an act of rivalry, was stolen by the people of Modena during a 14th-century raid on Bologna. If you want to see it, you may have to ask for the key to the tower at the Comune.

Most interesting is the town's Palazzo dei Musei. This contains the Biblioteca Estense which has a famous collection of illuminated manuscripts including the Bible of Borso d'Este. In the same building is the Galleria Estense, with a fine collection of paintings, including works by El Greco, Correggio, Velázquez and Tintoretto, as well as a bust of Francesco I d'Este by Bernini. Here, too, is the Museo d'Arte Medievale e Moderne e Etnologia.

i *Piazza Grande 17*

▶ *From Modena, return to Bologna on the SS9 – 39km (24 miles).*

The sculpted tomb of St Dominic in the Church of San Domenico, Bologna

Of Mosaics,
Sun & Sea

With one or two exceptions, the towns on this tour are the antidote that every trip needs to a surfeit of culture. Whereas the interior of Emilia-Romagna contains the cultural capitals, the coast has all the playgrounds. Restaurants, night-clubs and hotels are in good supply, particularly at Rimini. And there is still plenty of sightseeing to do.

2/3 DAYS • 258KM • 160 MILES

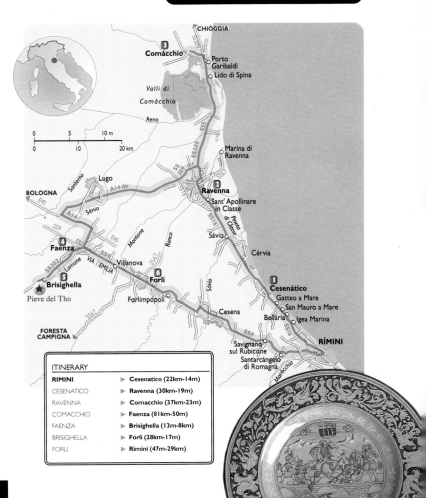

ITINERARY		
RIMINI	►	**Cesenatico (22km-14m)**
CESENATICO	►	**Ravenna (30km-19m)**
RAVENNA	►	**Comacchio (37km-23m)**
COMACCHIO	►	**Faenza (81km-50m)**
FAENZA	►	**Brisighella (13m-8km)**
BRISIGHELLA	►	**Forli (28km-17m)**
FORLI	►	**Rimini (47km-29km)**

i *Piazza Malatesta 28, Rimini*

▶ *From Rimini, the coast road, the **SS16**, leads north to Cesenatico.*

FOR CHILDREN

There are plenty of very safe beaches on this tour, where the water is shallow for a good stretch from the shoreline. In particular, San Mauro a Mare, about 4km (2½ miles) south of Cesenático, and Bellaria-Igea Marina (just further on) are ones to aim for. Gatteo a Mare, just south of Cesenatico, has a special games park for children.

---

❶ Cesenatico, Emilia-Romagna

Just a short way from Rimini on the Adriatic coast, Cesenático was built in 1302 as the harbour of Cesena, a town about 14km (9 miles) inland. It seems to have spent its days being destroyed by the enemy, each time being faithfully rebuilt. Cesare Borgia did much to prevent the sea knocking down the fortifications. These were built to the plans of Leonardo da Vinci, the originals of which are kept in the National Library in Paris.

Cesenatico nowadays is a seaside resort often crowded in the summer by people attracted by the fact that the beach gently slopes into the water and there

Colourful boats line the lively harbour in the town of Cesenatico

is good swimming. There are in fact about 6.5km (4 miles) of sandy beach, sometimes 200m (650 feet) in width, so there is room for everybody. While this stretch of beach has the usual array of tall hotels, there are also little shaded streets in the old town where there is a lively and colourful market.

The town was once a canal port and here you can still see the yellow and brown sails of the *bragozzi,* flat-bottomed boats with colourful designs painted on them. Brightly painted fishermen's houses with canvas canopies leaning out over the pavement line the waterfront. Hidden among these are the Antiquarium, the Seamanship Museum and a large variety of typical restaurants selling unpretentious local food.

ℹ️ *Viale Roma 112*

▶ *From Cesenatico, the SS16 goes straight towards Ravenna.*

2 Ravenna, Emilia-Romagna
This is the most important place in Italy for mosaics of the Byzantine era (5th and 6th

and they include the portraits of Emperor Justinian and his wife Theodora, located in the apse. Justinian offers a gift to the new church; his wife is covered in extravagant jewellery and both are surrounded by retinues of servants. The Mausoleum of Galla Placidia is a jewel-like little building. Inside is one of the most beautiful mosaics in the world. The interior is entirely taken up by this sumptuous mosaic – geometric patterns and flowers, as well as animals and religious imagery. There are also three hefty

greatest poet Dante died here in exile in 1321. There is also a variety of little museums, including the Museo dell'Arcivescovado which contains the exquisite 6th-century ivory throne of Maximian and the silver cross of Sant'Agnello. The Museo Dante tends to close rather erratically and you might not get in. The Accademia delle Belle Arti (Fine Arts Academy) has good Venetian paintings

Mosaic splendour fills Ravenna's Mausoleum of Galla Placidia

centuries). They adorn the interiors of the octagonal Church of San Vitale, the Mausoleo (mausoleum) di Galla Placidia, and the Church of Sant'Apollinare Nuovo, built by Theodoric. There are more in the Battistero degli Ortodossi or Neonian Baptistery (named after Bishop Neon who commissioned the mosaics) and the Oratorio di Sant'Andrea. Even if you see nothing else of the town of Ravenna but the mosaics, you will not go away disappointed. Those of San Vitale are the best

tombs, one of which contains the remains of Galla Placidia's second husband Constantius III. Galla Placidia was one of the patronesses of early Ravenna, though she was in fact buried in Rome.

Sant'Apollinare Nuovo has two long mosaic processions running the length of its nave – male and female martyrs. Other sights include, not far from the central Piazza del Popolo, Il Sepolcro di Dante (the tomb of Dante), housed in a little neo-classical mausoleum. Italy's

including works by Vivarini and Bellini.

> **FOR HISTORY BUFFS**
>
> The Church of Sant'Apollinare in Classe is worth the short detour from Ravenna, and completes the tour of Ravenna mosaics. In particular it has a wonderful apse with a depiction of the Transfiguration of Christ attended by Sant'Apollinare.

The Arch of Augustus in Rímini, where ghosts of the past rub shoulders with sun-seekers

i *Piazza Caduti per la Liberta 2/4*

▶ *From Ravenna, the SS309 goes north for about 32km (20 miles) to the turning for Comacchio, a further 5km (3 miles).*

❽ Comacchio, Emilia-Romagna

Comacchio is situated a few miles from the coast, just north of Ravenna. It is a kind of little Venice with the town sitting among a series of canals. Even its bridges, of which the most famous is the Trepponti which spans three of the waterways, have a Venetian look about them. But the resemblance stops here. Comacchio is a rural place, home to fishermen who sail down the canals, past the lagoon to the sea at Porto Garibaldi. It is famous for its eels: they are farmed in the nearby Valli di Comacchio and you can have them cooked with tomatoes or grilled and washed down with a Trebbiano wine called Vino di Bosco. You can watch the fishermen catch the eels in huge square nets suspended in the water. The season for eels is October to December. Grey mullet and bass, produce of the lagoons and canals of the area, are also often found on the menu at Comacchio, and you can visit the Peschiera (fish market),

housed in a restored 17th-century building. Until the beginning of the 16th century the town was a flourishing place with a healthy commercial life. Fearing competition, the Venetians destroyed it, but it was later rebuilt. Thus the look of the town today is fairly uniform because many of the buildings were constructed more or less at the same time. Find time to visit the churches of the Carmine and Del Rosario and the restored Cathedral of San Cassiano.

▶ *The quickest way to Faenza is to go back towards Ravenna on the SS309 and to continue on to the SS309dir, which quickly becomes the A14dir. Turn left on to the A14 and exit at the Faenza turn-off. Follow the signs to Faenza.*

❹ Faenza, Emilia-Romagna
Faenza has been one of the
most important centres of the
ceramic industry in Italy for
about 1,000 years and gave its
name to the type of glazed
pottery called faience. Early
faience ware is much sought
after and nowadays is the kind
of thing found gracing the cabi-
nets of international museums,
not least of which is the Museo
Internazionale delle Ceramiche
(International Museum of
Ceramics) in Faenza itself, one
of the most comprehensive
ceramics collections in Italy.
Here there are examples with
designs by Picasso, Chagall and
Matisse. Faience ware is a
majolica with characteristic
yellow and blue patterns. There
are traditional versions of it,
modernist reinterpretations of it
and you can eat off it, drink out
of it or simply put it on a shelf
and admire its colour and
texture. You can even decorate
your house with it as did the
owners of the Art Nouveau
Palazzo Matteucci, using
ceramic tiles of decorative
patternwork including flowers
and plants. There are shops
selling it all over town, and the
workshops are interesting to
visit. There is even an Institute
of Ceramics where works have
been documented and technol-
ogy tries to discover new and
exciting ways of manipulating
the raw material.

If you can tear yourself away,
visit the cathedral, which
contains some good
Renaissance sculpture, and the
Palazzo Milzetti with its 18th-
century Pompeian-style ceiling
decorations by Felice Gianni.

▶ *Close to Faenza is Brisighella,
13km (8 miles) to the southwest on the SS302.*

❺ Brisighella, Emilia-
Romagna
In the last century, the discov-
ery of the therapeutic efficacy
of the waters in the nearby
Lamone Valley put Brisighella
back on the map. It is a pretty
little town, dwarfed by the great

quarries that produced the clay
for the Faenza workshops. It
never grew much in size but it is
the proud possessor of one or
two interesting and unusual
monuments. Perhaps the most
noteworthy is the strange little
Romanesque Pievo del Tho, a
church which incorporates
Roman fragments.

Above the town is the 12th-
century castle, the Rocca, which
was built to guard the Lamone
Valley. It was radically modified
by the Venetians, who added
cylindrical towers. Nowadays it
contains the Museo del Lavoro
Contadino (Museum of Country
Life), covering the Lamone, the
Senio and Marzeno river
valleys.

▶ *Return to Faenza, then follow
the SS9 for about 15km (9
miles) as far as Forlì.*

❻ Forlì, Emilia-Romagna
Forlì, the administrative capital
of the Romagna, is another old
brick town with an ancient
Roman heritage. Once known
as the *Forum Livii*, it was an
important post on the old *Via
Emilia* which still bisects the

town. A large part of Forlì still
retains something of its old
character, but much of it
suffered under Mussolini.

Still, you can ignore the
surroundings and visit the interiors of the Romanesque
Basilica of San Mercuriale, the
cathedral and the Church of
Santa Maria dei Servi. The first
of these three churches has a
lovely red brick interior. If you
can get into the crypt, look out
for the remains of the 11th-
century church. The Cathedral
of Santa Croce has been much
rebuilt and most of what you
see now dates from the middle
of the 19th century. A piece of
the old fabric of the church
survives in the apse and is
adorned with a huge tempera
painting of the *Assumption* by
Cignani. In the Pinacoteca Saffi
(Picture Gallery), apart from the
work of local artist Marco
Palmezzano, there are paintings
by Lorenzo di Credi and
Fra Angelico. The Museo
Archeologico (Archaeological
Museum) contains the finds
from a variety of prehistoric and

View over Brisighella

Roman sites in and around Forli.

Ravenna's fine Basilica di San Vitale, a Byzantine-style church built in 547 in the city centre.

i | *Corso della Repubblica 23*

RECOMMENDED WALKS

South of Forli, in the Emilian Apennines, there is the famous Campigna forest, a vast parkland of beech, maple, fir, hornbeam and chestnut. This is an idyllic place to walk. Take the SS67 going south from Forli. At Rocca San Casciano (about 28km/17 miles), follow the signs to Santa Sofia, about 16km (10 miles). From there take the SS310 to Campigna (about 14km/8½ miles).

▶ *From Forli, take the SS9 back to Rimini, bypassing Cesena, a total distance of 47km (29 miles).*

SCENIC ROUTES

The road from Ravenna to Classe and to Cervia has a remote eerie flatness which is very typical of this stretch of the coast. Here there are pine groves. On the road from Brisighella to Faenza, the countryside is dramatically different around each of these towns; the former is deep in the Apennines, the latter on the plain. The road weaves through the Lamone Valley's pretty mountain scenery.

SPECIAL TO...

The Adriatic coast has a huge number of very popular beaches. The best among these are the Marina di Ravenna with its backdrop of pine woods and Cervia, with possibilities for windsurfing, sailing and other summer sports.

The Gentle
Veneto

This tour takes you through one of the most popular parts of the Italian peninsula. If travellers are not chasing the memory of a famous writer or painter, they are in search of the sublime beauty of Venice and its islands. Asolo, where the tour begins, claims Robert Browning as its most famous inhabitant. From Asolo you can visit the Renaissance villas among the vineyards that produce some of Italy's most characteristic white wines.

3 DAYS • 274KM • 169 MILES

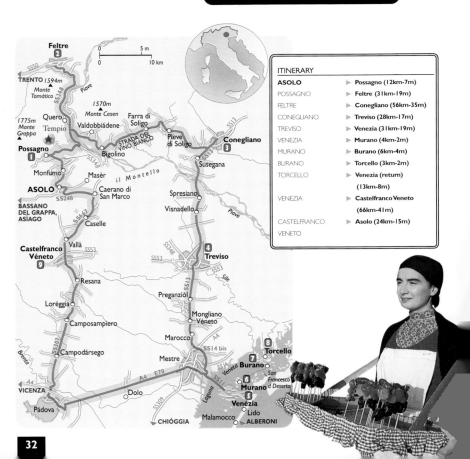

ITINERARY		
ASOLO	▶	Possagno (12km-7m)
POSSAGNO	▶	Feltre (31km-19m)
FELTRE	▶	Conegliano (56km-35m)
CONEGLIANO	▶	Treviso (28km-17m)
TREVISO	▶	Venezia (31km-19m)
VENEZIA	▶	Murano (4km-2m)
MURANO	▶	Burano (6km-4m)
BURANO	▶	Torcello (3km-2m)
TORCELLO	▶	Venezia (return)
		(13km-8m)
VENEZIA	▶	Castelfranco Veneto
		(66km-41m)
CASTELFRANCO	▶	Asolo (24km-15m)
VENETO		

▶ *From Asolo going north, follow the signs to Possagno.*

FOR HISTORY BUFFS

You cannot go on this tour and not visit at least one villa designed by the great architect Andrea Palladio. His designs, based on the architectural principles of the ancient world, were immensely influential throughout Europe and in the United States. Indeed, this influence is apparent in neo-classical buildings built even in the present century.

The Villa Barbaro at Maser, about 10km (6 miles) east of Asolo, is the very best of his houses. Still a private residence, it has fabulous frescos by Veronese, as well as original furnishings and lovely gardens. There are other villas; in fact you could go on a special villa route, seeing most of them.

❶ **Possagno,** Veneto
The first thing you will notice about Possagno is the huge mausoleum, the Tempio, of the sculptor Canova, who died here in 1822. You can see this building for miles around. It sits on a hill overlooking the town with the snow-covered heights of Mount Grappa looming behind it. Designed by Canova himself, the Tempio is based on the Pantheon in Rome. Canova's house is not far away, at the bottom of a wide straight road leading down from the Tempio. His rooms are preserved in the pretty courtyard house, now partly an art gallery, and there is a Gipsoteca (gallery of casts) where examples of his work, as well as full-scale plaster models for pieces now in museums or abroad, can be seen, including the *Three Graces*.

▶ *From Possagno, follow the signs for about 9km (6 miles) to the SS348, then branch north on this, along the River Piave, to Feltre, about 22km (13 miles).*

❷ **Feltre,** Veneto
You enter old Feltre, squatting on a low incline, through the Imperial Gate. From here, a road rises gradually to the Piazza Maggiore, passing on the way a series of palaces some of which, like the Casa Franceschini, have frescos by Morto da Feltre painted on their external façades. The Piazza Maggiore itself is full of old buildings, mainly from the 16th century. Apart from the Church of San Rocco and a lovely central fountain by Tullo Lombardo there are the remains of the town's old castle with its clock tower. Surveying the entire scene is an enormous column on top of which stands

Grand Canal, Venice's main thoroughfare, runs for two miles (3km) through the city

the Lion of St Mark, the symbol of Venice.

A large ornate palace to one side is the Palazzo Municipale, which has a striking Palladian portico of a type fairly common in this part of Italy. Beyond the piazza is the Palazzo Villabruna in which is the Museo Civico (Civic Museum). Here you will see paintings representative of the region's famous art history, in particular works by Cima da Conegliano and Gentile Bellini. The Museo Rizzarda contains a collection of wrought-iron work, much of it locally made by Carlo Rizzarda. Just below the spur on which Feltre is situated, and close to the site of the weekly market, is the Duomo (cathedral) with a 15th-century façade. Make a point of seeing the Byzantine cross of AD 524 housed here. It is carved with 52 scenes from the New Testament.

📋 *Piazza Trento e Trieste 9*

▶ *Go back to the SS348 and follow it south to Funer, at which turn left on to the Strada del Vino Bianco to Conegliano, a total of 56km (35 miles).*

3 Conegliano, Veneto
Conegliano is the centre for a wine-producing region. It was also the birthplace of the painter Cima da Conegliano, the great rival of Bellini. Preserved here is Cima's home, restored and filled with copies of his greatest work. In the Gothic Duomo is one of Cima's greatest works – an altarpiece dated 1493. Near by is the important Sala dei Battuti, a guildhall whose walls are covered in 16th-century frescos by, among others, Francesco da Milano. The details are extraordinary and the countryside scenery recognisably Venetian.

Above the town, standing on a cypress-covered hillock, is the castle, which has been turned into an art gallery. This is full of interesting works of art, including paintings by Palma il Giovane, a late 16th-century painter who once worked in Titian's studio, and sculptures by the Florentine sculptor Giambologna.

▶ *From Conegliano, the SS13 goes straight down to Treviso, about 28km (17 miles).*

4 Treviso, Veneto
Treviso is a bright, busy provincial capital, crossed by rapidly flowing canals that once fed the moat beneath the town's walls. There is plenty to see, although

None of Venice's grandeur on Burano, but plenty of colour

SPECIAL TO...

In Conegliano is the Strada del Vino Bianco (the Road of White Wine), a 42km (26-mile) wine route that encompasses some of the main vineyards between Conegliano and Valdobbiadene.
You can taste such wines as the *Prosecco di Treviso* and *Prosecco di Conegliano*, two delicious sparkling wines, at various stops along the way. There is also a Strada del Vino Rosso which starts at Conegliano.

---

the town suffered much damage during World War II. In the Duomo di San Pietro (St Peter's Cathedral), which has seven domes, is an *Annunciation* by the greatest Venetian painter, Titian, who died in 1576 at the age of 99. The 12th-century crypt is also interesting for its sea of ancient columns and its fragmentary mosaics. In the Museo Civico (Civic Museum) is the town's art gallery with works by Venetian artists such as Bellini, Guardi and Tiepolo.

Of Treviso's churches, perhaps the large Dominican Church of San Nicolò, with its fine apse and decorated columns, is the most interesting. In the restored 13th-century

Church of San Francesco you will see the tomb (1384) of Francesca, daughter of the poet Plutarch. Out in the streets of Treviso the arcades are full of cafés, and here and there you will see frescos painted on the walls of the older houses.

☐ *Piazza Monte di Pieta 8*

▶ *From Treviso, take the SS13 towards Mestre, about 18km (11 miles), then via the SS14 and the SS11 to Venezia. At Venezia you must leave your car in a specially provided garage.*

5 Venezia, Veneto
Venezia (Venice) is one of the great 'art cities' of Italy, and its churches and galleries are still crammed with magnificent paintings. To see the city's many treasures, you must take to the water – the *vaporetto* (water bus) is the main means of transport through the canal system and the lagoon. In Piazza San Marco (St Mark's Square) is the Basilica di San Marco, the chief glory of Venice, which was built after the original burned down in 976. Mosaics, coloured marbles, ancient columns and the famed bronze horses of St Mark are its chief attraction. The latter are copies of the 3rd-century BC originals, kept in the Basilica's Museo Marciano. Next door is the Palazzo Ducale (Doge's Palace) which took on its present appearance in about 1309. It has a lovely façade of lacy Gothic tracery and decorative brickwork. Look for the two reddish pillars on the front, said to have acquired their colour from the tortured corpses that used to hang there.

Behind the palace is the Ponte dei Sospiri (Bridge of Sighs) leading to the prison and just across the water of the Giudecca canal and standing on a separate little island, is the

Murano is known for its exceptional glassware which can be found all over the town

Church of San Giorgio Maggiore (1565), built by Palladio, one of Italy's most influential architects. Other great sights are the Ca' d'Oro, a former palace on the Grand Canal with a picture gallery, the Ponte di Rialto (Rialto Bridge) across the Grand Canal, and the Galleria dell' Accademia, the art gallery with some of the greatest masterpieces of Venetian art.

☐ *San Marco 71c*

SPECIAL TO...

In Venice the great Carnevale festival is held annually in the days preceding Lent, when the streets are thronged with people dressed in wild, extravagant costumes and masks. In the streets there are concerts and dancing and there are more formal concerts in the Teatro La Fenice (Fenice Theatre). Burned down recently, it is destined to reopen in 2000.

▶ *From Venezia take a vaporetto from Fondamenta Nuova to the island of Murano.*

BACK TO NATURE

The bird life of the Venetian lagoons is a high spot on this tour. Boat tours and ferries allow an interesting range of birds to be seen in the Valli Venete. Mediterranean gulls are a conspicuous feature of the area but also look for black terns and whiskered terns and waders and herons on any exposed areas of mud.

FOR CHILDREN

This tour does not especially favour children. However, the Lido, just southeast of Venice, is a popular holiday resort with sandy beaches, including two public ones.

6 Murano, Veneto
Murano has been famous for its glass-blowing workshops since the early 13th century. Many palaces in Venice contain elaborate multicoloured chandeliers from this island and nowadays you can visit the descendants of the glass-blowers in their forges and workshops. In the Museo

Vetrario (Museum of Glass) are the best examples of the work of the Murano glass-blowers and the Modern and Contemporary Glass Museum contains more up-to-date pieces. There are even fine pieces from Roman times. Glass objects can be purchased here in a large variety of shops. In the Church of Santi Maria e Donato, built at roughly the same time as St Mark's in Venice itself, you can see fragments of Murano glass in the 12th-century mosaic floor.

▶ *Murano and Burano are con-nected by boat. You can do a round trip that includes both, or else you can visit either on a single trip from Venice. The distance from Murano to Burano is about 6km (4 miles).*

Attila's Chair, outside Torcello's Church of Santa Fosca

7 Burano, Veneto
Lace-making is to Burano what glass-blowing is to Murano. All over the island you will find exquisite examples of it for sale. In the local Lacemaking School, the Scuola dei Merletti, you can watch women at work. This school was established late in the last century to rejuvenate the craft, which had all but died out. Burano is a very pretty island and its town, also called Burano, is like a miniature Venice. In the Church of San Martino is a *Crucifixion* by Tiepolo, the last of the great Venetian painters. While here, you could visit the little island of San Francesco del Deserto, about 20 minutes by ferry to the south of Burano. Here you can see the little monastery with beautiful gardens said to have been founded by St Francis of Assisi in 1220.

▶ *From Burano, the boat goes to the island of Torcello, a few miles further north.*

8 Torcello, Veneto
All that remains of this once great city, the first settlement in the lagoon in the 5th century AD, and once a serious rival to Venice itself, are two beautiful churches. One, the Byzantine-style Duomo di Santa Maria dell'Assunta, founded in 639 but rebuilt in about 1008, has splendid mosaics covering the floor as well as the walls. The *Last Judgement*, done by Greek artists in the 11th century, is particularly noteworthy. In the apse, the mosaic of the Madonna on a stark gold back-ground, is one of the finest examples of Byzantine art anywhere.

The other church, 11th-century Santa Fosca, is just as ancient. In the garden outside is a stone seat known as 'Attila's Chair', the exact origins of which are unknown. Near the cathedral is the Museo dell'Estuario which contains finds from the ruins of the old city and is worth a visit. There is a silver altarpiece from the cathedral and some Roman remains from the ancient city of *Altinum*, which once stood near the present-day town of Mestre (seen on the way to Venice). Malaria virtually wiped out the population, bringing life in Torcello to an end.

▶ *From Torcello, return to Venice. Here take the **A4** to Padua (35km/22 miles), then go north on the **SS307** to Castelfranco Veneto, about 31km (19 miles).*

9 Castelfranco Veneto, Veneto
This little town's claim to fame is that it was the home of Giorgione, one of the most mysterious and elsuive painters of the Venetian Renaissance. Little is known of him and few of his works survive (nobody knows why): those whose authorship has been authenti-

cated are very precious. You can see one in the town's duomo (cathedral). The *Madonna and Child with Saints*, often called the *Castelfranco Madonna*, dated 1504, has a typically lyrical Venetian landscape in its background.

The old town of Castelfranco was once surrounded by a battlemented brick wall. One chunk of this – the Torre Civica – survives in the centre of town, and there is another length of moated wall to the west. Visit the Casa del Giorgione (Giorgione's house); also see if you can get inside the pretty 18th-century Teatro Accademia.

▶ *From Castelfranco, the SS307 leads northwards to Caerano di San Marco, about 15km (9 miles), where you turn left on the SS248 to Asolo, a further 9km (6 miles).*

RECOMMENDED WALKS

There are some good, pretty walks in the foothills of the Dolomites around the little town of Asiago – about 32km (20 miles) from Bassano del Grappa, a town within easy reach of both Possagno and Asolo.
If you have time, spend as long as you can walking around the islands of the Venetian Lagoon – Murano, Burano, Torcello. Torcello in particular has little paths leading through the ghostly remains of what was once a large and important city.

Torcello's cathedral of Santa Maria Assunta is noted for its magnificent 11th- and 12th-century Byzantine mosaics

SCENIC ROUTES

The countryside is fairly flat on this tour. However, it has its scenic parts:
– the exit from Conegliano on the SS13: the profile of the town and its little mountain is idyllic;
– the scenery looking out over the Trevisian Plain from the castle at Asolo;
– the boat trip from Venice, to the islands of Murano, Burano and Torcello, with views of the lagoon and back over Venice.

Beyond Venice –
Inland Veneto

Many of the towns in this part of the Veneto have at least one architectural gem worthy of attention. Most often it is a church or a palace by Andrea Palladio, the greatest Italian architect of the 16th century. Verona, the starting point, is second only to Venice in the importance of its cultural treasures.

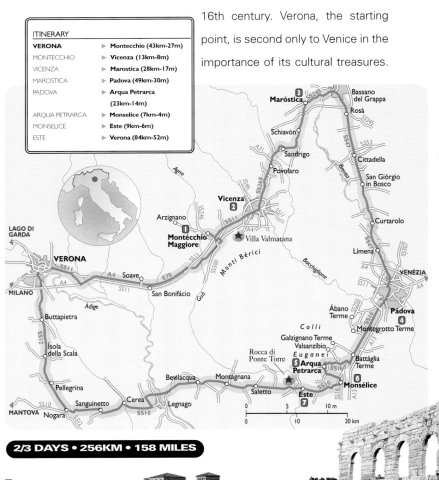

2/3 DAYS • 256KM • 158 MILES

i *Via Leoncino 61, Verona*

BACK TO NATURE

To the west of Verona is Lago di Garda, a fine place to forget art and architecture for a while and do some bird-watching. Herring gulls haunt the shores of the lake in the summer and great crested grebes and ducks can be seen on the open water. Migrant waders – notably sandpipers and plovers – can be found around the margins in spring and autumn.

▶ *Take the **A4** going east from Verona as far as the Montecchio Maggiore turning.*

❶ Montecchio Maggiore, Veneto

Montecchio Maggiore was one of the strongholds of the legendary Montagues of *Romeo and Juliet* fame. Nowadays the little town is a quiet backwater. The two castles here, now restored, are the town's chief monuments, but just outside Montecchio is the large Villa Cordellina-Lombardi, built in the Palladian style in about 1730. The building is now owned by the province of Vicenza and is used for conferences, but you can visit it and see the vast frescos by Tiepolo in the central hall. About 6km (3½ miles) away is the castle of Arzignano, whose mighty black stone walls are still intact.

▶ *Return to and take the **SS11** to Vicenza.*

❷ Vicenza, Veneto

Vicenza is known as the 'City of Palladio', due to the fact that many of its buildings were designed by the great architect, who was born here. Vicenza's Palladian works include the Basilica, the justice building, in the Piazza dei Signori. With classical statuary along the top and a two-tiered arcade along the front, it hides a much earlier collection of buildings. In the same square is his Loggia del Capitano, built in 1571 to celebrate the Venetian victory at the battle of Lepanto. The Corso Palladio contains Palladio's Palazzo Chiericati, now the Museo Civico (Civic Museum) housing an art gallery in which you can see Van Dyck's *The Four Ages of Man*. But Palladio's masterpiece is the Teatro Olimpico, which the architect modelled on the theatres of ancient Rome. Half-moon shaped, it has a permanent wood and stucco stage set of an imaginary city in fake perspective. This is supposed to be the ideal Renaissance dream city.

SPECIAL TO...

Vicenza holds the International Palladio Study Centre which offers summer courses in architecture. This is a very popular centre for Palladian studies and is good for a fuller understanding of the region's architecture. In the neighbourhood of Pádova are the thermal baths at Abano Terme, 9km (5½ miles) away, with 100 thermal swimming pools and a much venerated mud therapy. Others are at nearby Galzignano, Battaglia and Montegrotto.

Pádova's Church of Santa Giustina

ⓘ *Piazza Matteotti 12*

▶ *From Vicenza, take the **SS248**, going northwards for about 28km (17 miles) to Marostica.*

❸ Marostica, Veneto

Marostica preserves its medieval fortifications almost intact. Not a very big town, it is centred around a large oblong square called Piazza del Castello. In the square is the battlemented castle building, now the town hall, and all along the length of the walls are towers placed at regular intervals. The biggest, at the top of the hill up which the walls stretch, was supposed to have been the very last resort for the town's people in times of war.

South of Marostica is Cittadella, another remarkable town whose walls are circular and extremely high. They are punctuated by brick towers; from one of these, the Tower of Malta, political prisoners were once flung to their deaths.

▶ *From Marostica, continue to Bassano del Grappa, then branch directly south on the **SS47** via Cittadella to Padova.*

Old-fashioned craft fair, Piazza dei Signori, Vicenza

❹ Padova, Veneto

Shakespeare set *The Taming of the Shrew* in Padova (Padua), and although the city was badly damaged during World War II, much of its southern quarters retain the kind of setting that Shakespeare might have found appropriate for his play. Arcaded streets, fountains, orange brick churches and, above all, one of the oldest and most revered universities in Italy (founded 1222), survive to be looked at and walked through.

But the real treasure of this city is the Cappella degli Scrovegni, the 14th-century chapel of the Madonna dell'Arena, which contains the most revolutionary paintings in the early history of Renaissance art. Damaged in the 1998 earthquake, so far restoration has been speedy, but, as yet, only parts of the chapel have reopened.

Near by is the hermits' church, Chiesa degli Eremitani, with more early Renaissance works, this time by Mantegna. The Museo Civico (Civic Museum) in the old Eremitani convent of the Augustinians

contains Greek and Roman finds from the area. Tours are conducted around the seat of the university, the Palazzo del Bo'. Here you can see the old Anatomical Theatre (1594). Other places of interest are the Palazzo de Capitano in the Piazza dei Signori, with Italy's oldest astronomical clock (1344), and the domed Basilica di Sant'Antonio in whose treasury you can see, in a precious reliquary, the tongue and larynx of Sant'Antonio of Pádova, who was canonised in 1232.

ⓘ *Riviera dei Mugnai 8*

SCENIC ROUTES

The little country roads leading through the Euganean Hills around Arquà Petrarca, Monselice and Este are laced with vineyards. Volcanic mounds, they are quite out of character with the surrounding area, which is flat.

FOR CHILDREN

Try, if you are there in September, to take the children to see the open-air chess game at Marostica, called the Partita a Scacchi. The players, dressed in 15th-century costume, play on a 22m (72-foot) square board and the event is supposed to commemorate a contest for the hand of the daughter of the lord of Marostica. Plenty of local children are involved, dressed in Renaissance costume. As well as the chess match, there is a parade of younger people dressed as ambassadors, noblemen, bejewelled ladies, etc. This is a popular and lively spectacle.

> *From Padova, take the SS16*
> *south for about 18km (11*
> *miles) until the turning on the*
> *right, the SS16d for Arqua*
> *Petrarca. Follow the signs for*
> *about 5km (3 miles).*

5 Arqua Petrarca, Veneto
The second part of this town's
name derives from the fact that
it became the home, in his last
years, of Francesco Petrarca
(Petrarch), one of the greatest
early Italian writers. He died
here in 1374, and apart from
being able to visit his tomb in
the courtyard in front of Arqua's
parish church, you can visit his
house, the Casa del Petrarca, as
well. It contains furniture
contemporary with his period,
and it even has a stuffed cat
which you will be told belonged
to the great man himself.

The town itself thrives on the
memory of this illustrious past
resident. It is pretty, well
restored and has one or two
chapels worth a visit.

> *From Arqua Petrarca, a road*
> *leads to Monselice, 7km (4*
> *miles) to the southeast.*

RECOMMENDED TRIP

At Valsanzibio in the Euganean
Hills, just a few miles north of
Arqua Petrarca, is a magnificent
18-hole golf-course, good for a
game or a leisurely walk.
Close by is the Villa Barbarigo
with a lovely garden, park
and labyrinth all open to the
public.

6 Monselice, Veneto
Monselice dominates the lovely
Colli Euganei (Euganean Hills)
on the edge of which it stands.
Its position made it a natural
fortress which was none the less
fortified with castles and walls
in the Middle Ages. Not very
much of these survive because
the town lost its military func-
tion in the 15th century.
However, there is a lovely 16th-
century fortified palace in the
town, called the Ca'Marcello,

with a magnificent collection of
Renaissance arms. There is one
other palace at Monselice: Villa
Duodo. This was designed
towards the end of the 16th
century by Scamozzi, the most
important of Palladio's immediate followers. Only the gardens
may be visited.

Rising up the hill beside it is
the curious Via Sacra delle Sette
Chiese (the Sacred Way of the
Seven Churches), with seven
chapels spaced along it. This
was also designed by Scamozzi
and is linked to the town's
Romanesque duomo (cathe-
dral).

> *From Monselice, the SS10*
> *goes straight to Este, 9km*
> *(6 miles).*

7 Este, Veneto
Este is one of the more beautiful walled towns in this part of

public. Este was once protected
by other out-of-town strongholds.

One of these, the Rocca di
Ponte Torre, is the most interesting. It lies just outside town
on the west side. There is also
the town's Torre Civica (Civic
Tower), which was transformed
from a far earlier building in
1690 into a clock tower. In the
Duomo is a painting of St Tecla
by the artist Tiepolo.

One of Italy's best archaeological collections is in the
Museo Nazionale Atestino
here, housed within the Palazzo
Mocenigo. Note particularly
the 5th- and 6th-century bronze
statuettes.

> *From Este, continue along the*
> *SS10 for 53km (33 miles)*
> *until Nogara, at which branch*
> *north on the SS12 to Verona,*
> *31km (19 miles).*

The magnificent 1st-century
AD amphitheatre in Verona's
Piazza Brà has survived in remarkable condition despite a 12th-
century earthquake

the Veneto. Its fortifications –
crenellations and towers – date
from the 14th century. The
walls were once over 1,000m
(3,000 feet) long and there were
14 towers, of which only 12
remain. The castle became a
pleasure palace of the Mocenigo
family in the 16th century, and
today its park is open to the

FOR HISTORY BUFFS

If you want to see some of the
best preserved medieval fortifications in Italy, then go to the
little town of Montagnana,
15km (9 miles) west of Este
on the SS10. The walls were
built in the 13th century by
the Paduan tyrant Ezzelino da
Romano. Look out for the two
wonderful original gateways
into the town through the
wall. Also medieval, they look
like mini castles.

LIGURIA &TUSCANY

The Apennines, skirting the Gulf of Genova and the Ligurian coast, link the Maritime Alps on the Italian-French border with the mountains of Tuscany. But this, together with deep, wooded valleys and an idyllic climate, is all that Liguria and Tuscany have in common.

Liguria is better known as the Italian Riviera with, to the north of Genoa the Riviera di Ponente, famous for flowers and olives – and to the east the Riviera di Levante, with dramatic cliffs and pretty fishing villages. Justly famous, its attractions range from throbbing seaside resorts to lonely isolated coves hidden on one of the most spectacularly beautiful coastlines in Europe.

The great undiscovered secret of Liguria is, however, the hilltowns hidden among the Apennine valleys further inland. Built in inaccessible places in the Middle Ages, mostly as defence against Saracen attack from the sea, their little houses clustered together around the parish church are now mostly silent and empty. Yet, strangely, even the most under-visited of these is only, at the most, one and a half hours' drive from the coast. Mountain passes lead to them whilst providing incredible views down through the valleys to the sea.

Parts of Tuscany enjoy the same isolation as the Ligurian hinterland. And the beauty of this region is legendary. As the Apennines sweep down towards Firenze, much of the countryside is folded into hills and valleys which hide villages and castles, known only to the few. The Mugello, in the northeast of the region, is one of these places, characterised by thick woodland. By contrast, the Chianti region, producing Italy's most famous wine, between Firenze and Siena, is immensely popular and is a fixture on most travellers' itineraries.

It is difficult to appreciate that this peaceful landscape was, from the 11th to the 15th century, the backdrop to fierce wars between the independent city-states of the region before they were united as the Grand Duchy of Tuscany under the infamous Medici rulers. Remarkably, a great many towns and villages have preserved their cultural heritage intact. You can find, in remote country churches, paintings of the Madonna and saints from the very earliest days of the Renaissance, still in their original positions. Considering that so many wars, despots, invaders and calamities have each in their turn wrought havoc in this particular region, it is surprising that anything has managed to survive at all.

Firenze's Duomo

42

San Remo

There are two distinct parts to San Remo: a modern metropolis and a quaint medieval town. Vestiges of a more aristocratic period in its history survive in the grand old hotels lining the seafront, and the promenade backed by palms. But today, bustling, modern San Remo, with its glossy shops, cafés and its very popular Casino, has taken over. San Remo is a fairly costly place, but if you go into the old town (La Pigna) you will find less expensive restaurants. Up here the character of the old town has survived amongst the tangle of cobbled lanes and tunnel-like alleys.

Genova

Many travellers bypass Genova (Genoa), but by doing so, they miss out on not only one of the most lively cities in northern Italy but also on some unexpected monuments – especially those in the labyrinthine old quarter down by the port. In addition to the typically Genoese cathedral there are proud palaces which date from the 16th century when Genova was at the height of its power. For art lovers, the

Tuscany's Chianti region is justly famous for its wines

National Gallery in the Palazzo Spinolo contains some important work.

Pisa

Pisa contains some of the most magnificent buildings in Italy. Everyone knows about the Leaning Tower where Galileo conducted his experiments on the velocity of falling bodies, which, together with the cathedral, baptistery and the cemetery known as the Campo Santo (Holy Field) make up the Campo dei Miracoli (Field of Miracles) in the heart of Pisa. But what about the tiny Church of Santa Maria della Spina, one of the supreme examples of the Italian Gothic style? Pisa is full of surprises. In the Borgo Largo and Borgo Stretto districts there are ancient twisting alleys and an old market; here you will also find handsome squares and majestic palaces, such as the Palazzo dei Carovana and the Palazzo dell'Orologio.

Firenze

Firenze (Florence) is Tuscany's capital and the undisputed centre of the Renaissance. In its heart, the Piazza del Duomo, is the great Duomo (cathedral), crammed with paintings, sculpture and frescos by early masters, and the Baptistery, a strange little building in green-and-white marble with its famous and much imitated 15th-century sculpted bronze doors by Ghiberti. From the art in the Galleria degli Uffizi (Uffizi Gallery) to the numerous notable churches and palaces and the antique shops, markets and restaurants, Florence's reputation rests on the fact that it can offer everything that is best about Italy.

In Italy's small towns, the priest is an important figure

The Ligurian
Hilltowns

The Ligurian interior is wild and mountainous. The remote townships, once the home of rural communities, are empty now but are worth visiting for the magnificent views from them. By contrast, San Remo is a lively, if old-fashioned, resort full of 19th-century villas, hotels and places to swim and to eat.

ITINERARY	
SAN REMO	► Dolceacqua (22km-14m)
DOLCEACQUA	► Apricale (6km-4m)
APRICALE	► Pigna (10km-6m)
PIGNA	► Castel Vittorio (3km-2m)
CASTEL VITTORIO	► Triora (29km-18m)
TRIORA	► Ceriana (44km-27m)
CERIANA	► Taggia (19km-12m)
TAGGIA	► San Remo (11km-7m)

2 DAYS • 144KM • 90 MILES

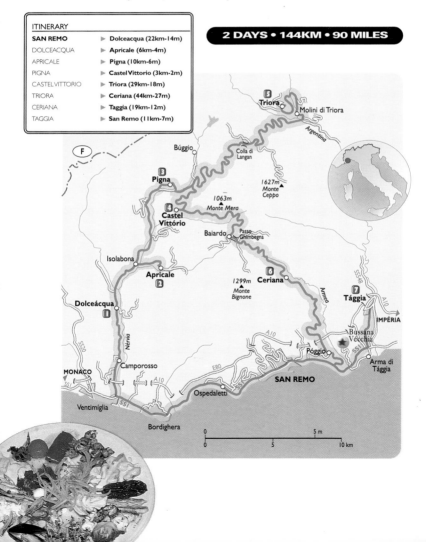

i *Largo Nuvolini 1, San Remo*

▶ *Take the coastal **SS1** going west from San Remo for about 12km (8 miles) to Bordighera, at which follow the signs to Dolceacqua, about 10km (6 miles) via Camporosso.*

❶ Dolceacqua, Liguria
This is one of the prettiest towns of the Ligurian country-side. A wide stretch of the River Nervia divides it into two parts: the higher section, dominated by the ancient castle of the Doria family, is the most interesting. If you happen to be in Dolceacqua in August, and are spending a few nights there, look out on the castle ramparts for the ghost of an unfortunate girl murdered by a Doria baron in the Middle Ages, when she refused him his *droit de seigneur*. The castle was partially destroyed by artillery fire in the Austrian War of Succession and

The Casino in San Remo, one of Italy's most elegant resorts

Remote Apricale is typical of Liguria's semi-deserted hilltowns

is now a ruin. The Doria moved into a small palace in the main square down by the Nervia, where Napoleon visited them in 1796.

Behind the palace, narrow medieval stone-paved streets, lined by tall houses, straggle up to the castle gates. The atmosphere is all the more evocative for the fact that cars are not allowed into the narrow streets. A curious single-arched medieval bridge links the two districts of the town, the section below the castle called Borgo, the other Terra. There are interesting little churches to visit in each. But the real reason for coming to Dolceacqua is to sample the local wine called *Rossese di Dolceacqua* – a favourite of Napoleon – which can be found for sale or for tasting in any of the little shops and bars slotted into the walls of the Borgo district.

▶ *Continue along the same unnumbered country road, along the Nervia River, branching right at Isolabona, for 6km (4 miles) to Apricale.*

2 Apricale, Liguria
You can see Apricale from miles around, lodged on the top of a hill covered in olive trees, way above the upper reaches of the Nervia River. Like most of the mountaintop settlements in the region, it was built on high as defence against attack from Saracen pirate raids in the Middle Ages. These were the scourge of Ligurian life at the time; if the Saracens struck, women and children were carried off and enslaved – or worse.

The ruined castle was another place that belonged at one time to the Doria barons. From this lair they could survey the comings and goings in the surrounding countryside. Not a great deal of it is left but its presence none the less gives Apricale, with its narrow dark alleys and streets, a dour air, all the more oppressive because much of the town is no longer inhabited. There is an interesting little Romanesque church dedicated to Sant'Antonio and there is also the Chapel of Santa Maria Alba.

▶ *Retrace your route to Isolabona on the Nervia River, then continue to Pigna.*

8 Pigna, Liguria

Pigna's name derives from the fact that, according to the locals, it resembles a pine-cone. Pigna's reputation as a picturesque town is matched by the views from the medieval gates across the valley to the little town of Castel Vittorio. In its tightly packed centre of old stone houses are the Romanesque Church of San Tommaso, the parochial Church of San Michele, and some pretty buildings in the main square in the local vernacular style. San Tommaso is in ruins, but enough architectural detail survives to be able to note that it was once an important building. San Michele is in better condition. Dating from 1450, it contains a painted wood altarpiece by Giovanni Canavesio hanging in the choir. You can see frescos, dated 1482, by the same artist, covering the walls of the Chapel of San Bernardino, not far away.

The oldest part of Pigna is also the highest. Up here is a small covered square which was used as an assembly point by the local parliament, with its old stone measures used in the sale of oil and grain.

▶ *Continue to Castel Vittorio.*

4 Castel Vittorio, Liguria

In the past this hilltown had a variety of names. It was known as Castel Dho, Castel Doy and Castelfranco, only becoming Castel Vittorio in the middle of the 19th century in deference to the ruling house of Savoy, one of whose members was Vittorio Emanuele XI, King of Sardinia and later the first king of a united Italy. Today it is more a village than a town, though it is recorded as having once possessed a fortress with four towers. None of this remains, but Castel Vittorio still merits a grinding detour in second gear to its high ramparts.

Look out for the openings

Pigna's chapel of San Bernardino has frescos by Giovanni Canavesio

under the houses where the locals kept their goats and pigs. You might well see this old tradition still being carried on. If you come to Castel Vittorio early enough in the morning you will see old women in black leading their livestock down into the terraced countryside. Chickens are shooed out into the streets and there is a pungent smell of dung and hay. In the winter, logs are dragged down the covered alleys and streets and bundled into the undercrofts for use while the countryside all around is clogged with snow.

▶ *Retrace your route back towards Pigna then continue in the opposite direction for 27km (17 miles) to Triora.*

5 Triora, Liguria

Triora is one of the most fascinating towns on the tour. It is in the upper valley of the River Argentina which it overlooks from its precipitous site, 1,240m (4,070 feet) above sea-level, on the side of Monte Trono. Like so many other remote towns in Liguria, it is practically empty, many of its ancient houses locked and deserted. However, it is an interesting place to wander through. Many streets are covered over with stone vaults, the upper limits of which have been blackened by the woodsmoke of the ages. Here and there you will see carved door lintels: some are decorated with figures of saints and there are others with past owners' initials.

Triora was an important walled fortress in the Middle Ages. It once had five towers but only three of these remain. In the centre of the town is a large square. It seems almost too big for a town of this size until you realise that beneath it is a vast cistern capable of holding enough water to enable the population of the town to withstand a siege of several months' duration.

Also in the square are two important churches: the Church of Our Lady contains one of the oldest dated paintings in the district, a panel called the *Baptism of Jesus Christ*, by Taddeo di Bartolo da Siena, 1398; the Church of San Giovanni Battista (St John the Baptist), smaller and older, has its own curiosity, a late 17th-century statue of its dedicatee, known to the locals more colloquially as San Zane. The statue is the centre-piece of an annual procession that takes place in the town in June.

▶ Return to Castel Vittorio, then follow the signs to Ceriana, 44km (27 miles).

6 Ceriana, Liguria
Ceriana was founded in Roman times by the Celiani family. It stands on a wooded promontory covered in olive, pine and chestnut trees and is full of interesting ancient monuments. Although this spot was inhabited way before the Middle Ages, Ceriana only enters the written records in the 11th century, when it is mentioned in the history of San Remo for the courageous part its population played in the struggles against Genova's supremacy.

Of special interest are the churches of SS Pietro e Paolo and of San Salvatore, both of which lie on the outskirts of the town. SS Pietro e Paolo, once called Santo Spirito, is early Romanesque, and has a lovely entrance portal. Inside, the church is divided in half by a low wall running across the nave. The front part was reserved for the men, the back for the women. San Salvatore is an immense building with outside buttresses supporting its weight. Ceriana still preserves its labyrinthine streets and alleys – often the coolest places to be at the height of the summer. Some are lined with arcades and most are still paved with flagstones.

▶ The country road leads back to the coastal **SS1** (follow the signs). Follow the signs to Taggia via Arma di Taggia a total distance of 19km (12 miles).

7 Taggia, Liguria
Being very close to the coast, Taggia was forever being attacked by the Saracens. In the 16th century, their attacks were so prolific that the prior of the local Dominican convent led a team of monks and townspeople in the construction of a massive fortress near the mouth of the River Argentina. This, and the defensive walls of Taggia itself, repelled the raiders so successfully that no subsequent raids were recorded there.

The castle, the walls and also the courageous prior's convent all survive today. Modern Taggia is surrounded by olive groves and fields of flowers (the cultivation of which is this area's particular plus point). Right at the centre of the town are characteristic streets (some of which are arcaded), long vaulted flights of steps, little Romanesque churches, one or two tiny baroque palaces and an assortment of carved stone portals.

BACK TO NATURE

In the hills and valleys immediately surrounding Triora, you will find dense but beautiful forests of chestnuts, pines and firs – good places for picnics. If you are lucky, walking through this remote landscape you will see wild boar (but take care, they can be very aggressive) and birds of prey including golden eagles.

FOR HISTORY BUFFS

Between Ceriana and Taggia is the ruined town of Bussana Vécchia. This was devastated in the 19th-century earthquake which killed a large proportion of its inhabitants.
Today it is officially a 'non-town' in the sense that it does not have electricity or running water provided by the local Comune. But you can visit it and poke about the quaint ruined streets and marvel at the fact that a colony of artists considers it safe enough to establish a community here.
Look in particular at the ruins of the parish church which collapsed on that fateful Ash Wednesday in 1887. Incongruously, there is a very good restaurant here.

Walk down the Via Soleri with its 15th- and 16th-century palaces; through the entrance portals you can glimpse ancient staircases and vaulted ceilings, most with old dappled glass in their windows.

Off the Via San Dalmazzo are two very steep streets which lead up to the castle. At the top of these you can still see a huge stone, said to have been rolled down the hill to crush invaders intent on climbing to the citadel.

The Convent of San Domenico (1490) lies just outside town. It has an interesting library and its church contains works by Giovanni Canavesio and the 15th-century Ligurian School painter, Ludovico Brea, who also painted the frescos in the library of the monastery. There are also various illuminated manuscripts and *incunabula* (books printed before 1501).

Castel Vittorio no longer has the fortress its name remembers

---

SCENIC ROUTES

Liguria is a very mountainous area and much of this tour is scenic. Particularly worth watching out for are:
– the approach to Triora on the road from Pigna; you come from the other side of the valley, above the Argentina River, level with Triora, then the road dives to the bottom of the valley only to rise gradually in a series of devious hairpin bends;
– around Apricale, where there are ever-changing distant views of other little hilltop villages and towns. Choose a particular view, park the car and sit and have a picnic among the wild flowers at the roadside.

[i] *Via Boselli*

▶ *Return to San Remo via the town of Arma di Taggia and the coastal **SS1**, a distance of 11km (7 miles).*

RECOMMENDED WALKS

Make your way to the Sanctuary of San Zane on the summit of Mount Ceppo on the other side of the Argentina River. Park the car here, where, apart from the magnificent views, there are acres of woodlands of chestnuts, beech, alder, Turkey oak and hazelnut in which to walk.

SPECIAL TO...

Taggia's mid-July festival of Saint Mary Magdalen is centred around the life-giving powers of the lavender blossom. Two men perform a Dance of Death in which the saint is 'brought back to life' by the miraculous perfume of the blossom, thus renewing the fertility of the countryside.

The Riviera
di Levante

The shoreline of this part of Italy is the most popular riviera on the peninsula. It is also the most beautiful. Away from the clamour of the bigger ports, there are hidden villages. These are places where you could sit all day on a restaurant terrace, washing down seafood with sparkling local wine. Genova (Genoa), on the other hand, is Liguria's biggest city, though its old centre still has the flavour of a small seaport. It has big department stores as well as little traditional markets where the locals all know each other.

3 DAYS • 267KM • 166 MILES

ITINERARY

GENOVA	▶	**Camogli** (23km-14m)
CAMOGLI	▶	**Portofino** (14km-9m)
PORTOFINO	▶	**Rapallo** (8km-5m)
RAPALLO	▶	**Monterosso al Mare** (69km-43m)
MONTEROSSO AL MARE	▶	**Vernazza** (17km-11m)
VERNAZZA	▶	**Portovenere** (27km-17m)
PORTOVENERE	▶	**Genova** (109km-67m)

i *Via Roma II, Genova*

▶ *Take the coastal **SS1** from Genova to Recco, branching off right on the minor road to Camogli, 23km (14 miles).*

1 Camogli, Liguria

Camogli is one of a series of little fishing ports which dot the Ligurian coastline. Tall, brightly painted houses crowd on to the quay overlooking rows of fishing boats and small yachts. Space being at a premium along this steep crowded coastline, everything is tightly packed together. Streets are narrow and tortuous and some are really only flights of steps tunnelled beneath the buildings. The tangy smell of the sea is everywhere and so are the fishing nets, buoys, and the up-turned, brightly painted dinghies, while strollers are constantly tripping over the lines being repaired by old, bronzed seamen. Explore the town in the morning, then lunch on the terrace of a restaurant, of which Camogli has many.

The Museo Archeologico contains all the finds from old Camogli, beginning with the very earliest settlement on this seaside spot (Bronze Age). There are also a number of items taken from the water, including rare Roman silver coins from about the 3rd century BC. The Museo Marinaro (Maritime Museum) concentrates on the maritime traditions of the town. It illustrates various aspects of Camogli's once-important fleet. There are journals, navigational equipment, maps, pictures, prints and votive offerings. There are also objects from Roman ships. A Garibaldi section is devoted to this famous national figure and his followers.

Perched on a rock near the port is the 12th-century Castello Dragono (Dragono Castle). It once provided for the defence of the town and now it contains the Acquario, a seawater aquarium full of indigenous fish in specially re-created 'natural' habitats.

Genova's 17th-century Palazzo Reale (Royal Palace), Via Balbi

▶ *From Camogli, continue to rejoin the **SS1** for a short distance before branching off right to Santa Margherita Ligure, about 9km (6 miles), at which turn right on to the coastal **SS227** for Portofino, about 5km (3 miles).*

SPECIAL TO...

Camogli holds its annual fish festival on the second Sunday in May. Here fish are cooked in the largest frying pan in the world, then freely distributed to all and sundry.

---

2 Portofino, Liguria

Portofino is one of the tiniest ports on the coast. It is also one of Europe's costliest playgrounds. Previously a meeting place for sailors and coral fishermen, whose former homes have been transformed into sumptuous weekend retreats, Portofino is nowadays the holiday haunt of leading lights of Italian society. Prices in the local restaurants and bars, of which there are many, are, not surprisingly, extremely high. But you can always buy a *cappuccino* and sit for hours in the sun in the village's only square. There is no telling what celebrity might stroll by.

Portofino's good fortune has always been due to its exceptional position. Even in Roman times it was an important base. Its little harbour is protected by an arm of land which stretches out, practically encircling it. At the very end of this are the remains of the 16th-century Castello di San Giorgio. Surrounded by gardens, the position of the old fortress is idyllic. Having been there, it is an easy walk to the Church of San Giorgio, which is a fairly recent rebuilding of an ancient chapel. Today its fame rests on the fact that it contains what are supposed to be the mortal remains of the patron saint of England, St George. They found their way here when returning crusaders were washed ashore with them in a

storm. Needless to say, bits of St George languish in other churches around Europe, but this does not worry the people of Portofino who celebrate his feast day (23 April) with a huge bonfire in the main square. The little Oratorio dell'Assunta dates back to the 14th century and has Gothic and Renaissance elements. There is also the parish Church of San Martino to look into, an early 16th-century building that contains some interesting works of art.

[i] *Via Roma 35*

BACK TO NATURE

Parco Naturale del Monte di Portofino protects one of the few remaining unspoilt coastal stretches of the Gulf of Genoa. The promontory is cloaked in *macchia* (like the French *maquis*) vegetation, comprising aleppo and maritime pines with a fragrant understorey of tree heathers, cistuses, rock-roses, junipers, strawberry trees and orchids. The bird life includes Dartford, subalpine and Sardinian warblers.

FOR HISTORY BUFFS

The Abbey of San Fruttuoso can be reached on foot (a long walk from Portofino) or by boat (also from Portofino). It is a very secluded spot. The surrounding countryside and religious buildings were given to the state by the Doria family to whom they had belonged for centuries as a way of protecting them from developers. The abbey itself was founded in 711. In the 13th century the monastic complex was transformed into a secular abbey and became the traditional burial spot for members of the Doria family.
There is one commoner who was allowed to be buried here – Maria Avegno, who drowned in 1855 during a noble attempt to help a shipwrecked English vessel.

SPECIAL TO...

In Portofino there are regattas and boating activities during the summer months.

▶ *Go back to Santa Margherita Ligure and on to Rapallo, 8km (5 miles).*

3 Rapallo, Liguria

Rapallo is another ancient seaport once important for its local coral fishermen. Today, however, it is the major tourist and bathing resort on this stretch of the Ligurian Riviera. People favour its mild climate and its long sunny promenades overlooking the beaches. The size of the town, and its popularity, have attracted a whole range of summer cultural events. These and the town's museums are welcome relief from suntan oil and the ridiculously warm Ligurian sea water. In the Museo Civico (Civic Museum), you can examine collections of local pillow-lace. This art was one in which the people of Rapallo excelled. They still do, in fact, and you can see examples of it for sale in many shops in the town. The 17th-century examples are particularly important. See other specimens in the Museo Pizzo al Tombo, whose exhibits are more magnificent. In particular, it contains the very rare and precious liturgical works of lace belonging to Rapallo's parish churches. A school for lace-making ensures that the craft will never die in Rapallo.

Despite the town's image as a modern holiday resort, it has some ancient monuments, including the Church of Santo Stefano, a pre-1000 parish church rebuilt in the 17th century and recently restored, and the Oratory of Santissima Trinità. Other places of interest include the fortress built to deter the Barbary pirates. There is also the Church of San Francesco, with a lovely sculptural group by Maragliano, and the much restored 16th-century Collegiate Church of San Gervasio e Protasio.

ℹ️ *Via Diaz 9*

Portofino's colourful waterfront, setting for Italy's high society

▶ *Continue along the SS1 for about 48km (30 miles) until the village of Carrodano Inferiore, then follow the signs back down to the coast to Monterosso al Mare, about 21km (13 miles).*

4 Monterosso al Mare, Liguria

Monterosso al Mare is the first town in a series with four others in what is called the Cinque Terre (Five Lands) region. Vernazza, Corniglia, Manarola and Riomaggiore (all within the next 15km/9 miles) are noted for their wine, their seafood catches and their wonderful secluded positions crammed to the side of precipitous hills falling dramatically down to the sea.

All the towns, Monterosso included, are quite difficult to reach both by sea (in bad weather) and by land. Monterosso is perhaps the most important of the five. Its little port is usually full of brightly painted fishing boats. It has a lovely 14th-century parish church dedicated to St John the Baptist, two ancient oratories – degli Neri and Santa Croce, and a castle on the hill near the town, built as defence against the pirate menace.

▶ *Vernazza is a few kilometres further down the coast from Monterosso – use the winding cliff road.*

5 Vernazza, Liguria

Vernazza is also a port – of sorts. Tiny and ancient (it was founded by the Romans), it is still used by the local fishermen. In the port is the old fortress whose benign existence nowadays is celebrated by the fact that it contains a restaurant. Vernazza's fine 14th-century parish church, with octagonal bell tower, is dedicated to St Margaret of Antioch.

From Vernazza it is easy to reach Corniglia, the tiniest of the Cinque Terre, and Manarola is another fishing village with a harbour and very steep, cobbled

lanes leading down to the sea. This is perhaps the most picturesque of the Cinque Terre, with its seamen mending nets, cats lying in the sun, brightly painted houses and wonderful countryside all around. You cannot take your car into the village, the streets are too narrow and too steep. So leave it in the car-park specially provided for the purpose.

▶ *Continue along the little cliff road for about 15km (9 miles) to the large industrial town of La Spezia, at which take the slightly bigger SS530 to Portovenere, about 12km (8 miles).*

SCENIC ROUTES

On the winding road from Manarola to Portovenere (about 10km/6 miles), look out for the Sanctuary of the Madonna di Montenero on the way. There are incredible views down the steep mountainside to the sea way below.
For the same reasons, the road from Manarola to Corniglio (about 6km/4 miles) and from Monterosso al Mare to Vernazza is quite stunning.

RECOMMENDED WALKS

The most scenic part of the Ligurian coastline, on this tour, is that of the Cinque Terre. You could actually walk parts of it. From Vernazza to Corniglia, there is a good path around the cliffs. That would take about an hour and a half. From Manarola to Riomaggiore, there is another one, known as 'Lover's Way'. It, too, is a pretty walk.

6 Portovenere, Liguria

Portovenere is a bit like Portofino, though not nearly as expensive. There are one or two hotels here and a great many

The charming, steep cobbled streets of Manarola run down to the sea and its delightful harbour

restaurants and bars. Another lovely Ligurian Riviera town, this one was fortified by the Genoese in the early 12th century; it has a ruined fortress and remote, windswept sanctuary to be visited. The latter is dedicated to St Peter (San Pietro), the patron saint of fishermen, and is supposed to stand on the site of an ancient temple dedicated to Venus, who may have given her name to the town itself. She, too, was the protectress of fishermen. The sanctuary is one of the most beautiful churches – more of a chapel really – along the Ligurian coastline. Built in 1277, it is constructed in black and white marble. The other coloured marble that shows through dates from a 6th-century building that once stood on the spot. From the

sanctuary you can see across to the little islands of Palmaria and Tino.

Just below the sanctuary, very slippery steps lead down to the rocky shoreline and a cove associated with Lord Byron – it is thought to be the spot from which he swam across the sea to Lerici. Look in the Church of San Lorenzo and see the town's most precious relic, the Madonna Bianca (White Madonna), which is said to have floated into town in the 13th century, encased in a cedar log (also on view).

FOR CHILDREN

The little beach at San Fruttuoso (see For History Buffs) is very small and should be safe for young children to bathe from. Its scale means that toddlers cannot wander out of sight.

▶ Trace your route to La Spezia, then follow the **SS1** to Carrodano where you join the autostrada **A12** back to Genova, a distance of 109km (67 miles).

SPECIAL TO...

The Cinque Terre (Five Lands) are noted for wines which are among the best you will find anywhere in Italy.
Two produced here are DOC (*Denominazione d'Origine Controllata*) wines, considered to be of particular reputation and worth. The *Cinqueterre Bianco secco* is a dry white, good with seafood and liver. *Cinqueterre Sciacchetra* is rarer: it has a golden colour and varies from being sweet to almost dry. There are lots of others: look out for *Vermentino*, *Albarola* and *Trebbianco*.

Treasures of
Tuscany

Most of the towns on this tour made a contribution to the unique artistic achievements of Toscana (Tuscany). A rich heritage of monuments survives covering a time-span ranging from the Etruscan period to the Renaissance. Pisa, one of the region's principal cities, competes with Florence as a showcase for the region's artistic accomplishments.

3 DAYS • 314KM • 194 MILES

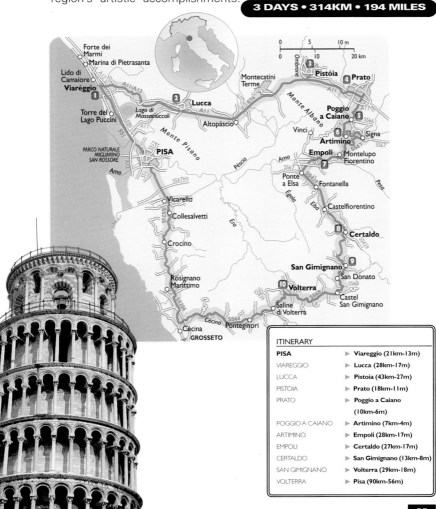

ITINERARY		
PISA	▶	**Viareggio (21km-13m)**
VIAREGGIO	▶	**Lucca (28km-17m)**
LUCCA	▶	**Pistoia (43km-27m)**
PISTOIA	▶	**Prato (18km-11m)**
PRATO	▶	**Poggio a Caiano (10km-6m)**
POGGIO A CAIANO	▶	**Artimino (7km-4m)**
ARTIMINO	▶	**Empoli (28km-17m)**
EMPOLI	▶	**Certaldo (27km-17m)**
CERTALDO	▶	**San Gimignano (13km-8m)**
SAN GIMIGNANO	▶	**Volterra (29km-18m)**
VOLTERRA	▶	**Pisa (90km-56m)**

[i] *Piazza Duomo, Pisa*

▶ *From Pisa, take the* **SS1** *going north for about 21km (13 miles) to Viareggio.*

[] **Viareggio,** Toscana

This coastal resort's scale is matched by its popularity in summer. The biggest resort on the north Tuscan coast, it has two pretty promenades beside the sea, a tremendous sandy beach and the kind of night-life that people drive miles to indulge in. It has a small dock-yard dominated by a 16th-century tower and in the centre of the town is a museum housed in the old Palazzo Comunale. Lido di Camaiore, Marina di Pietrasanta and Forte dei Marmi are other popular bathing resorts along the coast, the latter, in the shadow of an 18th-century fortress, being the most fashionable.

[i] *Via G Carducci 1*

▶ *From Viareggio, take the* **A11** *about 28km (17 miles) to Lucca.*

The skyscrapers of San Gimignano: once there were scores of towers

[] **Lucca,** Toscana

Strangely, this is one of the more under-visited Tuscan cities, travellers preferring to stop in Pisa or Florence. Lucca is small and compact – mostly contained within massive walls – and is undoubtedly one of Italy's most beautiful cities. It has the most impressive bastions in Italy and three of its early gates are still intact. Porta San Pietro (St Peter's Gate), on the south side, has preserved its portcullis, Porta San Donato is decorated with statues of San Paolino and San Donato, while Porta Santa Maria, the oldest, is decorated with a 16th-century sculpture of the *Madonna and Child*. The city you walk – or cycle (as most people do) – through today has preserved its Roman street plan, betraying its origins. The outline of the now vanished amphitheatre is preserved as the Via dell'Anfiteatro which, lined with medieval houses, follows its original shape. The Romanesque and Gothic Duomo di San Martino (cathedral), is a masterpiece in the Pisan style. In it you can see a crucifix said to have been carved in New Testament times by the Jewish high priest Nicodemus and supposedly an accurate portrait of Christ.

Other places to be seen are the Pinacoteca Nazionale, housed in the Palazzo Mansi, with paintings commissioned by the Medici family, including some by Bronzino; the Museo Guinigi which contains good paintings and sculpture; and the new Museo della Cattedrale.

i *Piazza Guidiccioni 2*

▶ *From Lucca, the **A11/E76** runs directly to Pistoia, about 43km (27 miles).*

RECOMMENDED WALKS

North of Lucca (take the SS12 going up the River Serchio) is the mountainous Garfagnana region. At Borgo a Mozzano, go left along the SS445 to Barga – a pretty town with good views, and a good starting point for walks into the Garfagnano.

---

❸ Pistoia, Toscana
Pistoia's reputation rests on its Piazza del Duomo, the medieval square at its ancient heart. It is overshadowed by a Romanesque cathedral, a 14th-

century baptistery and two magnificent Gothic palaces. In the Duomo (cathedral) you can see a clutch of paintings and sculpture by Tuscan artists, and the Dossale di San Jacopo (Altar of St James), made of solid silver. Started in 1287 and not completed until the late 15th century, it weighs over a ton. Adjacent is the Museo San Zeno, with other treasures. The Gothic Palazzo del Comune, just beside the cathedral, has a huge collection of paintings, some of which you should go out of your way to see, for instance the *Madonna and Child* by Domenico Beccafumi.

Beyond the magnificent heart of this city, famous in the past for the manufacture of weaponry, are countless churches. Among the most characteristic is San Bartolomeo in Pantano, where you can see a remarkable pulpit which stands on the backs of humans and lions. The pulpit in the Church of Sant'Andrea, by Giovanni Pisano, is one of Tuscany's finest, with scenes from the Life of Christ depicted on it.

i *Piazza Duomo 4*

▶ *From Pistoia, the **A11** continues to Prato, about 18km (11 miles).*

❹ Prato, Toscana
Prato is a centre for textiles. As such it has been important for the last 600 years, though its stature nowadays is obscured by its more illustrious neighbour, Florence. Its principal attraction is the Duomo (cathedral), a great green and white striped building. The choir is decorated with frescos by Filippo Lippi, a 15th-century monk who abducted a nun by whom he had a son called Filippino, also a great painter. If you have time to wander about Prato's quiet, deserted streets, look in at the fortress built by the Emperor Frederick II, the Castello dell'Imperatore. The Galleria Comunale (Communal Gallery) in the Palazzo Pretorio contains

The rolling countryside between San Gimignano and Volterra

Prato's Romanesque Duomo with its green and white marble stripes

more Lippis, both father and son, while the Museo dell'Opera del Duomo (Cathedral Museum), in addition to yet more Lippis, contains the fine panels carved by Donatello for the pulpit which stood at the cathedral's west front. The Museo Pittura Murale contains minor artworks from churches in and around Prato.

▶ *From Prato, follow the signs going south for about 10km (6 miles) to Poggio a Caiano.*

5 Poggio a Caiano, Toscana
Poggio a Caiano is a small rural town, no more distinguished than any other in Tuscany except that in its midst is a colossal late 15th-century Medici villa built by Guiliano da Sangallo for Lorenzo il Magnifico (the Magnificent). Its (mostly empty) rooms, open to the public, have frescoed scenes painted to the glorification of members of the Medici family by Andrea del Sarto and his assistants; incidents in Roman history are depicted as events in the lives of Cosimo il Vecchio (the Old) and Lorenzo il Magnifico. There are lovely views from a wide terrace, on a colonnade that encircles the villa – you look down into formal gardens and a park.

▶ *Follow the signs to Artimino – about 7km (4 miles) away on a ridge above Poggio.*

6 Artimino, Toscana
Artimino is famous for another magnificent Medici villa, this one built a little later (1594) for Ferdinand I de Medici by Bernardo Buontalenti. The villa faces Artimino village, standing a little way outside of it at the end of a long tree-lined avenue. Its position is spectacular – from its front windows you look out over the valleys and hills beyond.

Artimino, more a hamlet really, is a walled enclosure in which only a handful of families now live. Its other notable monument is a Romanesque church, a short way out of the village, on the opposite side of the ridge from the route by which you approached Artimino. It is a pleasant, short walk to this building which seems to have been constructed from the stones of a nearby Etruscan cemetery (7th-century BC), discovered only in 1970.

▶ *Follow the signs to Signa then, having crossed the Arno, continue west on the SS67 to Montelupo Fiorentino. After that, it is only about 7km (4 miles) further to Empoli.*

7 Empoli, Toscana
The oldest part of Empoli dates from the Roman era, though today's town centre grew up around the Church of Sant'Andrea (sometimes known as the Collegiata) in the 12th century. This little church has a beautiful, typically Florentine Romanesque façade – when in Florence, compare it with the Church of San Miniato al Monte – in green and white marble. To the right of the church is the Museo Collegiata where you can see paintings by the ever prolific Filippo Lippi and other important Renaissance artists, such as Masolino and Lorenzo Monaco.

While you are here you should also look at the Church of Santo Stefano, which was built by Augustinian monks. Most of the church's works of art have gone for safekeeping to the Collegiate Museum. Still *in situ*, however, is a *Madonna* by Masolino.

▶ *Take the cross-country road going southwest until you run into the SS429. Certaldo is 22km (14 miles) further on the latter.*

this church are two museums, one of which contains local ecclesiastical works of art, jewels and vestments, the other, the finds from nearby Etruscan sites.

If you can absorb any more religious artworks, go to the Museo Civico (Civic Museum) in the Palazzo del Popolo adjacent to the cathedral. Here in the Pinacoteca (art gallery) are more works by Gozzoli and Filippino Lippi. From the piazza, the Via Matteo, littered with fine medieval buildings including the Church of San Bartolo, leads down to the Church of Sant'Agostino with more frescos by Gozzoli.

> **SPECIAL TO...**
>
> San Gimignano has scores of wine shops all over town in which you can buy the local brew – in particular the white *Vernaccia di San Gimignano*, a wine with an ancient pedigree, drunk by Dante and Boccaccio.

8 Certaldo, Toscana
Certaldo is one of the most dramatic hilltowns in the region. Its silhouette is the kind that immediately springs to mind when you think of a medieval Tuscan hilltown – orange-red buildings, towers and castellations crammed together on the pinnacle of a defensive outcrop. It has two principal buildings: the crenellated Palazzo Pretorio and the Casa del Boccaccio. The Palazzo Pretorio's outside walls are covered in coats of arms, made of majolica or painted on to the wall surface, belonging to the local notables of long ago. Those on the façade above the entrance are still very brightly coloured. The Casa del Boccaccio was the home, until he died, of one of Italy's greatest writers, Giovanni Boccaccio (1313–75). Author of the *Decameron*, he had a profound influence on the English poet Chaucer. His home is preserved as a museum.

Boccaccio was buried in the Church of Santi Michele e Jacopo – he himself wrote the inscription on his tomb.

> *Cross the Elsa River and follow the signs to San Gimignano, about 13km (8 miles).*

9 San Gimignano, Toscana
San Gimignano is known as the City of Towers; though only a dozen or so remain out of an original 70 or more, it is for these that it is remembered even today. They were built for protection by the feuding families of San Gimignano. The town is easily seen at a leisurely pace in one morning. Enter at the medieval Porta San Giovanni, the gate which opens the way to the heart of town. Here in the Piazza del Duomo is the town's largest church, the Collegiata, in which are spectacular frescos by early Renaissance artists including Benozzo Gozzoli. Attached to

> *Take the road via the hamlet of San Donato to Castel San Gimignano, then go west on the SS68 to Volterra.*

10 Volterra, Toscana
Once a rival to Florence, Volterra was one of the most important centres in Italy for over 2,000 years. It was already an inhabited site in the 9th century BC, and was most favoured by the Etruscans for its defensive hilltop position. Their presence survives in the Museo Etrusco Guarnacci, one of the most important of all Etruscan museums, whose collection includes carved sarcophagi and a large array of funerary urns. To continue the leaps through history, you can visit the remains of the Roman occupation of the town: the ruins of an amphitheatre survive, as do those of the baths.

The rest of the town is predominantly medieval. Enclosed by fearsome brooding

BACK TO NATURE

Parco Naturale Migliarino San Rossore lies to the west of Pisa. This large area of coastal forest – mainly stone pines – together with *macchia* (scrub) vegetation and wetlands, is excellent for birds, butterflies and reptiles.

FOR HISTORY BUFFS

Rather more off the beaten track, near the village of Artimino, (or go from Empoli, whichever is more convenient) is Vinci, birthplace of Leonardo da Vinci. It has a castle and a museum dedicated to the great painter, sculptor, architect and engineer, whose birthday (15 April) is celebrated there by annual festivities.

SCENIC ROUTES

Particularly scenic is the steep road between Artimino and Poggio a Caiano: Artimino is on the top of the hill, Poggio a Caiano at the bottom, on a small hillock.
Just before you reach Artimino, stop and look back down to Poggio a Caiano. The A12 between Viareggio and Lucca is a beautiful motor-way in a country noted for the functionalism of its main routes. As you leave Lucca, look to the right at the rugged Apuan Alps.

walls (in which you can see the best preserved Etruscan gate-way in Italy – the Porta dell'Arco), it has a large 15th-century castle, the Fortezza Medicea, and the oldest town hall in Tuscany, the Palazzo dei Priori, which dates from 1208.

Despite its heavy Etruscan influences, Volterra has fine Roman remains

This contains Volterra's art gallery, the Pinacoteca Comunale, whose prized possession is an *Annunciation* by Luca Signorelli. Other places to see are the 15th-century cathedral, with its fine frescos by Gozzoli, and the earlier octagonal baptistery.

▶ *From Volterra, continue along the **SS68** towards the sea, then branch on to the **SS206** which goes back to Pisa.*

The Cradle of
the Renaissance

The city of Firenze (Florence), the cradle of the Renaissance, was the brilliant new world which succeeded the murk of the Dark Ages. Visiting Florence first gives a foretaste of the other great monuments of art and architecture to be seen in such places as Siena and Arezzo.

3 DAYS • 456KM • 282 MILES

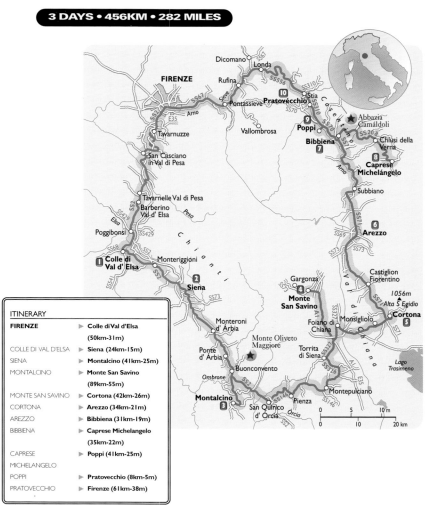

i *Via Manzoni 16, Firenze*

▶ *From Firenze, take the **SS2** going south for about 43km (27 miles) to Poggibonsi. Two kilometres (1 mile) further on, branch right to Colle di Val d'Elsa.*

❶ Colle di Val d'Elsa,
Toscana

Colle di Val d'Elsa is a small town sloping down the side of a steep ridge. There are two parts to it: the Colle Alto (upper town) was always the religious and administrative centre, while the Colle Basso (lower town) was home to artisans and their workshops. While the buildings in the former are still almost uniformly Renaissance, the latter has changed with the times, and today there are factories producing excellent glassware and crystal.

In the upper town, the Castello is still walled by grim fortifications in which is a massive castellated gate called the Porta Volterrana (or Porta

Siena's main square, Piazza del Campo, is one of the finest in Italy

16th-century bronze crucifix over the altar – and ancient administrative buildings, including the Palazzo dei Priori (now the Civic Museum) and the Palazzo Vescovile (the museum of religious art). The most interesting museum is the little Antiquarium in the Piazza del Duomo, containing a collection of objects from the Casone Necropolis, in use from the late Iron Age to the last days of the Romans. Colle di Val d'Elsa was the birthplace of the architect Arnolfo di Cambio (died *c*1302), who designed the bell tower – the Campanile – of the cathedral in Florence. His house is marked with a plaque.

FOR HISTORY BUFFS

From Colle di Val d'Elsa, go to Monteriggione (about 8km/5 miles), a fortified hamlet that survives with its walls and 11 of its huge towers intact. It has a little church and sits on its own like an island in a sea of olive groves.

---

❷ Siena, Toscana

After Florence, Siena is the most interesting city in Tuscany. Its most memorable characteristic is the Campo, a sloping semi-circular piazza dominated by the mighty Palazzo Pubblico. This late 13th-century Gothic building is topped by a 102m (335-foot) high tower, the Torre del Mangia, from the top of which there are amazing views of the surrounding countryside. Nearer at hand, it looks down over the Campo crammed with the tables of open-air cafés, and other important Sienese landmarks, including the Duomo (cathedral), sited at the city's highest point. This Romanesque building was added to over the centuries and restored in the 19th century. The most ambitious part of it is the polychrome marble façade designed in the 13th century by Giovanni Pisano. There is also a magnificent rose window in the upper façade, which was added in the next century, and the pinnacles of the gables are decorated with 19th-century mosaics. This remarkable decorative display is matched inside by black and white bands on the columns and walls. Before leaving the building look at Nicola Pisano's fantastic pulpit, 1265–8, with New Testament scenes in relief. One of Siena's greatest works of sculpture is in the Battistero San Giovanni (baptistery) under the cathedral. This is a baptismal font, the bronze relief panels of which are by some of the greatest exponents of Renaissance art – Ghiberti, Donatello and Della Quercia.

As with Florence, it would take days to explore Siena fully. Nearly any church you see is worth entering, though San Francesco, with 14th-century frescos by the Lorenzettis, is among the best. For a closer look at the original works from the cathedral go to the Museo dell'Opera del Duomo (cathedral museum). The Pinacoteca Nazionale (art gallery) is in the 14th-century Palazzo

Nuova). Beyond, crammed in among dark stone alleyways lined with brooding medieval houses, are the Duomo (cathedral) – go inside and see the

▶ *From Colle di Val d'Elsa, the road leads in a southeast-wards direction towards Siena, a distance of about 24km (15 miles).*

The 'icing sugar' fantasy of Siena's magnificent cathedral

Buonsignori; here there is an excellent survey of Sienese art from its beginnings to the 17th century. Pre-eminent here are the works of Guido da Siena, the best of the earliest Sienese painters, and the work of Pietro and Ambrogio Lorenzetti. Others to look out for are the works of Beccafumi, born 1484, a High Renaissance artist and contemporary of Raphael, and the works of Il Sodoma, born 1477, the leading mannerist painter in Siena. You can see other works by him in the nearby Church of Sant' Agostino.

While in Siena make sure you wander through the back streets, away from the main tourist spots, and see its medieval houses, ancient alleyways and little churches. The Church of San Domenico contains the head of Saint Catherine in a golden reliquary. She, like St Francis, received the *stigmata*. Not far away is Casa di Santa Caterina (Saint Catherine's house), now a museum and a shrine to this mystic reformer, one of the co-patrons of Italy. Also near by is the medieval Fonte Branda, a fountain which was once an important source of water for Siena's inhabitants.

If you have time, go out of Siena on the SS2, south, and after about 27km (16½ miles) branch right on the SS451 to the remote Abbey of Monte Oliveto Maggiore which is still inhabited by monks. Chief among its treasures is the huge cloister with a fresco cycle depicting the life of St Benedict, partially by Luca Signorelli (born *c*1441), and by Il Sodoma. There is a lovely early 15th-century church here, and the entrance gate is decorated by fine della Robbia terracottas. The abbey is set in a striking position and is considered one of the chief attractions of the Sienese locality (you could go here on the way to the next town, Montalcino).

[i] *Via di Città 43*

Taking a quiet moment from the daily chores in Cortona

▶ *From Siena, take the SS2 south as far as Buonconvento, about 27km (17 miles) then, about 2km (1 mile) further on, branch on to the smaller country road that leads to Montalcino.*

3 **Montalcino,** Toscana

The most memorable thing about Montalcino is the number of wine shops scattered around what is a rather small town. They make sight-seeing difficult because their attractions are hugely popular. Montalcino is the home of the famous *Brunello di Montalcino* and perhaps the best place to taste this wine is in the café housed in the old Rocca, the 14th-century castle at the top of the town.

Montalcino is a hilltown surrounded by medieval walls. Its precipitous streets straggle up to a lovely medieval Palazzo Comunale in the Piazza del Popolo, while higher up is the Romanesque Church of Sant'Agostino with a good rose window in its façade. There are two collections of Sienese paintings in the town, one in the Museo Civico (Civic Museum), the other in the Museo Diocesano (Diocesan Museum).

Montalcino is a good place from which to visit a collection of other lovely, typically Tuscan towns and villages. It should take an extra afternoon or morning. One of these, Castelnuovo dell'Abate, just 8km (5 miles) to the south, has the lovely 12th-century Benedictine Abbazia di Sant'Antimo which is supposed to have been founded by Charlemagne. Just to the north of Montalcino, also about 8km (5 miles), is the little town of Pienza, famous for having been the birthplace of one of the greatest popes of the early Renaissance, Pius II (Aeneas Sylvius Piccolomini). During the Pope's lifetime it became something of a centre for art. See the magnificent façade of Pius' family home, the Palazzo Piccolomini which was designed by Bernardo Rossellino in 1460, one of the great Renaissance architects, with significant works in Florence. He was also responsible for Pienza's cathedral. To the east of Montalcino is San Quirico d'Orcia, another well preserved town with a good Romanesque church.

▶ *Return to the SS2, turn right and continue southeast for about 14km (9 miles) on this road to San Quirico d'Orcia. From here, take the SS146 to Pienza and Montepulciano and then follow the signs to the A1 via the SS326 and the SS327. Go north on the A1 for 14km (9 miles) to the exit for Monte San Savino.*

4 **Monte San Savino,** Toscana

Monte San Savino is another of Tuscany's most characteristic hilltowns. It is a quiet, pretty place that comes alive early in the morning, the shopping hours, and late in the afternoon when everyone takes their evening stroll. The most interesting things to see here are the monuments that were either designed or restructured by Andrea Cantucci, a sculptor who was born here in 1496, and subsequently nicknamed Sansovino. His is the Loggia dei Mercanti in the Corso Sangallo and he was responsible for altering the 14th-century Church of Sant'Agostino. Some of his sculptural works can be seen in Santa Chiara. It was Antonio da Sangallo the elder, an architect who built some of the masterpieces of Renaissance architecture, who designed the Palazzo Comunale early in the 16th century.

Not far from Monte San Savino (take the SS73), is the little walled village of Gargonza. Turned by its owners into a hotel, it was once frequented by Dante and is an interesting and beautiful spot to stay. It has a little church dedicated to the saints Tiburzio and Susanna, and the whole clutch of buildings behind their north wall is dominated by a medieval tower.

▶ *Go back down the A1 for 14km (9 miles) as far as Val di Chiana, then follow the signs via Foiano di Chiana and Monsigliolo to Cortona.*

5 Cortona, Toscana
Cortona, one of the oldest towns in Tuscany, is also one of the highest. The views from its ramparts are among the best in the region. There is a lot to see and do here but be prepared for your calf muscles to bear the brunt of your sightseeing. Cortona is perched on the side of Monte Egidio and all the streets, like the medieval Via del Gesù with its overhanging houses, and the steps leading to and from the central piazza, are immensely steep. The Duomo (cathedral), poised above a steep drop to the valley below, is perhaps the least interesting building in this lovely medieval town. Originally Romanesque, it underwent later alterations that left it leagues behind the 13th-century Church of Sant'Agostino, and the 14th-century San Niccolò, which contains a *Deposition* by Luca Signorelli. More works by Signorelli, who was born in Cortona, can be found in the Museo Diocesano (Diocesan Museum) alongside other precious Renaissance paintings, most notably those by Fra Angelico and Pietro Lorenzetti. Relics of the Etruscans can be seen in the museum in the Palazzo Pretorio, while the Etruscan walls, nearly obliterated by the Roman and medieval ones, can be seen around the Porta Colonia (the Colonia Gate).

At the top of the town is the forbidding Fortezza Medicea, not far from the Basilica di Santa Margherita da Cortona, which contains a fine Gothic tomb. Cortona is a lovely place to be in the late afternoon when the townsfolk emerge after their siesta. They loiter in the main square eating ice-creams and gossiping, or else indulge in the universal Italian pastime – *la passeggiata*. This is the leisurely evening stroll backwards and forwards up the piazza, down the other side, then along one of the side streets and back again. Overlooked by ancient buildings, this scene can not have changed much over the centuries.

▶ *From Cortona, return to the SS71, west of Cortona, which leads to Arezzo, about 29km (18 miles) further on.*

6 Arezzo, Toscana
Arezzo, birthplace of the poet Petrarch, is another Tuscan city with a medieval air about it. Piazza Grande is its most magnificent square, lined with an assortment of medieval houses, some of which are attached to castellated towers. The piazza slopes downwards from Giorgio Vasari's 16th-century loggia – built in the style of an ancient Greek stoa or portico – of the Palazzo delle Logge on the right of which is the Palazzo della Fraternità dei Laici topped by a clock tower. Just below this building, also on the right, is the apse of the Romanesque Church of Santa Maria della Pieve. The entrance to this church is at the other

side, by way of a most extraordinary façade consisting of a three-tiered loggia. Inside is Pietro Lorenzetti's famous polyptych (1320) of the *Madonna and Saints*. The Gothic Duomo is further up the hill past the Palazzo Pretorio, whose façade is decked with the coats of arms of imperial and Florentine governors of the city. The best things about the cathedral, begun in 1277, are the 16th-century stained glass, by the Frenchman Guillaume de Marcillat, and the tomb of Bishop Guido Tarlati, who died in 1327, an enormous sculpted monument set with 16 relief panels.

Above all, do not miss the Church of San Francesco which contains one of the finest fresco cycles to have emerged from the Renaissance. The work of the great Piero della Francesca, it depicts the *Legend of the Cross*, and is generally accepted as one of the world's greatest paintings. Piero, a follower of the Florentine school of painting, produced his masterpiece between 1452 and 1466, but its drama, colour and light speak across the centuries.

Other places to visit are the Casa del Vasari, the house of the painter and early art critic Giorgio Vasari (1511–74) which is now a museum; the remains of a Roman amphitheatre down near the station; and the Museo Archeologico next door, containing the relics of the city's more ancient past, including good Etruscan items.

ⓘ *Piazza Risorgimento 116*

▶ *From Arezzo, take the* **SS71** *going north to Bibbiena for 31km (19 miles).*

7 Bibbiena, Toscana
Bibbiena is in the heart of the Casentino area of Tuscany, the lovely wooded valley in which the River Arno rises. It is the biggest town in the area, a typical hilltown where the pace of life is slow and easy. Here is the 15th-century Church of San Lorenzo which contains terracottas attributed to the school of della Robbia.

The 12th-century Church of SS Ippolito e Donato has a triptych painted by Bicci di Lorenzo (1435), as well as the remains of some late medieval frescos. Most interesting of all is the 16th-century Palazzo Dovizi, with a dramatic façade lining the main street in the centre of town. This was the home of Cardinal Bibbiena (1470–1520), friend of the painter Raphael.

From Bibbiena (take the SS208) it is easy to get to the Abbey of La Verna, high above the town, the site of which was given to St Francis in 1213; it was here that he received the *stigmata* (Christ's wounds).

▶ *Take the* **SS208** *to Chiusi della Verna, from where follow signs to Caprese Michelangelo, a total of 35km (22 miles).*

8 Caprese Michelangelo, Toscana
This tiny hamlet, birthplace of Michelangelo, occupies a rock site with the source of the Tevere (Tiber) River that runs through Rome, just to the east, and the upper reaches of the Arno River to the west. Everything there is to see here has something to do with Michelagniolo di Lodovico Buonarroti – Michelangelo – perhaps the greatest artist that Italy ever produced. You can

Pieve di Romena church near Pratovecchio, a Romanesque gem

visit his birthplace among the chestnut trees; the Casa del Podestà, where his father was the Florentine governor, is now a museum. There are also the remains of a castle and the little Chapel of San Giovanni Battista where Michelangelo is said to have been baptised.

▶ *From Caprese Michelangelo, return to Bibbiena. Turn right on the SS70, which leads after 6km (4 miles) to the turning for Poppi.*

9 Poppi, Toscana
You can see Poppi from miles around. It stands high above the plain of Campaldino, where an important battle was fought in 1289 (at which the poet Dante was present). Dante's bust faces the piazza in front of the Palazzo Pretorio which dominates the town and the countryside. This was once home to the Guidi counts who, in the Middle Ages, dominated the entire Casentino hill region. Today it houses some frescos from the 15th century and a chapel decorated a century earlier. Poppi is very pretty indeed. Its main street is arcaded and lined with medieval houses. Nothing stirs here, not even the cats lying in the sun when you walk past.

From Poppi cross over to the Abbey of Camaldoli, about 8km (5 miles) to the north. Its buildings date mostly from the 17th and 18th centuries – visit the monks' old pharmacy, and also the little baroque church about 2.5km (1½ miles) above the abbey. Here, housed in cells, lived (and still live) hermit monks in complete isolation.

i *Piazza Amerighi*

▶ *From Poppi, return to and turn left on to the SS70. Turn right within 2km (1 mile) on to the SS310 to Pratovecchio, a further 6km (4 miles).*

10 Pratovecchio, Toscana
Pratovecchio, like other places in the area, is associated with the poet Dante. It serves as a base from which to visit places of interest in the immediate vicinity. For example, a short way out of town is Stia, from whose lofty position you can see right over Casentino to Poppi and Caprese Michelangelo. In the centre of this village, and at its highest point, are the remains of a castle which also belonged to the Guidi counts and in which Dante was imprisoned for a while.
Near by, and just above Pratovecchio, is the Castello di

Enjoying a quiet moment in Montalcino's Piazza del Popolo

Romena, once a fortified village but now in ruins, and a country church called the Pieve di Romena, one of the most beautiful Romanesque buildings in the region. Ask for the key at the neighbouring farmhouse, go inside, and examine the carvings on the columns lining the nave.

▶ *From Pratovecchio continue north on the SS310. After 2km (1 mile), branch left on to, and follow, the SS556 via Stia until it cuts the SS67 which leads back into Firenze.*

FOR CHILDREN

Show the children true Tuscan cooking. Take them to a barbecue Tuscan style (by doing so you are following the real tradition of Tuscan cuisine) and eat juicy wild boar sausages or a steak *alla Fiorentina* grilled on the open flame. The latter is a steak on the bone with a drop of olive oil added once it is cooked. Fish, too, is delicious. Follow the whole lot with the best ice-cream in Italy – from Vivoli's in Florence.

UMBRIA & THE MARCHES

Even though it is so close to Tuscany, Umbria is remarkably under-visited. It is green and fertile, a land of saints and artists, a gentle region whose towns have on the whole been left alone by the march of progress. The Marches (so called because they were a border province of the Holy Roman Empire), lying just to the east and bordering the Adriatic Sea, are a lesser version of the same thing. But whereas Umbria has been opened up by the great central valley running through its midst from Città di Castello to Todi, the hilly landscape of The Marches has been miraculously preserved from development, since a large portion of its terrain is difficult to negotiate. Access to The Marches is easier by way of the coastal autostrada; as a result, few visitors to the region venture beyond the easily reached coastal resorts to explore the ancient cities further inland.

It is the Apennines, the mountainous backbone of Italy, that are responsible for the region's varied scenery. They continue their southward march from Firenze towards Perugia in Umbria, becoming increasingly more rugged as they approach The Marches. But by the time they reach the coast the landscape has transformed itself entirely into a gently rolling coastal belt which falls away to the sandy beaches of the Adriatic.

Most of the Umbrian towns you will visit have, hidden in the gloom of a church or palace, a fresco of a dewy-eyed Madonna or a scene of the life of a local saint, on a wall or inside a niche. Umbria was hit badly by the earthquake of 1998, and while many country villages were damaged, restoration is currently being undertaken very quickly. Churches are reopening one by one; this is the most sophisticated task of restoration ever undertaken in Italy.

But if Umbria is under-visited, then The Marches region is Italy's best kept secret. Quiet, small towns, packed with magnificent art and architecture, punctuate the mountain valleys, just waiting to be discovered by the more adventurous traveller. And in the north, in Urbino, the region can boast a city on a par for beauty and interest with such towns as Lucca or Siena in Tuscany.

Left: sunflowers clothe the Umbrian landscape

Perugia

Perugia, capital of Umbria, is a treasure-house of art, centre for industry and commerce, medieval hilltown, and home of two universities. As Umbria's major city – and surrounded by motorways – its old character could have been ruined, but this is not so. Indeed, the dominant face that it presents to the world is its medieval one. Perúgia was a flourishing commercial centre in the Middle Ages, and its major buildings, the Duomo, the Palazzo dei Priori and the Corso Vannucci lined with fortified palaces (now shops and cafés), date from this period or shortly after. The narrow cavernous back streets contribute to this old-world character. In addition, Perugia has the region's finest paintings in the Galleria Nazionale dell'Umbria (National Gallery of Umbria) in the Palazzo dei Priori.

Ancona

Ancona, the capital of The Marches region, was the ancient Greeks' northernmost Adriatic settlement. Its oldest quarters sit on a promontory which juts out into the Adriatic, with the half-moon of the harbour below. Although much of it was destroyed during World War II, with further damage caused by an earthquake and landslide in 1972, a large-scale restoration effort has meant that there is once again plenty to see and do here. There are one or two churches with fine Romanesque façades (Santa Maria della Piazza is one, with entertaining carvings), and the cathedral was built on the site of a very much more ancient temple of Venus.

Urbino

Urbino is dramatically placed overlooking the Metauro River. It is a perfect – and rare – example of a Renaissance city that has survived intact, complete with surrounding walls. Dominating all is the huge Palazzo Ducale (Ducal Palace) that seems, even though it was never finished, almost like a city within a city. Started in 1444, this was once home to the Montefeltro dukes of Urbino whose cultured court was the envy of the rulers of many other Italian city-states during the Renaissance. At the time, it contained an enviable art collection and, although the Montefeltro family no longer exists, a part of the collection does and you can see what survives in the palace, now, in part, an art gallery – Galleria Nazionale delle Marche. Raphael, one of the greatest artists of the later Renaissance, was born in Urbino in 1483, and you can visit his home. A quiet walk around the town, preferably after dark, through the cobbled lanes lined with ancient houses, is an evocative experience, transporting you back in time very nearly to the period of the Montefeltro family.

The little church of Santa Maria Maggiore once served as Assisi's cathedral

The Green
Heart of Italy

Umbria is best observed from the ramparts of the ancient hill-towns crammed into its central valley. Its hills and lower slopes are covered with olive groves, pines and grapevines and the towns in this magical region are among the most evocative in Italy. Perugia is an imposing city with a grand central square, Gothic cathedral and magnificent 13th-century fountain.

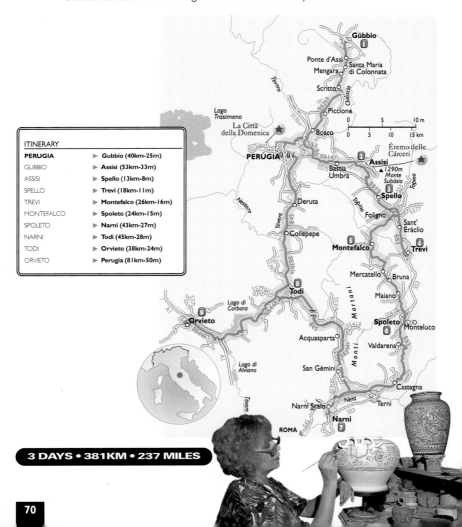

3 DAYS • 381KM • 237 MILES

FOR CHILDREN

La Città della Domenica is a Disney-style playground 8km (5 miles) west of Perugia, just off the SS75bis. The 200-hectare (500-acre) park has a zoo, archaeological zone, games rooms, bumper cars and a variety of buildings based on fairy-tale themes, such as 'Snow White's House'.

▶ Take the **SS298** going north-east from Perugia to Gubbio.

❶ Gubbio, Umbria
Beautifully situated at the mouth of a gorge and rising up the slopes of Mont'Ingino, Gubbio has managed to preserve much of its medieval appearance. In the Middle Ages it was one of the fiercest and most warlike places in Umbria, and the 14th-century Palazzo dei Consoli, a massive Gothic battlemented structure of dressed stone, in Piazza della Signoria, still dominates the town. It now houses a museum and art gallery. Among its many exhibits are the famous *Tavole Eugubine* (Gubbio Tablets), seven 2nd- to 1st-century BC bronze plaques with inscriptions in Umbrian and Latin, which are the most important evidence extant of the Umbrian language. The Palazzo Ducale, built in 1476 for Federico da

Steep winding streets in the hilltop town of Spello

Montefeltro, Duke of Urbino, by Luciano Laurano, has a delightful Renaissance court-yard and charming rooms with unusual architectural fashions, carved doors and 16th-century fireplaces.

As you wander through the town look out for the Porte del Morto (Doors of Death or Deadman's Gates). Many houses still have two doorways. The lower one, according to tradition, was where coffins were removed from the house after death. In the lower part of the town is the Gothic Church of San Francesco, whose simple façade is adorned with a great

Fine frescos in Todi's Romanesque and Gothic Duomo, Piazza del Popolo

rose window, creating a striking effect. Inside is a notable fresco depicting the *Life of the Virgin*, painted by Ottaviano Nelli in the early 1400s.

Gubbio's 1st-century AD Roman theatre is one of the largest surviving of its kind. It is in an excellent state of preservation, and in the summer provides dramatic performances.

[i] *Piazza Oderisi 6*

▶ *Return towards Perugia on the SS298. Just before Perúgia turn south on the SS3bis, then on to the SS75 eastwards for a short distance before taking the SS147 to Assisi.*

2 Assisi, Umbria
Nestling on the slopes of Monte Subasio, Assisi has hardly changed since St Francis, born here in 1182, the son of a wealthy merchant, walked its streets, and its ancient character has helped to preserve his cult. Little, winding, stone-paved streets, lined with old houses, lead from the base of the town to the various monuments. Almost everything worth seeing is in some way associated with the saint. Art-lovers should head for the Basilica di San

Francesco, which consists of two fine 13th-century churches, one on top of the other. Here there are frescos celebrating the life of St Francis. Most important is the series of 28 by Giotto, the first major artist of the early Renaissance, in the basilica's upper church. Earthquake damage here was severe. The upper church is closed until further notice, but the rest of the basilica can be visited. More exquisite are the scenes from the life of St Martin by the Sienese painter Simone Martini (1322) in the Chapel of St Martin in the basilica's lower church. In addition, there are a number of relics belonging to the saint, among them his sandals and his patched grey cassock.

You cannot avoid the religious life in Assisi: the streets are full of nuns and monks and there are several other churches well worth visiting, including the 13th-century Santa Chiara which enshrines St Clare's body still intact. Even though she died nearly 750 years ago, her

SPECIAL TO...

In Gubbio, the Corsa dei Ceri (Feast of Candles), takes place every year on 15 May and begins with a picturesque procession through the streets to the Abbey of Sant'Ubaldo on Mont'Ingino, just outside the town. The festival is centred round a dramatic race in which three teams of sturdy men each carry a huge, heavy, candle-shaped pillar up the hill to the abbey in honour of St Ubaldo, whose mortal remains are preserved in an urn beneath the main altar. Legend has it that the venerable saint intervened in a battle against Perugia, giving the victory to the outnumbered Gubbians. If you don't care to walk, the abbey can be reached by car or funicular.

body, blackened by time, lies open to view in the crypt. One of St Francis' earliest and most enthusiastic supporters, St Clare founded the order of the Poor Clares.

It is well worth the stiff walk up Via San Francesco to the Piazza del Comune. Here you can see the remains of the Temple of Minerva, a good example of Roman architecture dating from the 1st century AD and now the Church of Santa Maria della Minerva. There are also several fine medieval buildings: the Palazzo del Capitano del Popolo, and the Torre and Palazzo del Comune, the latter containing the Pinacoteca Civica (Civic Picture Gallery).

[i] *Piazza del Comune 12*

▶ *Take the road southeast from Assisi to the SS75, which runs for 3km (2 miles) before the turning to Spello, 13km (8 miles) from Assisi.*

FOR HISTORY BUFFS

For those interested in the life of St Francis, and who have the stamina, a walk up Monte Subasio, offering magnificent panoramas of the surrounding countryside, brings you to the Eremo delle Carceri, the saint's favourite retreat. The hermitage, cut out of the rock, is set in the dense woodland covering the mountain, 5km (3 miles) behind Assisi. Most of the miracles recounted in St Francis' *Fioretti* ('Little Flowers') took place in these woods.

---

3 Spello, Umbria
Clinging to the southern slopes of Monte Subasio, Spello has changed little since the Middle Ages. History lies all around you here, as you will find if you pick your way through its streets: if not Roman, then it is bound to be medieval or, at the very latest, Renaissance. The town was under the influence of the Romans for much of its history.

Look for the Porta Venere, a fine old Roman gateway which survives in the town's walls. Near the station you will find another, the Porta Consolare, with three statues from the Roman theatre whose ruins can be seen just before entering the town.

Steep winding streets lead from it and up into the town, past higgledy-piggledy medieval shops and houses to the centre and the Church of Santa Maria Maggiore. The church's magnificent Cappella Baglioni (Baglioni Chapel) contains frescos (1501) by Pinturicchio, which tell the life of the Virgin in a fresh and lively way. An important Renaissance artist, whose work

can be seen in the Sistine Chapel in the Vatican, Pinturicchio was assistant to Perugino. The church itself is a hotch-potch of different periods – the front door is Renaissance, the carvings above it Roman and the interior is unexpectedly baroque.

▶ *Rejoin the SS75 heading southwest and turn right on to the SS3 round Foligno to Trevi, about 18km (11 miles) away.*

4 Trevi, Umbria
Magnificently situated on the slopes of a steep hill, dominat-

Ancient Narni, on Umbria's border, was once a fortress-city

ing the Spoletino plain, Trevi is set so high that on approaching it you cannot see it from the car windows. It is a lovely, undiscovered place whose pavements are speckled with mosaic-like arrangements of cobbles, while a maze of winding streets and blind alleys is contained within two sets of medieval walls. The 14th-century Palazzo Comunale in Piazza Mazzini, the site of the town's Pinacoteca (art gallery), contains a mixture of Renaissance paintings by Pinturicchio and Lo Spagna, Roman remains, sculptures and ceramics. You can see Lo Spagna's fresco of the *Life of St Francis* (1512) in the Church of San Martino in Via Augusto Ciufelli on the edge of town. This is thought to be his best painting and it has a contemporary view of Assisi in its background.

Also worth a visit is the 12th-century Church of Sant' Emiliano with its richly decorated altar by Rocca da Vicenza, and if you still have time, take a walk below the town to the Church of Santa Maria delle Lacrime, with its beautiful doorway and fine Umbrian

A modern sample of Gubbio's centuries-old pottery industry

School pictures, including one by Perugino.

▶ *Return to Foligno via the SS3, then follow signs to Montefalco.*

5 Montefalco, Umbria
The pretty little walled hilltown of Montefalco – 'Falcon's Mount' – once boasted more saints than any other town in the region, earning itself the title of 'a little strip of heaven fallen to earth'. With a population of only 6,000, this was quite a feat!

The Church of San Francesco, founded in 1336, contains 15th-century frescos by Benozzo Gozzoli, and work by other Umbrian painters. These frescos are considered so important that the building is no longer used as a church but has become a museum.

Other churches to see are the Gothic Church of Sant'Agostino with its fine selection of Renaissance frescos by local artists, and the baroque Church of Santa Chiara di Montefalco. Here you can see the crumbling remains of Santa Chiara's heart. Montefalco is a tranquil, peaceful place, often called the 'Balcony of Italy'; you should sit in one of its cafés and sample the famed *Sagrantino* wine or

take in the delightful views of the surrounding countryside.

▶ *Head across country, via Mercatello and Bruna, to Spoleto.*

6 Spoleto, Umbria
Spoleto, shadowed by its 14th-century Rocca (castle), is a very old city, rich in evidence of a history that began centuries before the Roman occupation. It has survived sieges, earthquakes, plagues, a period of misrule by the notorious Lucrezia Borgia and World War II bombing. The Duomo (cathedral), built in 1067 but restored in the 12th century, with its splendid doorway and Renaissance porch surrounded with mosaics, is without doubt the most beautiful in Umbria, though the churches of San Gregorio Maggiore, Sant'Eufemia and San Pietro come close. Be sure to visit them all, particularly the latter (just out of town), with its extremely early relief sculptures.

Among Spoleto's many Roman ruins is a partially restored theatre in the vicinity of Piazza della Libertà, which is still used for concerts, and the 1st-century AD Arch of Drusus, in an excellent state of preservation. The imposing Ponte delle Torri (Bridge of the Towers) was erected in the 13th century as an aqueduct over a river gorge (pedestrians only now), and links the town with neighbouring Monteluco. Built of stone, with 10 arches, it is 230m (755 feet) long and 81m (265 feet) high and was probably constructed on the foundations of an earlier Roman aqueduct.

Spoleto can get very busy at peak times, so it is best to plan your visit to avoid these. It is one of the liveliest towns in the region, helped by the annual Festival dei Due Mondi (Festival of the Two Worlds) that takes place here. The festival, in June and July, presents the latest trends in art, music,

theatre, painting and sculpture against the magnificent setting of the ancient town.

The Duomo in Orvieto: detail from the much-admired carved façade

ℹ️ *Piazza della Libertà 7*

▶ *Take the **SS3** south. Bypass Terni, and head for Narni, entering on the **SS3ter**, 43km (27 miles).*

7 Narni, Umbria
Narni, crammed on its hilltop, is so constricted that it has hardly

expanded since Roman times. This solid, stone-built town has an interesting, though ruined, 14th-century Rocca (castle), with fine views in most directions, and the odd-looking Palazzo del Podestà, which was created by joining three fortified tower houses together. Now it houses the local art gallery whose greatest treasure is a *Coronation of the Virgin* by the 15th-century master Ghirlandaio. See the fine inlaid choir stalls and early marble screen in the Romanesque Duomo (cathedral), which, with the Podestà Palace, provides a splendid backdrop to the Corso dell'Anello, a spectacular costumed pageant enacted each May, when horsemen representing the town's rival quarters joust for a coveted prize.

Just below Narni, on the line of the ancient Via Flaminia, are the ruins of the Roman Ponte d'Augusto (Bridge of Augustus) which was originally 120m (400 feet) long and carried the road almost 30m (100 feet) up over the River Nera.

▶ *From Narni, head back towards Terni, turning north on **SS3bis** to Todi, about 45km (28 miles).*

8 Todi, Umbria
Todi occupies a triangular site, still partly surrounded by its rings of Etruscan, Roman and medieval walls, on a ridge above the Tevere (Tiber) valley. The Piazza del Popolo, at the centre of town, is the kind of place where you could sit all day in the sun at one of the cafés and do nothing but watch the world pass by. On one side of the piazza is the Romanesque Duomo (cathedral), on the site

of a former Roman temple to Apollo, while the remaining sides are bounded by a variety of other medieval buildings, in particular the 14th-century Palazzo del Capitano. The sleepy charm of this place is enlivened early in the evening when the residents pour into the piazza for the daily stroll and a chat: then it seems like a drawing room with a party in progress.

You should not leave Todi without visiting Santa Maria della Consolazione, inspired by Bramante's plan for St Peter's in Rome. This domed church on the plan of a Greek cross, is much admired as one of the finest creations of Renaissance architecture. Started in 1508, it took over 100 years to complete.

i *Piazza Umberto I*

▶ *Leave Todi on the **SS448**, and head southwest, around the Lake of Corbara, to Orvieto.*

❼ Orvieto, Umbria
Orvieto's commanding position on a great square rock makes it an amazing sight, visible from miles around. An ideal site for a fort, it was first settled by the Etruscans (who called it *Volsinii*), but they could not withstand the might of the rising new power, and eventually Orvieto fell to Rome. It is a dark, brooding town, dominated by its glorious Gothic-style Duomo (cathedral), which was started in the late 1200s, supposedly to the designs of Arnolfi di Cambio, famed for his Duomo and Palazzo Vecchio in Florence. It was built in alternate courses of black basalt and greyish-yellow limestone, and decorated by the finest artists of the day, to commemorate the Miracle of Bolsena (when the Host started to bleed during a celebration of Mass in the town of Bolsena). The façade, adorned with elaborate sculptures and coloured mosaics, was designed by Lorenzo Maitani of Siena. To appreciate fully, you should view it in bright sunlight, when the effect is quite stunning. Inside, magnificent frescos in the lovely Cappella della Madonna de San Brigio are largely the work of Fra Angelico and, later, Luca Signorelli. The town abounds in interesting monuments: the 11th-century Palazzo Vescovile, an old papal residence; the 12th-century Palazzo del Capitano del Popolo; and the churches of San Domenico, San Lorenzo, Sant'Andrea and San Giovenale are among the best buildings.

Orvieto is famous for its wine, particularly the whites. Signorelli, when painting the Duomo, is said to have asked

---

---

that part of his contract be paid in wine, and the rock beneath the city is honeycombed with caves used to ferment the grapes for the Orvieto vintages.

i *Piazza del Duomo 24*

▶ *Take the **SS448** back towards Todi, then turn left on to the **SS3bis** to Perugia.*

BACK TO NATURE

While you are travelling in Umbria you will undoubtedly notice the kind of countryside which naturalists call *macchia* (*maquis*). This is the characteristic Mediterranean habitat of evergreen trees with a shrubby understorey. As well as its distinctive wild flowers, including several species of orchid and the much more easily spotted, but no less pretty, rock-roses, this habitat contains such creatures as praying mantids, wall lizards and green lizards (look for them basking in the morning sunshine) and lots of snakes (don't worry, they are likely to see you a long time before you see them and beat a quiet retreat!). You probably will not see, but will almost certainly hear, Scop's owls. Their call, delivered for most of the night – usually from trees – is a quite uncanny and unnatural sound, likened by some to sonar bleeps.

View over the heart of Perugia, capital of Umbria

Italy's Best
Kept Secret

It takes hours to get through the Marches region of central Italy on the little country roads but there are breathtaking views. Ancona is the biggest port in the region, running along a natural promontory in the shadow of Monte Conero. Severely damaged by World War II bombs and in a later earthquake, its charms are well hidden.

3/4 DAYS • 406KM • 252 MILES

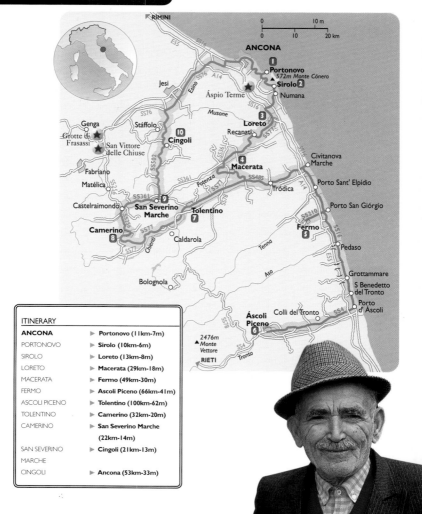

Though mountainous, the Marche region is extremely fertile

i *Via Thaon de Revel 4, Ancona*

▶ *Take the coast road from Ancona going south for about 11km (7 miles) to Portonovo, which itself is 1km (½ mile) off the main road.*

1 Portonovo, Marche
One of the most beautiful stretches of coastline along the Adriatic begins just south of Ancona. Called the Riviera del Conero, it is made up of sheltered beaches which alternate with cliffs dropping straight down into the ocean. The first port of call among the pines and the holm-oaks lodged into the crevices of this area, is Portonovo, a minute settlement whose major attraction, apart from its shoreline and attendant campsites, is the ancient Church of Santa Maria di Portonovo. Built in 1034, it sits among the olives and the scrubland not far from the shore. This Romanesque building is in very good condition and you can clearly see Byzantine influences on its design. It has always been regarded as an architectural gem – the poet Dante mentions it in his *Divina Commedia* (*Divine Comedy*). Also at Portonovo is a reconstructed Napoleonic fortress erected in 1808 and an early 18th-century watch-tower, where the writer Gabriele D'Annunzio often stayed.

▶ *Return to the main road, which winds further south to Sirolo, 10km (6 miles).*

SPECIAL TO...

At Camerino, not far from Portonovo and Sirolo, is Aspio Terme, one of The Marches' important thermal springs. There are six of them on this spot – cold salt-bromo-iodic water good for the treatment of jaded livers, dodgy stomachs and biliary tract diseases.

---

2 Sirolo, Marche
Monte Conero, 572m (1,877 feet) separates Portonovo from Sirolo which is bigger and better equipped as a holiday place. There is a handful of hotels, restaurants and one or two night-clubs and, because this is still the Riviera del Conero, there are also little coves and places to swim. Sirolo has a medieval fortress of the Counts Cortesi, and the local Franciscan convent, now a villa, has two elms planted, according to legend, by St Francis himself on a visit to the town in 1215. In the Church of the Sacrament you will find a lovely local painting of the *Madonna of the Misericordia*, about 1500.

Not far away at Numana, about 1.5km/1 mile further south, go to the Santuario del Crocefisso (Sanctuary of the Cross) and see the venerated Byzantine *Crucifixion*.

FOR CHILDREN

Children would enjoy playing on the beaches at Sirolo. Like many others along this shore, Sirolo's beaches fall gently down to the sea so that the water is shallow for some way out.

▶ *From Numana follow the signs to the SS16. Turn left on to the SS77 for 5km (3 miles) before taking the turn-off for Loreto.*

3 Loreto, Marche
This town has the incredible reputation of being the point at which the Madonna's house, transported by angels from Nazareth to Italy, came down to earth late in the 13th century. This much-venerated relic, which is a simple brick building

thing is built of terracotta-coloured brick, and the homogeneity of its appearance is the town's most striking feature. But there are a host of monuments, mostly Renaissance and baroque. Apart from the 11th-century Duomo (cathedral), there is the even earlier Santa Maria della Porta – look for the Gothic doorway. The Basilica della Misericordia has an interior by Vanvitelli. The Art Gallery adjoining the Church of San Giovanni contains works by local 'Marchegiani' artists, as well as a *Madonna* by Carlo Crivelli, whose style of painting was influenced by Mantegna.

i *Via Garibaldi 87*

FOR HISTORY BUFFS

In the Via Manzoni in Macerata is the Palazzo Compagnoni-Marefoschi, scene of the marriage in 1772 of the 'Young Pretender' to the British throne, Bonnie Prince Charlie, to Louise of Stolberg. Charles, at 52, was no longer 'young' or 'bonnie', and the marriage was a failure.

containing traces of medieval frescos inside, is the final destination of a pilgrimage undertaken by thousands of Italians each year. The Santa Casa (Holy House) is kept in the Santuario della Santa Casa (Sanctuary of the Holy House) and is placed directly under its dome. It is worth noting that the church's baroque façade is one of Italy's finest. Nobody knows who designed the façade, but a whole host of other great names worked on the building: for instance Giuliano da Sangallo was responsible for the cupola and Bramante (one of Italy's greatest Renaissance architects) designed the side chapels.

In the Piazza della Madonna in front of the building is a beautiful loggia designed by Bramante in 1510, and in the middle of the square is a large fountain by Carlo Maderna, one of the architects of St Peter's in

Rome. The sanctuary is brimming over with great works of art. Look out for the frescos by Angelica Kauffmann, who was a founder member of the London Royal Academy, in the right transept chapels. Bramante designed the beautiful marble screen in front of the Santa Casa itself and there are statues by Baccio Bandinelli.

i *Via G Solari 3*

▶ *From Loreto, take the SS77 across country, via Recanati, to Macerata, about 29km (18 miles).*

4 Macerata, Marche
Macerata is one of the oldest university towns in Italy. It crowns a series of low hills and is a quiet place, full of bookshops and hidden restaurants, with narrow streets and stairways. Mostly medieval, every-

▶ *From Macerata, go southeast for about 6km (4 miles) to the SS485, then head back towards the coast for 21km (13 miles). Branch south again on the SS16 for 15km (9 miles) to Porto San Giórgio before turning right on to the SS210, which leads up to Fermo, 7km (4 miles) further.*

5 Fermo, Marche
Fermo is a very pretty hilltown poised above the Adriatic. It has tremendous views over Monti Sibillini and the Gran Sasso peaks in the Abruzzo to one side, and to the sea on the other. As in Macerata, almost everything is of terracotta-coloured brick, in this case primped and cleaned in recent restoration programmes.

Fermo was a relatively important town during Roman times.

In the Via degli Aceti you can see the remains of the 1st-century Piscina Epuratorio, an underground reservoir designed to hold and to clarify rain water. Above ground again, the Duomo has a lovely façade of the 13th to 14th centuries – although most of the rest of the building was rebuilt in the 18th century. Look at St Thomas à Becket's chasuble, woven from Moorish silk in 1116. It was left here by a bishop of Fermo to whom à Becket presented it. In the Palazzo Comunale is a small gallery which contains a painting of the *Nativity* by Rubens. On this building's façade is a weird statue of Pope Sixtus V, once a bishop of Fermo. Other places of interest are the Teatro dell'Aquila (1780) and the Church of San Domenico (1233).

[i] *Piazza del Popolo 5*

▶ *From Fermo, return to the coastal **SS16** and continue south along the coast for 32km (20 miles) until Porto d'Ascoli, at which branch inland on the **SS4** and continue to Ascoli Piceno.*

❻ Ascoli Piceno, Marche
Ascoli Piceno is one of the great towns of The Marches region. There is a lot to see, most of it confined to the Piazza del Popolo, which lies at the centre of town. The early 13th-century Palazzo del Popolo has a later façade by Ascoli Piceno's best known artist, Cola dell'Amatrice. Also in the square is the Church of San Francesco (about 1262) with a statue of Pope Julius II over the south door, and there is the Franciscan Chiostro Grande (Great Cloister) of the mid-16th century, which is now used as a market. The Loggia dei Mercanti was built by the Wool Corporation in the early 1500s.
In the Piazza dell'Arringo you will find the Duomo della Sant'Emidio (cathedral), a largely 12th-century building

with an unfinished façade, also by Cola dell'Amatrice. Look in the chapel on the right of the nave and you will see a beautiful painting by Carlo Crivelli – thought to be his finest work. The treasury contains a silver altar-frontal and an opulent silver reliquary by Pietro Vannini. Beyond the cathedral is the Palazzo Comunale gallery containing works by, among others, Titian and Crivelli.

[i] *Piazza del Popolo 1*

▶ *Retrace your route to, and join, the **SS16** travelling northwards to Civitanova, at which take the **SS485** going inland past the turning to Macerata, continuing for 19km (12 miles) to Tolentino.*

SPECIAL TO...
In Ascoli Piceno a festival is held in August in which local townsfolk don the costumes of 15th-century musicians, soldiers, lords and ladies, and parade through the medieval streets of the town before the tournament known as the Quintana. In this jousting tournament, in which the rules go back to the 14th century, horsemen ride at a figure representing a Saracen.

Palazzo del Popolo, a 13th-century town hall with a graceful Renaissance courtyard, in the heart of Ascoli Piceno

RECOMMENDED WALKS

To the north of Ascoli Piceno, beyond its walls, is the valley of the River Tronto, a pleasant area for walks and picnics – ideal for the family as the terrain is gentle.

7 Tolentino, Marche

Tolentino's medieval centre is far more interesting than its outskirts, which are mostly modern. An ancient bridge known as The Devil's Bridge leads the way to the Basilica di San Nicola da Tolentino, the main reason for visiting the town, which has a beautiful early 15th-century portal by Nanni di Bartolo. In the crypt beneath the church is the tomb of St Nicholas of Tolentino who died in 1305. A great many miracles were attributed to him and in a large chapel on the right side of the basilica you can see his statue by Giorgio da Sebenico. In the cloisters is a small museum of majolica and silver. In the Palazzo Bezzi is the Museum of Caricatures, a collection of hundreds of satirical cartoons from all over the world.

► Continue west from Tolentino via the **SS77** for 23km (14 miles) to a turning on the right for Camerino, a further 9km (6 miles).

8 Camerino, Marche

At Camerino is a massive fortress built by Cesare Borgia, one of the most hated figures of early Italian history. There are also the remains of the Rocca Varano, an early 13th-century castle built by the Varano family, who held the fiefdom of Camerino for about 300 years until 1539. Churches to see include the Duomo (cathedral) San Venanzio with its beautifully executed Renaissance doorway, and the little Church of the Annunziata. The Museo Diocesano

(Diocesan Museum), in Camerino's main square, has a *Madonna* by the Venetian artist Tiepolo, while the town's other museum, the Museo Civico, is filled with works by the local 15th-century painter Girolamo di Giovanni.

► The **SS256** leads northwards towards Castelraimondo. Shortly before Castelraimondo, turn right on to the **SS361** through the town and along the Potenza river, to San Severino Marche, 22km (14 miles).

9 San Severino Marche, Marche

The 16th-century anatomist Bartolomeo Eustachi was born in San Severino Marche. He is best known as the man after whom the Eustachian tube (in the ear) was named, but there is not much in the town to remind you of this fact. You will, however, see the work of a local painter who achieved great fame at the beginning of the 15th century – Lorenzo Salimbeni, who was also born here. Some of his frescos can be seen in the old cathedral, in the old upper town. While you are there, have a quick look into the cloister, then go back down to the Church of San Lorenzo and the Duomo Nuovo (new cathe-

dral), in the lower town. The Duomo Nuovo contains a striking painting of the *Madonna* by one of the great Mannerist painters Pinturicchio. Look in at the art gallery in the Palazzo Comunale where there are works by yet another great 15th-century painter born here – Lorenzo d'Alessandro.

► The **SS502** goes north from San Severino Marche to Cingoli.

St Nicholas' Basilica's 13th- to 14th-century cloisters, Tolentino

10 Cingoli, Marche

Cingoli is a very ancient town famous for its views. Crammed on to the top of a hill, its nickname is 'The Balcony of The Marches'. There is no single great masterpiece to be viewed here, but the little town's small early Renaissance palaces, particularly the Palazzo Castiglione in the Corso Garibaldi and those in the Polisena Quarter, appeal, with their carved entrance portals, their old window surrounds and their general air of antiquity. Narrow stone-paved streets, cupolas and belfries are the predominant characteristics of the town. Look into the church of San Francesco, the proud possessor of a lovely 16th-

BACK TO NATURE

Migrant birds – especially song-birds and birds of prey – pass through Italy each spring and autumn on their way to and from their breeding grounds in northern Europe and the wintering grounds in Africa. Many species follow the coast on their journeys and the Ancona headland is an excellent observation area. Unfortunately, countless millions are shot or trapped in Italy for 'sport'. Warblers and turtle doves suffer particularly badly.

an ancient vaulted structure founded in 1100 by the Benedictines. It contains frescos from the 15th and 16th centuries, and a *Flagellation* by Sebastiano del Piombo, one of the greatest of the Venetian painters and a contemporary of Michelangelo.

[i]   *Via Luigi Ferri 17*

▶ *From Cingoli, the SS502 continues northwards (for 20km/12 miles) towards Jesi. Turn right on to the dual carriageway, which goes back to Ancona, about 33km (20 miles).*

SCENIC ROUTES

For the loveliest coastal views, nothing in The Marches will beat the Riviera del Conero, its cliffs and sheltered coves contrasting with the uninteresting straightness of the east Italian seaboard elsewhere. From Camerino, to the south of Cingoli, you will be able to see the great Gran Sasso ranges of mountains which actually lie in the south of the Abruzzo. The most scenic part of this tour is undoubtedly to be seen from the SS502 in and around Cingoli, about 650m (2,130 feet) above sea-level.

century wooden crucifix, and the church of Sant'Esuperanzio,

San Severino Marche, a modest town but worth a halt

The Northern
Marches

In the 15th century many of the towns in this part of The Marches were in the orbit of the powerful Federico di Montefeltre, Duke of Urbino. Monuments to his reign are scattered around the region. Luckily he was an enlightened individual and there is little from the time of his rule that is not worth visiting or contemplating.

3/4 DAYS • 410KM • 255 MILES

The countryside around Urbania has changed little over the years

wards for 16km (10 miles) leaving it at the Cattolica exit. Join the SS16 travelling south for 5km (3 miles) before branching right on the minor road to Gradara.

FOR HISTORY BUFFS

The Rocca in San Leo once housed, in its prison, the infamous Giuseppe Balsamo, better known as Count Alessandro di Cagliostro, a con-man who, in the 18th century, duped countless gullible people all over Europe into believing that he had discovered a way of turning base metals into gold. Ugly women came to him in the belief that he could make them more beautiful. He was eventually condemned for freemasonry and ended up in San Leo where he died in 1795.

SPECIAL TO...

The provinces of Urbino and Pesaro hold annual weekend 'gastronomia' events, in which chosen restaurants in a variety of locations (San Leo is one) agree to produce a specific menu of local dishes on an agreed date. This keeps obscure culinary traditions going and usually results in a delicious feast. Check the details in the local tourist office.

i *Piazza Rinascimento 1, Urbino*

RECOMMENDED WALK

One very pleasant walk from Urbino – go west for about half and hour – is to the little Church of San Bernardino which is thought to have been designed by Bramante. Inside are the black marble tombs of the Montefeltro dukes.

▶ *The best way to San Leo from Urbino (about 52km/32 miles) is to go cross-country via Sassocorvaro, Macerata Feltria and Montecopiolo.*

❶ San Leo, Marche
San Leo is accessible by a single road cut into the rock. It is a tiny place, poised way above the Marecchia river on a kind of rocky lump. Its castle, the Rocca, in its present state dating from the 15th century, is even higher, dramatically placed on the edge of a cliff overlooking the town. Remarkably well preserved, the little town confines most of its interesting monuments in and near to the central Piazza Dante. The 12th-century Duomo (cathedral) was erected in honour of St Leo. Its interior is dark, solid and unadorned, its mighty structure in a wonderful state of preservation. La Pieve (the parish church), which backs on to the main square, is the oldest church in the vicinity (9th-century possibly). San Leo has good restaurants and the seats in the square's cafés are great for a couple of hours' coffee-drinking and watching the world go by.

▶ *From San Leo, follow the signs to San Marino, then towards Rimini on the SS72 (about 39km/24 miles). Then take the autostrada A14 south-*

❷ Gradara, Marche
You will be able to see the whole of Gradara in about two hours. The old town only contains about 25 buildings and a fortress, the whole lot contained within 14th-century walls which are mostly still intact. You can go inside the castle and see the rooms in which one of the great tragedies of medieval Italy was enacted. The beautiful young Francesca fell in love with her very ugly,

and older husband's younger brother, Paolo. This was almost inevitable, as Paolo had stood proxy for his older sibling at the marriage ceremony. A servant reported the two young lovers to the husband, who murdered them. You can visit the scene of the murder – an event immortalised by Dante in the *Divine Comedy* and by Tchaikovsky in his fantasy overture *Francesca da Rimini*.

Once you have strolled around the castle, peered over its walls to the patchwork countryside all around, and looked in at the glazed terracotta relief by Andrea della Robbia (1435–1525) in the castle chapel, you will have seen all there is to see in Gradara.

▶ *Return to the **SS16** and travel southeast to Pesaro.*

8 Pesaro, Marche

Pesaro is proud of the reputation of Rossini, the composer, who was born here in 1792. It preserves his birthplace at Via Rossini 34, which you can visit, and it holds a series of annual concerts and operas during the annual Rossini festival held towards the end of the summer. You can also go and look at his spinet and his manuscripts in the Conservatorio in Piazza Olivieri.

Pesaro is a large, bustling city, a seaside resort brimming over with people in the summer, as well as a commercial centre. It has some quirky old streets in its older quarters but, because of heavy bombing during World War II, which laid waste large tracts of the city, its monuments are no longer very exceptional. However, the Museo Oliveriano contains local finds from the Etruscan and Roman periods – inscriptions, bronzes, coins; and the Museo Civico has some lovely majolica as well as a *Coronation of the Virgin* by Giovanni Bellini.

ⓘ *Viale Trieste 164*

▶ *From Pesaro, the **SS16** leads to Fano, about 12km (7 miles) away.*

4 Fano, Marche

Fano is much better preserved than its less fortunate neigh-bour. It was an important Roman town and you can still see the Arco d'Augusto (Arch of Augustus), a triumphal arch dating from the 1st century AD. Nearby buildings were constructed over the centuries using material stolen from this Roman relic. In particular, and interesting in its own right, is the 15th-century pawnshop, the Logge di San Michele, at the end of the street named after the arch. The old Church of San Michele, another structure made from recycled antique building materials, preserves a relief carved on to its façade showing what the arch looked like in the 15th century.

In the Church of Santa Maria Nuova are fine altarpieces by Giovanni Santi, Raphael's father, and Perugino, Raphael's teacher. In fact there is also, preserved here, a little panel painting supporting the work of the young Raphael (Raffaelo Sanzio) himself. The Museo Civico (Civic Museum) is equally well endowed with

A massive fortress defended Gradara in medieval times

precious works of art: apart from pieces by Santi Senior, there are works by Domenchino (1581–1641), and the 17th-century artist Mattia Preti.

▶ *Continue along the SS16 for 14km (9 miles) to Marotta, at which branch inland on the SS424 and follow the signs to Corinaldo.*

⑤ Corinaldo, Marche
Corinaldo is a walled medieval village famous as the centre of production of the *Verdicchio* wine, one of the most popular Italian white wines. Behind its 15th-century walls, in which you can still see massive bastions, towers and old gateways – such as the Porta Nuova and the Porta di Sotto – the village is intact and compact, hardly spreading down the hillside at all. From the Porta di Sotto a massive stairway takes you into the village, ascending steeply between the little houses and lateral alleys. It is a quiet place whose churches Sant'Agostino and San Francesco are the most interesting. The latter dates from the 17th century and contains paintings by Claudio Ridolfi.

▶ *The quickest way to Jesi is to go back to the SS16 and continue along it for 24km (15 miles) as far as Rocca Priora, then branch inland on the SS76 and continue to Jesi.*

The cloisters of the Church of Santa Maria Nuove in Fano

⑥ Jesi, Marche
Jesi sits on the plain by the River Esino. Another walled town, it has houses built outside the walls. It is a picturesque place, best known as the birthplace of the Emperor Frederick II (1194–1250) whose empire included Germany and Sicily. If you look on the external façade of the Palazzo Comunale, you will see, carved on a piece of stone, the text of a letter Frederick wrote to the townspeople confirming Jesi's ancient privileges. This old curiosity is not Jesi's only treasure, however.

In the Palazzo Pianetti, which contains the local Pinacoteca (art gallery), you will see a set of paintings by Lorenzo Lotto (1480–1556), which are some of this artist's finest works. While you are in Jesi, you should look at the 14th-century frescos in the Church of San Marco, just outside the town walls.

▶ *Follow the SS76 for about 42km (26 miles) to Fabriano.*

FOR CHILDREN

When bored with the countryside and 'Great Art', youngsters can go skating at Jesi and Fabriano.
Boating at Pesaro is another attraction, while places for riding can be found at Urbino, Urbania, Jesi and Fabriano.

---

⑦ Fabriano, Marche
The paper watermark was invented in Fabriano and this little town has been an important centre for paper-making since the Renaissance. Today banknotes are manufactured here. In a small local museum, housed in the old Convent of San Domenico, you can see how the watermarks are made and also examine a variety of equipment used for doing it over the centuries. The town was the home of Gentile da Fabriano (1370–1427), whose paintings were important examples of the International Gothic style that was to influence the Florentine Renaissance. You can examine some of his work in the art gallery in the Palazzo Vescovile (Episcopal Palace), which also contains the more precious pieces from local churches. The baroque Church of San Benedetto has an extravagant gilt and stucco interior comparable to the elaborate decoration of the nearby Oratorio del Gonfalone (Oratory of the Gonfalone). In particular, this building has a deeply coffered ceiling of the 17th century, with figures of gilded saints and tiny figures of the Apostles. There is gold everywhere – quite out of proportion with the building's very tiny scale.

▶ *From Fabriano, a country road leads northeast to join the SS360 after 15km (9 miles). Continue northeast on the SS360 for a further 10km (6 miles) to Arcevia.*

⑧ Arcevia, Marche
Arcevia sits on a spur of land about 535m (1,755 feet) above sea-level. The site has been inhabited since prehistory, though the oldest remains in evidence today are those from the late Middle Ages to the Renaissance.

As usual, the town is fortified, and its 15th-century walls are mostly intact. Walk down the Via Ramazzani and take in the façades of a range of small coun-

10 Fossombrone, Marche
Fossombrone lies on the lower slopes of a hill near a crumbling fortress and the River Metauro. For a town of its size, it has a remarkable number of things to visit and admire. First of all there are the ruins of the old Roman town. Called *Forum Sempronii* (which, corrupted, gives 'Fossombrone'), they lie about 3km (2 miles) down-stream in San Marino. Until World War II, there were also two Roman bridges but these were destroyed by bombs. There are five churches includ-ing the Duomo (cathedral) and there is an elegant Palazzo Vescovile (Bishop's palace) dating from the 15th century, as well as a museum housed in a mansion which once belonged to the dukes of Urbino.

▶ *From Fossombrone, the SS73bis leads directly to Urbino, about 19km (12 miles).*

Part of the 14th-century walls enclosing the old town of Jesi

try palaces – in particular the Palazzi Anselmi, Pianetti and Manneli-Pianetti. The parish Church of the San Medardo, rebuilt in 1644, can be regarded as the local art gallery, so precious are its contents. Here you can see works by Signorelli, della Robbia and Ridolfi, as well as a variety of works by minor local artists. Giovanni della Robbia's glazed terracotta altar (1513) is the most stunning piece. Sitting on it is the Madonna crowned beneath glazed fruit and flowers. Behind her is the blue glaze, so typical of the della Robbia family's work.

▶ *Make your way from Arcevia via Pergola, about 27km (17 miles), to the SS424 and follow the signs to Cagli, 19km (12 miles). Here, take the SS3 as far as Acqualagna, about 9km (6 miles), then follow the signs to Urbania, a further 17km (11 miles).*

9 Urbania, Marche
About the size of Arcévia, Urbania is a centre for the production of blue jeans – which seems an unlikely activ-ity for this small walled medieval town. Its other activ-ity is the production of majolica (a type of earthenware with coloured decoration on an opaque white glaze), a craft for which it has always been famous. However, it is for neither of these that people tend to come to Urbania. For here, in the old Palazzo Ducale (Ducal Palace), is the famous library of the dukes of Urbino, which is full of drawings and engravings. The palace also contains an art gallery and a small museum. Look in also at the Chiesetta dei Morti (the Little Church of the Dead) where rows of mummies lie embalmed in the shadows.

▶ *Retrace your steps to the SS3, joining it once again at Acqualagna, and continue northeast for 16km (10 miles) to Fossombrone.*

SCENIC ROUTES

This is one of the most scenic tours in Italy. In particular, look out for the sudden views from the road, towards San Leo and Gradara as you approach them.
At dusk, the views from the parapets of Urbino are magical and in the half light the landscapes of local Renaissance painters are never far from the mind.

BACK TO NATURE

The Adriatic Sea is not only a beautiful stretch of water popular for seaside holidays, but is also rich in wildlife. Shorelife is difficult to observe because of the poor tidal range, but out to sea, Cory's and the Mediterranean race of Manx shearwaters can be seen along with gulls, cormorants and dolphins.

LAZIO, CAMPANIA, ABRUZZO

Lazio is centred on Italy's capital, Roma (Rome), home to half the region's population. The landscape surrounding this ancient metropolis ranges from the hills and mountains of the Apennines to the most important lakes in the southern half of Italy – Bolsena, Bracciano, Vico and Nemi. Each of these was once a volcanic crater and the countryside all around them shows signs of turbulence. To the west of Rome is a plain which extends southwards along the Tyrrhenian Sea and here are Lazio's sandiest beaches.

The ancient origins of Italy are closely linked with the history and fortunes of Lazio. Those mysterious early Italians, the Etruscans, had important settlements in the area. Abutting Lazio on the east side is the Abruzzo region where the Apennine peaks reach as high as 2,000m (6,500 feet) above sea-level. This is an essentially rustic zone, a large chunk of which is protected by legislation as a National Park. Much of Abruzzo is territory unseen by conventional travellers to Italy. Close to Rome and easily accessible (there are two motorways), it has none of the star attractions of a Florence or a Milan. Yet hidden in the hills of its awe-inspiring landscape, the region offers glimpses into a fascinating version of normal Italian life.

Campania, Lazio's neighbour to the south, is often known simply as 'the Naples countryside'. Centred on this sprawling city, the region presents two distinct faces to the world – an idyllic coastal belt along the Tyrrhenian Sea and, inland, rough mountain terrain. The Romans considered the Bay of Napoli one of their country's most beautiful spots. The emperors had their villas on its coast and scattered among its islands, and some of the principle attractions of Campania today are those left behind by the Romans. In the brooding shadow of Mount Vesuvius, coastal Campania is still a stunning part of Italy.

A few kilometres inland, however, the contrasts are enormous. Here the mountains and valleys are less visited; travellers, spoiled by the coastal luxuries, never make it to the ancient cities of the Campanian countryside, well worth the effort of the trek inland.

Roma

The ancient capital of the Roman Empire (and now the capital of Italy) was built on seven hills – the Palatine, the Capitoline, Esquiline, Viminal, Caelian, Aventine and Quirinal. Much of its ancient construction survives; you could easily spend a week just visiting the ruins of such imperial splendours as the Colosseum, the Forum and the Baths of Caracallá. In fact, you could divide Rome up into historical periods, spending a week investigating each one. The city centre is full of baroque churches and convents of great magnificence, and countless palaces. Renaissance and baroque, some of them are now galleries or museums; and then there is the Vatican City with Bernini's magnificent Piazza San Pietro (St Peter's Square) and the huge and sumptuous Basilica di San Pietro. The Vatican museums give access to Michelangelo's Sistine Chapel, but they include many other museums and galleries with paintings and sculpture from all periods. Visitors will also find that Rome is a noisy, breathlessly busy city.

Napoli

Napoli (Naples) has one of the most important archaeological collections in the world housed in the Museo Archeologico Nazionale (National Museum). Here are displayed treasures and everyday items – silver and gold objects, household utensils and gladiator's weapons – from Pompeii, Ercolano and all the other ancient sites which proliferate throughout the Campania region. But Naples is also a great seething metropolis where daily life takes place against an ever-present background cacophony of car horns and revving engines. Anarchic

Left: the Colosseum, Rome

traffic jams, headily scented vegetable markets, a vast royal palace (Palazzo Reale) from the 17th century, overdecorated baroque churches the like of which you will never see anywhere else on the Italian mainland – all are facets of this unforgettable city. And here you can dine at pavement cafés on the best pizzas you will taste anywhere – this now universal fast-food dish was Naples' most important gastronomic contribution to the world. A word of warning: Naples is an unruly city as far as traffic is concerned. Buy a detailed map of the city but do not be clever and take short cuts: you are bound to find yourself hopelessly lost after a very short time.

Pescara

Pescara is the Abruzzo's biggest resort. It is also its most popular watering hole,

and you can visit his birth-place – Casa Natale. But apart from this and the very odd Fish Museum, Pescara's principle attractions are down on the beach and the promenades, beyond the 19th-century holiday villas and the pine trees.

L'Áquila

L'Áquila, capital of Abruzzo, was founded by the Hohenstaufen Emperor Frederick II, and the city took the name of the imperial symbol – the eagle. It is well endowed with fine buildings, and the more precious items from its history and from the region have been gathered together in the excellent Museo Nazionale d'Abruzzo (National Museum of Abruzzo), housed in the Castello. From L'Áquila you

The popular resort of Sorrento, on the dramatic Amalfi Coast

partly because it has a very good jazz festival. Gabriele D'Annunzio, poet and dramatist, was born here in 1863,

get the finest views of the Gran Sasso peak of the Apennines which is over 2,000m (6,560 feet) high.

The Apennines
& the Adriatic

This tour takes in maritime Abruzzo, which consists of a coastal plain fringed by thick pinewoods and long sunny beaches. Pescara has 16km (10 miles) of sandy shoreline. Just inland, beyond the fertile valleys close to the sea, are the rugged mountains of the region – you can see the vast Gran Sasso range to the west.

4 DAYS • 373KM • 229 MILES

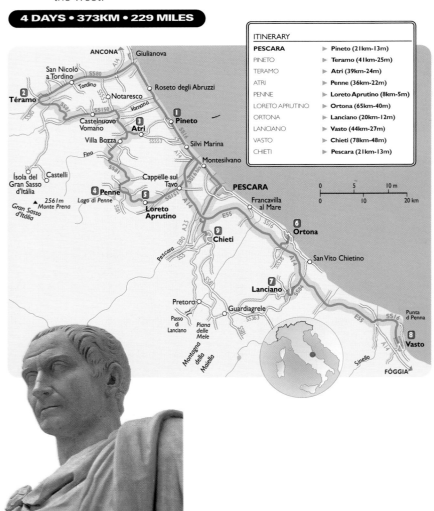

ITINERARY		
PESCARA	▶	**Pineto (21km-13m)**
PINETO	▶	**Teramo (41km-25m)**
TERAMO	▶	**Atri (39km-24m)**
ATRI	▶	**Penne (36km-22m)**
PENNE	▶	**Loreto Aprutino (8km-5m)**
LORETO APRUTINO	▶	**Ortona (65km-40m)**
ORTONA	▶	**Lanciano (20km-12m)**
LANCIANO	▶	**Vasto (44km-27m)**
VASTO	▶	**Chieti (78km-48m)**
CHIETI	▶	**Pescara (21km-13m)**

i *Via N Fabrizi 172, Pescara*

▶ *From Pescara, take the coastal SS16 to Pineto.*

❶ Pineto, Abruzzo

Pineto is one of the prettiest resorts on the Abruzzo coast. Its wide, sandy beach is lined with pines about five trees deep, so that in the heat of summer you can be near the sea without boiling on the sand all day. Many people come here for the camp sites, though if you cannot find places in these there are a great many others to choose from, lining the coastline practically all the way from Pescara to Martinsicuro, about 35km (22 miles) further north from Pineto. There are seafront hotels, some with swimming pools, night-clubs and restaurants where the speciality is *brodetto alla pescarese*, an extremely hot, peppery fish stew. Otherwise, Pineto's chief attraction is the Torre di Cerrano, a tower built by the Emperor Charles V as defence against the threat of the Ottoman Turks in the 16th century.

i *Via G Mazzini*

▶ *From Pineto, continue along the SS16 for 16km (10 miles) as far as Giulianova, at which branch inland on the SS80 in the direction of Teramo, about 25km (15 miles).*

❷ Teramo, Abruzzo

Teramo is the capital of the northern chunk of the Abruzzo. Its special attractions, apart from the amazing views to the Gran Sasso, are its two cathedrals. The earlier Duomo di Santa Maria Aprutiensis is full of assorted decorative bits and pieces – such as the ancient frescos of angels and some splendid Lombard carvings. The 'newer' (12th-century) cathedral has a lovely Romanesque entrance portal, which incorporates sculpture, a rose window and mosaics. Its chief interior attractions are the 15th-century altarpiece by Jacobello del Fiore and a silver altar frontal of the same date by a local artist Nicola da Guardiagrele, which depicts scenes from the New Testament. This artist was obviously much in favour at the time: his work can also be seen on the façade of the building,

One for the connoisseur of hilltowns: Loreto Aprutino

in the statues of the Archangel Gabriel and the Virgin Annunziata balancing on the tops of columns borne by lions. Teramo was originally a Roman city: bits of its ancient past pop up everywhere.

You might have noticed the remains of a Roman house (*domus*) incorporated within Santa Maria, but near the 'new' cathedral are the more modern buildings that grace Teramo's streets these days. Look out for the Casa dei Melatini, a well-preserved 14th-century house, and the old Franciscan Church of the Madonna delle Grazie which houses a painted wooden *Madonna and Child* by Silvestro dall'Aquila, one of the region's most important 15th-century sculptors. The Museo Civico (Civic Museum) in the Villa Comunale contains more works by local artists of the 15th century.

i *Via del Castello 10*

▶ *From Teramo, take the SS81 going southeast for 14km (9 miles) until it cuts the SS150.*

Continue east along this for 13km (8 miles) until a turning on the right for Atri, a further 12km (7 miles).

FOR CHILDREN

About 29km (18 miles) south of Teramo, just off the motorway, is the village of Castelli in whose Institute of Ceramic Art you can see a 100-figure ceramic crib. Highly detailed, this is a remarkable example of the art of crib-making, popular all over the south of Italy, and is fascinating for children.

❸ Atri, Abruzzo

Still in the shadow of the Gran Sasso massif, Atri is another ancient place that was once a Roman colony. You can survey relics of this era of its past among the excavations in the piazza and in the crypt of the Cattedrale dell'Assunta (Cathedral of the Assumption). In the gloom beneath this building are the remains of a Roman *piscina* (pool). The cathedral itself contains some excellent 15th-century frescos of the *Lives of the Virgin and Jesus* by Andrea Delitio, one of the most renowned local painters, and there is an interesting 16th-century tabernacle. But the real treasures of this town are to be found in the cathedral museum – ivories, statues, majolicas and an interesting array of fragments from the much more ancient church that preceded the cathedral.

A wander around Atri should also take in the churches of Sant'Agostino and Sant'Andrea and the courtyard of the Palazzo Acquaviva, once the home of the Dukes of Acquaviva, which dates from the 14th century.

SPECIAL TO...

In Atri is the Parade of Carts, when traditional carts are drawn through town carrying singers and dancers in costume.

▶ *From Atri, the best way to get to Penne is to go across country. Leave the town the way you entered, and after 1.5km (1 mile), follow the signs on the left to Villa Bozza from which follow the signs to the* SS81 *and Penne, about 36km (22 miles) in all.*

RECOMMENDED WALKS

Near Atri, on the outskirts of the town, in fact, and within easy walking distance from it, are the strange *calanchi* rock formations – you cannot miss them. The odd geology of the area has also given rise to caves which were once inhabited by humans.

❹ Penne, Abruzzo

Penne is a small town that sits on a low rise not far from the Lake of Penne. Surprisingly for its size it is full of miniature but majestic palaces and mansions, some baroque, others Renaissance. Just by the Porta San Francesco, the town's main gate, is the Palazzo Castiglione with two tiers of balconies wrapped around with wrought iron. Further up among the old brick-paved streets and alleys is the Palazzo del Bono (in the Via

Pineto's beautiful beach is typical of the Abruzzo coast

The impressive campanile of Atri's Cathedral of the Assumption

Pansa), a lovely two-storeyed Renaissance palace. There is a homogeneity about Penne: churches, houses, palaces and streets are all built of the same material, a reddish brick, which gives the town a warm glow. Penne's cathedral is perhaps the town's least interesting building. It was destroyed in World War II, then rebuilt, but it does have an interesting crypt which has survived from the earlier building. The 18th-century Church of the Annunziata is far more interesting; with its columned façade it is considered to be the most perfect church of its period anywhere in the region.

▶ *Loreto Aprutino is 8km (5 miles) to the southeast.*

5 **Loreto Aprutino,** Abruzzo

Everybody who comes to Loreto Aprutino comes to see the *Last Judgement* fresco in the Church of Santa Maria in Piano.

Here the dead are seen heaving themselves out of their graves, some to end in Hell, the others in Paradise. A centre for the production of olive oil, this is one of the region's prettiest hill-towns; the cottages that make up the bulk of the town are squeezed among churches, whose bell towers can be seen from afar.

At the summit of the town is San Pietro Apostolo with a good Renaissance portal. Near by is the Palazzo Acerbo in which is a small museum housing a stunning collection of antique Abruzzesi ceramics with examples from the very early Middle Ages to the 18th century.

▶ *Take the SS151 towards the coast, branching left on to the SS16bis at Cappelle sul Tavo. Join the A14 north of Montesilvano at the Pescara Nord junction and follow the autostrada south to the exit for Ortona.*

6 **Ortona,** Abruzzo

Most of Ortona was reconstructed after two of the most horrific battles fought during World War II – the battles of the Sangro and Moro rivers in November–December 1943. The Duomo (Cathedral) has been partially rebuilt since, but its lovely 14th-century portal was unscathed. The Palazzo Farnese, begun in 1584 for a visit to the town by Margaret of Parma, also survived. Although unfinished, it is the town's best building, its architect having been Giacomo della Porta, notable as a follower of Michelangelo. Ortona is now the region's largest port with the usual kind of raffish, tangy character to match, particularly in the Terravecchia quarter beside the remains of the Aragonese castle. While the restaurants here are good, you will probably find it more pleasant at the resort of Francavilla a Mare, just 6km (4 miles) to the north, a more popular place to stay and to relax.

▶ *Rejoin the A14 travelling south to the next exit (Lanciano). Lanciano is 7km (4 miles) to the southwest along a minor road.*

7 **Lanciano,** Abruzzo

Lanciano was an important market town with international trade in the Middle Ages. Its medieval nucleus survives, known as Lanciano Vecchia, at the centre of which are the churches of Sant'Agostino and

Penne's main gate

San Biagio. However, in the Città Nuova, the 16th-century 'new town', the Church of Santa Maria Maggiore is far more interesting. Dating mostly from the early 14th century, it has two perfect rose windows and a huge Gothic portal lined with highly decorative columns. Its most spectacular interior fitting is a 15th-century crucifix. The Duomo (cathedral), with its 17th-century belfry, actually sits on the remains of a Roman bridge, dating from the time of the Emperor Diocletian and restored in the 11th century. The only town gate to survive from medieval times is the Porta San Biagio.

FOR HISTORY BUFFS

A few kilometres beyond Lanciano is Guardiagrele, whose most famous inhabitant, Nicola da Guardiagrele, produced some of the region's finest works in gold and silver in the 15th century. In the church here is a silver crucifix by this artist.

▶ *From Lanciano return to the A14 and travel south to the Vasto Nord turn-off. Take the SS16 and follow the signs to Vasto, a distance of 44km (27 miles).*

SCENIC ROUTES

Fine views can be seen on the route via Orsogna from Lanciano to Guardiagrele and the approach to Loreto Aprutino from the Penne side.

8 **Vasto,** Abruzzo

The fine old town of Vasto is dominated by a huge 13th-century fortress which looks on to the Piazza Rossetti, the centre of town and the site of a former Roman amphitheatre. It sits on the edge of the medieval town whose limits are still marked out in part by walls, punctured occasionally by old gates. The aspect of the town changes as you pass from the newer part to the old: whereas the streets are wider and more elegant outside the Porta Santa Maria or Porta Nuova, inside

the walls, beyond these gates, they are narrow and tortuous, full of strange little squares and old doorways. The older precincts contain the more interesting churches, particularly San Giuseppe (the cathedral) and Santa Maria Maggiore. The 13th-century cathedral has a good Gothic portal.

The remains of another church, San Pietro, can be found not far from the Palazzo d'Avalos. In the lunette of the entrance portal – all that remains of the church – is an interesting sculpture of the crucified Christ wearing a regal crown rather than the usual crown of thorns.

Vasto has a Museo Civico (Civic Museum) whose section on the Roman antecedents of the town is the most interesting. One last fact about the town – in the Piazza Diomede is a statue of the English Pre-Raphaelite poet and painter Dante Gabriel Rossetti, whose family originated in Vasto.

▶ *Rejoin and travel north on the A14 until the Pescara Ovest-Chieti turn-off, 78km (48 miles).*

🔟 **Chieti,** Abruzzo

Chieti has a number of star attractions which make it an indispensable part of the tour. You should set aside two hours to see the excellent Museo Archeologico degli Abruzzi (Archaeological Museum), whose chief exhibit, the peculiar-looking *Warrior of Capestrano*, is an over-lifesize figure probably dating from the 6th century BC, accompanied by an as yet undeciphered inscription. Substantial parts of the town's Roman baths have survived, including a room which retains its mosaic pavement.

The Roman theme continues throughout the town with the ruins of three small temples, a large rock-cut cistern (the former reservoir) and the intact original early town layout (of the Civitella district, the oldest section of Chieti). If you examine these then look at the Roman artefacts in the museum, you should be able to build up a good picture of ancient Chieti. Another important period of Chieti's history is represented by the Gothic Cathedral of San Giustino, which contains a silver statue of St Justin.

SPECIAL TO...

Chieti's Good Friday Procession is one of Italy's oldest Easter ceremonies. Participants in the torchlight procession wear the black tunic and grey mantle of penitents.

RECOMMENDED WALKS

From Passo di Lanciano, a small resort in the Abruzzo massif between Chieti and Lanciano, it is possible to enjoy mountain walking in the Maiella range, which reaches over 2,700m (9,000 feet).

BACK TO NATURE

From Chieti and Lanciano it is not far into the mountains of Abruzzo. The area is rich in woodlands, including the pinewoods of Piana delle Mele and Valle delle Monache. Here, look for birds of prey, including perhaps even a red kite or a golden eagle soaring overhead, and warblers, nightingales and other songbirds among the trees themselves.

ℹ️ *Via B Spaventa 29*

▶ *Return towards the A14 and follow the signs to Pescara, about 21km (13 miles).*

The Aragonese castle at Ortona dates from the 15th century

Abruzzo – the
Remote Interior

Although geographically not very far from some of Italy's biggest cities, the Abruzzo is a largely untamed region. This tour introduces you to Italy's natural environment at its wildest. Centred on the area between southern Italy's highest mountain, the Gran Sasso, and the Abruzzo National Park, most of the smaller towns on this tour have managed to escape the march of progress.

3 DAYS • 362KM • 226 MILES

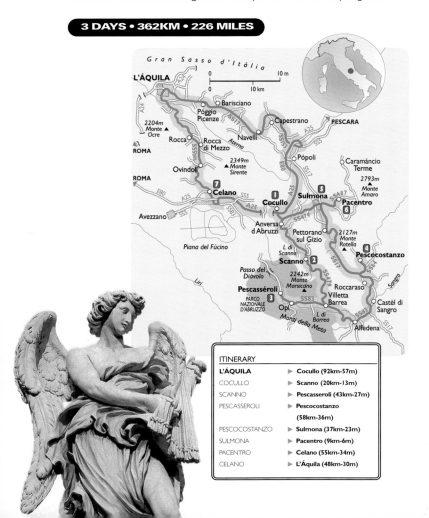

ITINERARY		
L'ÁQUILA	▶	**Cocullo (92km-57m)**
COCULLO	▶	**Scanno (20km-13m)**
SCANNO	▶	**Pescasseroli (43km-27m)**
PESCASSEROLI	▶	**Pescocostanzo**
		(58km-36m)
PESCOCOSTANZO	▶	**Sulmona (37km-23m)**
SULMONA	▶	**Pacentro (9km-6m)**
PACENTRO	▶	**Celano (55km-34m)**
CELANO	▶	**L'Áquila (48km-30m)**

i *Piazza Santa Maria di Paganica 5, L'Áquila*

▶ *From L'Áquila, take the SS17 for 34km (21 miles) until Navelli, at which bear left via the SS153 to the SS5. Turn left and after 2km (1 mile) join the A25 at the Bussi junction. Travel in the direction of Roma for 30km (18 miles) until Cocullo, which lies just 3km (2 miles) off the autostrada.*

❶ Cocullo, Abruzzo
Cocullo is a small rural town full of ancient mud-coloured houses clinging to the side of a hill beneath the spire of a church. It has one main street, a single piazza and an important sanctuary dedicated to San Domenico Abate. The town's patron saint and a hermit who, like St

Autostrada viaduct near Scanno gives access to the mountains

Francis, made 'friends' with animals, he used to live in a cave that still exists beneath the sanctuary. The sanctuary itself contained the painted wooden statue of the hermit which, in 1981, following an earthquake, was transferred further up the hill, to an ancient chapel whose miniature pilastered façade faces the main piazza.

SPECIAL TO...

Cocullo holds the Processione dei Serpari which takes place in the town every year on the first Thursday in May. Snakes (non-poisonous) are collected from the surrounding countryside then flung at the statue of San Domenico Abate. Those that cling on are carried around the town entwined around the statue – the aim is to touch one. If you do, the villagers say you will have a longer life.

▶ *Cross over the A25 and go south, following the little country road via Anversa degli Abruzzi to Scanno, 20km (13 miles).*

❷ Scanno, Abruzzo
Scanno, which overlooks the attractive Lago (Lake) di Scanno, is one of the most popular places in the region, especially for summer holidays. There are hotels, and places to swim, eat and relax. At the same time, Scanno itself is a perfectly preserved medieval hilltown. The old town sits apart from the modern outskirts, partly because it crowns the pinnacle of a low rise on the side of a hill. A map on a signboard as you enter the town suggests a route through its centre (very small). This will take you past Santa Maria della Valle, a medieval church built on the remains of a pagan temple, the 16th-century Fontana di Saracco (Saracco Fountain) and the little Church of Santa Maria di Constantinopoli, which contains a fresco of the *Madonna Enthroned*, signed 'De Ciollis AD 1478'.

There are other churches squeezed into oddly-shaped little squares as well as Renaissance and baroque houses and small noble palaces. There are also ancient mansions in whose windows you sometimes catch glimpses of old women in costume mending clothes or embroidering. Other characteristic features are the external staircases on to steep streets, arches and dark passages. Scanno has much else to offer: superb landscape views; folklore; local arts and handicrafts, such as lace-making and the production of gold and silver jewellery (beautiful filigree earrings for example); and a handful of delicatessen which cater for tourists, selling local wine, bottled peppers, sausages and local cheeses.

▶ *From Scanno, follow the SS479 south for about 7km (4½ miles) to Villetta Barrea*

The hilltop above Celano is topped by a massive castle

at which turn right on to the SS83, following the signs to Pescasseroli, 16km (10 miles).

SPECIAL TO...

In Scanno, the women's costumes are little different from medieval garb. They take the form of long patterned dresses and turban-like headdresses. The older women often still wear them for every-day work, but many younger ones bring them out of wraps only for special occasions.

8 Pescasseroli, Abruzzo
Pescasseroli lies within the confines of the Parco Nazionale d'Abruzzo (Abruzzo National Park). Although its principal attraction is as the starting point for walks and expeditions into the mountains and valleys of the park, it does also have a handful of interesting buildings. The parish church has been added to over the years, having started life in the 8th century as part of a monastery. It has a simple Gothic entrance portal

and inside, in the Cappella della Madonna Nera (Chapel of the Black Madonna), is a very early wooden statue of the Madonna carved from black wood. In the Strada Valle del Fiume is one of the town's earliest remaining houses and one or two slightly later characteristic baronial palaces.

In the Piazza Benedetto Croce is the Palazzo Sipari, birthplace of Pescasseroli's most famous inhabitant, the philosopher Benedetto Croce, who was born here in 1866. The Casa Comunale preserves his manuscripts. As you wander through the town, look out for old, carved stone doorways and windows – in particular notice the Gothic mullioned window in the Piazza Umberto I which is thought to have come from Pescasseroli's castle. For winter visitors there are ski runs in the nearby mountains – on Monte Ceraso and Monte Vitelle.

ⓘ *Via Piave*

▶ *Go back via Villetta Barrea, continuing on the SS83 to its junction with the SS17. Follow this road northwards for about 15km (9 miles), at which branch off on the SS84*

and follow the signs to Pescocostanzo, about 5km (3 miles).

FOR CHILDREN

Organised riding lessons can be had at equitation centres in and around Pescasseroli in the Abruzzo National Park. Also available are guided rides on horseback through the countryside – for adults and children.

BACK TO NATURE

Accessible from Pescasseroli via the Sangro Valley, the Parco Nazionale d'Abruzzo is a region of wooded slopes and mountains offering a last refuge for the Italian race of the European brown bear and chamois as well as the European wolf.
The alpine meadows are a riot of colour in the spring and summer and golden eagles, goshawks and peregrines are regularly seen. Mountain birds are well represented at high altitudes.

FOR HISTORY BUFFS

At Alfedana, on the way to Pescocostanzo, are the ruins of the ancient Samnite town of *Aufidena* – you can see the cyclopean walls (built with enormous stone blocks) above the river and the ancient necropolis. The Samnites were an ancient Italian people who flourished in the 4th century BC. They came into conflict with the Romans, who eventually crushed them in 82 BC.

4 Pescocostanzo, Abruzzo
The collegiate Church of Santa Maria del Colle (or Collegiata) in Pescocostanzo, is one of the most beautiful churches in the

Corso Ovidio in Sulmona: the poet Ovid was born here

Abruzzo – even though it was badly damaged during World War II. Having been started in

the 13th century, it was rebuilt after an earthquake 200 years later. Nowadays its most beautiful components are the late 17th-century wrought-iron gates to the Chapel of the Sacrament, and the gilded and painted wooden ceiling of the nave. Look out for the medieval wooden statue of Santa Maria del Colle incorporated in a niche of the high altar.

Pescocostanzo is an unusual place: it seems bland, even uninteresting at first, but it has a surprising number of worth-while buildings. The principal piazza has a 16th-century Palazzo Comunale and there is an array of mansions in the Corso Roma – Palazzo Grilli and Palazzo Mansi in particular – and in the Via della Fontana are Palazzo Colecchi, Palazzo Ricciardelli and Palazzo Mosca. You sometimes see local women wearing the town's traditional costume – bright red skirts, lace aprons and dark bodices in

brown, blue or black, decorated with gold thread. Local handicrafts here are the same as those in Scanno. Once a wealthy town, Pescocostanzo was at one time controlled by Vittoria Colonna, patroness of Michelangelo and a member of the great Roman Colonna family.

[i] *Piazza Umberto I*

▶ *Return to the SS17, then continue northwards via Pettorano to Sulmona.*

SCENIC ROUTES

Perhaps the most scenic parts of this tour are the following:
– the first 10km (6 miles) of the road by which you leave Scanno, going south. You might be forgiven for thinking yourself in Scotland;
– the famous Passo del Diavolo (the Devil's Pass), just north of Pescasseroli. Although this is not strictly part of the tour route, it is worth a detour to drive at least a section of it. The pass takes you through part of the Parco Nazionale d'Abruzzo (Abruzzo National Park).

5 Sulmona, Abruzzo
Sulmona is the biggest town (apart from L'Áquila) on the tour. Its situation at the centre of a small plain surrounded by high mountains is perhaps what visitors find most attractive about it, and it makes an ideal base for excursions into the Abruzzo national park. As the birthplace of Ovid, the great Roman poet (43 BC–AD 17), however, and with its complement of old buildings, it has a decidedly antique air. The church and palace of Santa Maria Annunziata are perhaps the finest buildings. Originally a mixture of Gothic and Renaissance styles, the exteriors were rebuilt in baroque style early in the 18th century. The palace is the finer. Its façade has richly carved elements, statues

– in particular the lunette figures of the *Madonna and Child*, once gilded and painted – and delicate tracery (see the first-floor windows). Today the palace houses the town's museum with local paintings and goldsmiths' work.

Running through the centre of town is the old aqueduct, constructed in the mid-13th century. It wends its way through Piazza Garibaldi on Gothic arches, adjacent to the Church of San Francesco della Scarpa. Sulmona's best-known product is confetti, not coloured paper but sugared almonds which are handed out at weddings and christenings.

i *Via Roma 21*

▶ *Take the **SS487**, going east to Pacentro, 9km (6 miles).*

6 **Pacentro,** Abruzzo
Pacentro is just one of a clutch of pretty hilltowns in the vicinity of Sulmona. Its ancient centre focuses on the Castello Cantelmo with its handful of surviving towers. Beneath these and the church steeple, the rustic houses, a collection of sandy-coloured blocks, sit crammed together, linked by tiny weaving passages and alleys.

Further north is Caramancio Terme, a hilltown resort with sulphur baths. It lies at the very heart of the Maiella mountains. Caramancio has a lovely parish church, Santa Maria Maggiore, with a fine late 15th-century portal and reliquary by local master Nicola da Guardiagrele.

▶ *From Pacentro, return to Sulmona, then take the **SS479** via Anversa degli Abruzzi in the direction of Roma for 20km (12½ miles), exiting at the Aielli-Celano turn-off, and follow the signs to Celano.*

7 **Celano,** Abruzzo
Celano is another lovely hilltown, this time overlooking the Fucino Basin, the most fertile

piece of Abruzzo countryside, in antiquity a lake. The little town clusters beneath the Castello Piccolomini, which was begun in 1392. This imposing building was restored after an earthquake (along with Celano's churches) earlier this century and today has regained its appearance as a formidable example of a feudal power base, in this case of the Piccolomini family. Not far from Celano is the Gole di Celano, a spectacular, narrow and very deep gorge – or canyon – containing a torrent. It runs down from the direction of Monte Sirente towards the town.

▶ *From Celano, take the **SS5bis** back to L'Áquila, 48km (30 miles).*

RECOMMENDED
WALKS

The best walks on this tour are to be had in the Parco Nazionale d'Abruzzo (Abruzzo National Park). Pick up trail maps at Pescasseroli – there are special trails as well as refuge huts should you want to stay overnight.

Market day in L' Áquila

Roman
Country Retreats

The upper echelons of Roman society have always relaxed in villas and secluded countryside retreats just outside Roma (Rome). There are all kinds of villas and castles from Emperor Hadrian's ruined country palace at Tivoli to Pope John Paul II's country house at Castel Gandolfo. But there are also more 20th-century forms of relaxation available on the beaches at Ostia, Gaeta and Sperlonga. Rome itself has a variety of palaces and villas that can be visited.

4 DAYS • 483KM • 300 MILES

ITINERARY		
ROMA	▶	**Tivoli** (32km-20m)
TIVOLI	▶	**Anticoli Corrado**
		(28km-17m)
ANTICOLI CORRADO	▶	**Subiaco** (21km-13m)
SUBIACO	▶	**Gaeta** (201km-125m)
GAETA	▶	**Sperlonga** (16km-10m)
SPERLONGA	▶	**Castel Gandolfo**
		(98km-61m)
CASTEL GANDOLFO	▶	**Frascati** (19km-12m)
FRASCATI	▶	**Ostia** (40km-25m)
OSTIA	▶	**Roma** (28km-17m)

i *Via Parigi 5, Roma*

▶ *From the centre of Roma,
the **SS5** goes east for 32km
(20 miles) to Tivoli.*

❶ Tivoli, Lazio

Tivoli sits on a wide spur of
Monte Ripoli just before Lazio
becomes really mountainous.
The town grew up as a strategic
point on an ancient route from
the east to Rome. Today it is
largely associated with the Villa
Adriano (Hadrian's Villa), built
by the Emperor Hadrian.
Construction began at his acces-
sion to the imperial throne and
continued until AD 134. Here
the Emperor set about recon-
structing buildings he had seen
on his foreign travels, such as
the Canopic Temple at
Alexandria and Plato's Academy
in Athens. But this huge villa,
the biggest ever in Italy, also
contained libraries, baths,
temples and theatres, and there
was even a little private palace
built on an island in a huge pool
and surrounded by a colonnade.
The richness of the complex is
demonstrated by the enormous
quantity and excellent quality
of the sculpture which has been
found on this site over the
centuries. Most of it has ended
up in the Vatican Museum in
Rome.

During the Renaissance other
villas were built at Tivoli by rich
cardinals. The most sumptuous
is the Villa d'Este, built by
Ippolito d'Este. The gardens
here are more elaborate than
the actual buildings; a river was
diverted to provide water for
countless fountains and a huge
variety of cascades and pools.
The Villa Gregoriana is another
place worth a visit, with a fine
waterfall by the great architect
and sculptor Bernini, formed by
the diversion of the River
Aniene.

i *Largo Garibaldi*

▶ *Continue along the **SS5** from
Tivoli for 23km (14 miles)
until the turning on the right
to Anticoli Corrado.*

❷ Anticoli Corrado, Lazio

This is a lovely hilltown poised
dramatically on an eminence
dominating the countryside all
around. It has remained
completely unspoilt by the
passage of time and has for
years been the destination of
painters in search of sublime
landscape scenes. Anticoli
Corrado's houses are mostly
medieval with small windows
and outside staircases. The
Church of San Pietro preserves
fragments of its early mosaic
floor.

▶ *From Anticoli Corrado return
to the **SS5** and turn right.
Shortly after, branch right and
follow the winding country
road (**SS411**) southeast, past
the hamlet of Agosta to
Subiaco, a total of 21km
(13 miles).*

Ceiling fresco from St Benedict's monastery church at Subiaco

The impressive Roman ruins of Ostia Antica

SCENIC ROUTES

The road from Anticoli to Subiaco goes through one of the most mountainous parts of Lazio. Look at the views, up to the left, to Monte Simbruini. Particularly fine is the approach to, and views from, Anticoli Corrado. From here you can see over the artists' landscape to the village of Saracinesco and Marano Equo.

3 Subiaco, Lazio

One of an isolated group of interesting little places on the edge of the Simbruini mountains, Subiaco has some very ancient buildings, most of which have something to do with St Benedict. This saint retired here late in the 5th century to write his *Rule* which was to heavily influence Christian monasticism. Subiaco originally had 12 monasteries organised by Benedict. Much later, in the atmosphere of piety and learning that these engendered, the first printed books in Italy were made (1464). While not much remains of the early illustrious period of St Benedict himself, there is the Monastery of Santa Scolastica (Benedict's sister) which has three cloisters. Of St Benedict's own monastery, San Benedetto, high upon a rocky site, all that remains are two churches, one carved out of the rock, with frescos of varying ages.

Subiaco is a quiet, interesting place and well worth the visit. While you are there, you could visit the nearby gorge of the River Aniene, where there is a lake with a waterfall that might have been the work of the Emperor Nero who once had a villa at Subiaco (*Sublaqueum*).

▶ *Retrace the route via the SS411 to the SS5. Head for Roma, but after 9km (6 miles) join the A24 at the Vicovaro-Mandela junction, continuing towards Roma. About 22km (14 miles) along the autostrada, turn on to the A1 heading towards Naples. Continue on the A1 for 106km (66 miles) until the Cassino turning. Follow the signs to Gaeta via the SS630.*

4 Gaeta, Lazio

The old town of Gaeta sits at the very end of a promontory jutting out into the Tyrrhenian Sea. This ancient centre still stands behind its old walls and remains largely medieval. There is plenty to see here, and it might be an idea to stay, as the beaches, the restaurants and the daily life of this seaside town are lively and varied. Apart from the Duomo (Sant'Erasmo), there is a 13th-century fortress and a maze of little ancient alleys and streets harbouring churches, old doorways and quirky little squares full of cats. The cathedral itself has been rebuilt at various times

Fountain in Tivoli's Villa d'Este

but its campanile (bell tower), with its decorative upper parts, is from about 1148.

A great rock known as Torre d'Orlando (the Tower of Orlando) dominates Gaeta and on it is the circular mausoleum of the Roman consul Lucius Munatius Plancus, who died at Gaeta in 22 BC. Mount Orlando divides ancient Gaeta, called *Sezione Erasmo*, from the newer part of town. This is the Porto Salvo, consisting of a series of narrow, straight streets of brightly painted houses and lots of wrought-iron balconies.

ⓘ *Piazza Traniello*

FOR HISTORY BUFFS

Near Gaeta (20km/12 miles going south on the SS213) are the remains of *Minturnae*, a Roman town founded in 295 BC. You can visit the excavations which include an aqueduct, theatre and forum, and the Antiquarium which contains memorable sculptures. Closer to Gaeta, just before Formia, is the so-called Tomb of Cicero. The great orator and writer was killed in 43 BC near his villa at Formia. Both of these monuments have the added attraction of being very near to beaches.

▶ Take the **SS213** from Gaeta to Sperlonga, 16km (10 miles).

🄻 Sperlonga, Lazio

The coastline from Gaeta to Sperlonga is beautiful, with many coves and promontories. Like Gaeta, Sperlonga sits on a spur of land that juts out into the Tyrrhenian Sea. Its centre is consistently medieval. Near by is the Grotta di Tiberio (Tiberius' Cave), where the emperor is said to have made merry in his own particular way. There is also the emperor's villa, and some good classical sculpture in the Museo

Archeologico Nazionale di Sperlonga.

▶ From Sperlonga, continue along the **SS213** to Terracina, then take the **SS7** for 80km (50 miles) to Castel Gandolfo, leaving the **SS7** and following the signs from Albano Laziale.

🄶 Castel Gandolfo, Lazio

Castel Gandolfo is where the Pope has his summer residence. Both town and papal palace are poised on a ridge above Lago (Lake) Albano and both come alive each year from July to September when the papal court transfers itself there from the Vatican City. All year round, however, the Swiss Guards are pacing up and down at the palace entrance, which faces a

large square full of cafés and little shops. Entry to Castel Gandolfo, which takes its name from the castle built on the site of the present papal palace by the Gandolfi dukes in the 12th century, is via a magnificent 16th-century doorway. After resting in the square by the palace, visit the Church of San Tommaso di Villanova by Bernini, inside which are frescos by Pietro da Cortona. Both Bernini and da Cortona were among the founders of the Roman high baroque style.

From any number of points around the town you can look down over Lago Albano, a lake of volcanic origin that was chosen in the 1960s as the venue for the Olympic Games' rowing competitions. The

retreats have been a part of Frascati's landscape since ancient Republican times when wealthy Romans settled at nearby *Tusculo*, an even more ancient city, now ruined, some distance up the slope behind modern Frascati.

The villas at Frascati date mostly from the 16th and 17th centuries. Most are still private and are not normally accessible, but some, like the Villa Falconieri, can be visited with prior permission. One of the greatest late baroque architects, Borromini, was responsible for parts of its design, though it was unfinished at the time of his death.

The Villa Aldobrandini is the most spectacular here. Around 1,600 plans were made to bring water to the villa and a large cascade and water theatre were constructed. You can see the villa from the road and at odd times it is open to the public. The town itself has a pretty cathedral (San Pietro) built in 1598.

Frascati is also famous for its white wine, which has a touch of almond flavour in its after-taste.

☐ *Piazza G Marconi 1*

installations built at the time are still in use and it is a lovely place to swim. All around are thick woodlands of oaks and chestnuts and there are also some ancient remains in the form of the Bagni di Diana (Baths of Diana) and the Villa dell'Imperatore Domiziano (Villa of the Emperor Domitian) – follow the yellow signs from the centre of town to find these.

☐ *Piazza Libertà 5*

▶ *From Castel Gandolfo, rejoin and continue along the SS7 to Frattocchie (about 4km/2½ miles) then branch right across country for about 9km (5½ miles), past the SS511, to the SS215, turning right for Frascati.*

7 Frascati, Lazio

This little country town is famous not for the buildings in its centre, but for the country retreats in the hills surrounding it. Although Frascati itself is medieval, the existing villas are much later. However, villa

▶ *From Frascati, return on the SS215 to the GRA encircling Roma and continue clockwise on it for 18km (11 miles)*

Gaeta's popular beach on the Tyrrhenian Sea

and there is one, the Casa di Diana (House of Diana), which still has its first floor intact, which is very unusual.

You could spend hours in Ostia Antica. There is a lot to see but make sure you pick up a map of the city before you go and plan a route around it. The Museo Ostiense contains the portable artefacts from the site.

The Lido di Ostia is the closest seaside resort to Rome and as such is very popular. However, over the years it has become immensely crowded and commercialised, and the water and sand are often dangerously polluted. A safe bet for swimming in the area are the beaches east and west of Sperlonga, to the southeast.

until the turning left to the **SS8**, *bound for Ostia and the sea.*

Some of the houses have lovely mosaic floors – see the Casa di Apuleio (House of Apuleius) –

▶ *From Ostia, the* **SS8** *goes directly back to the centre of Roma.*

8 Ostia, Lazio

Ostia, the port of Rome, offers two contrasting attractions: the archaeological site of Ostia Antica and Lido di Ostia.
The old port of Ostia Antica, now Italy's best preserved Roman town after Pompeii, was established in about 338 BC when Rome needed to establish a settlement to supervise naval traffic and protect the mouth of the Tevere (Tiber) from raids by Tyrrhenian pirates. But old Ostia saw further construction right up to the 4th century AD, when it was abandoned.
A visit should start perhaps at the Porta Romana (the Roman Gate), past the statue of Minerva Victoria and the forum. There are some re-erected columns of temples in the forum and a little further on are the Terme di Nettuno (Baths of Neptune) with their installations for heating. There is also a small restored theatre capable of holding 3,000 spectators.

View over the quiet, medieval town of Subiaco

The Roman
Countryside

North of Roma (Rome) the countryside is contorted into weird shapes by the prehistoric upheavals that took place beneath the earth's surface. It has a dour brooding aspect, heightened by the fact that the ancient towns in this area are built of local purple-black volcanic rock.

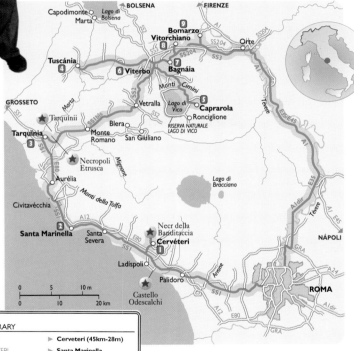

3 DAYS • 362KM • 226 MILES

ⓘ *Via Parigi 5, Roma*

▶ *From Roma, take the SS1 going west towards the coast for 28km (17 miles) until the turning inland for Cerveteri.*

❶ Cerveteri, Lazio

Under the name of *Caere*, Cerveteri was one of the richest Etruscan towns as long ago as the 7th century BC. Today, however, what you see is largely medieval. Its old walls still exist as does the Rocca (castle) of the Orsini, later altered for the Ruspoli family. But it is for the Etruscan remains that Cerveteri is important. A great deal survives here from the period including an extensive necropolis, the Banditaccia Necropolis, that has yielded important treasures – jewellery and other elegant gold objects. The Banditaccia Necropolis was laid out like a town and if you get a map on entering the site, you can walk down its principal streets and visit a great number of old family burial chambers including the Tomba dei Rilievi (Tomb of the Reliefs) which is covered in painted bas-reliefs of cooking utensils and other household objects. Another, called the Tomba degli Scudi e delle Sedie (Tomb of the Shields and Chairs) reflects the appearance of an Etruscan house. This is a rare find. You will never see the actual remains of an Etruscan house anywhere because they were built of wood, plaster or terracotta, and they never survived. Look out for the Castello Odescalchi at Ladispoli. The Odescalchi family were a prominent Roman family whose castles litter the countryside around Rome.

▶ *From Cerveteri, return to, and turn right on to the SS1 which hugs the coast for 20km (12½ miles) until Santa Marinella.*

❷ Santa Marinella, Lazio

Santa Marinella is a pleasant beach resort that provides a very welcome diversion off the

Formal beauty in the garden of the Villa Lante, Bagnaia

exhausting trail of the area's history. But even this place is located on Roman foundations, though there is a big castle here which was built by the Odescalchi family during the late Renaissance period.

▶ *Continue along the SS1 for 30km (19 miles) to Tarquinia.*

❸ Tarquinia, Lazio

Modern Tarquinia stands on a hill not far from Etruscan *Tarquinii*, which was built on another hill to the east. There is a lot to see in both places. Perhaps you could visit the newer town first: there are some pretty churches and picturesque medieval streets, particularly around the Church of San Pancrazio. The Romanesque Church of Santa Maria Castello (begun in 1121) has a lovely façade by Pietro di Ranuccio. The Museo

Nazionale Tarquiniese, housed in the 15th-century Gothic Palazzo Vitelleschi, contains an extraordinary collection of objects, including sarcophagi from the Etruscan and Roman periods as well as the celebrated terracotta winged horses from a temple frieze dating from the end of the 4th century BC. The best of the 5th-century BC tomb paintings from the Etruscan period are also kept here: these include 'the Chariots', 'the Ship' and 'the Sofa'.

No visit would be complete, however, without seeing at least some of the old tombs themselves. The necropolis is all that has survived from the old city, and on the walls of the tombs you will see some of the best art ever produced by these mysterious people. If time is short, make for the tombs of 'the Lionesses', 'the Augurs' and 'the Leopards'.

Piazza Cavour 1

FOR HISTORY BUFFS

On the way from Tarquinia to Tuscania, drop in on the tombs and catacombs cut out of the rock at Blera, about 12km (7½ miles) south of Vertralla. Nearby San Giuliano has one of the most important rock necropolises in the area; one tomb has a chamber decorated with reproductions of the wooden beams of a genuine habitation.
Some of the tombs date back to the 8th century BC.
The town to which the necropolis belonged was connected to Blera in Etruscan times by roads, cut into the soft rock. Magnificent rock-cut tombs can also be seen at Norchia, north of Blera, characterised by great façades with false entrances.

▶ It is 5km (3 miles) southeast to the **SS1bis**. Follow this to Vetralla, 32km (20 miles), then change to the **SS2** for 13km (8 miles) to Viterbo. Follow the signs to Tuscania, 26km (16 miles) westwards.

SCENIC ROUTES

On the approach to Tuscania, the landscape is unusual – flat and with bamboo – quite unlike any other part of Lazio. The views from the ramparts of Bomarzo are spectacular. Look for Vitorchiano to the southwest.
On the stretch of the A1 from Orte to Rome, look back and see the characteristic Lazio hilltowns littering the landscape.

❹ **Tuscania,** Lazio

Tuscania is another town of great antiquity, though the visible remains of its past are confined, for the most part, to the medieval period. Here you can view the Etruscan past in

the Museo Archeologico (Archaeological Museum). You can also see a section of the ancient road, the Via Clodia, that once connected Rome with the Etruscan cities further north, in Tuscany.

But the real treasures of the town are the fascinating little churches of San Pietro and Santa Maria Maggiore. Both are very ancient foundations (8th century), added to in the 11th, 12th and 13th centuries.

Romanesque San Pietro is one of the most important churches of its age in Italy and is especially noteworthy for its unusual sculpted façade – look at the shallow relief figures and plants around the rose window above the central door. There are early sculpted panels on the interior and an ancient crypt constructed using columns, some of which are Roman.

Santa Maria Maggiore also has some excellent, early sculpture, including the work on its entrance portal, a lovely rose window and an old pulpit.

▶ Go back to Viterbo, then follow the signs south, in the direction of Lago di Vico (Lake Vico), to Caprarola – from Viterbo a distance of 19km (12 miles).

❺ **Caprarola,** Lazio

The main reason for coming to Caprarola is to visit the vast 16th-century Villa Farnese, built for the Farnese family (Pope Paul II, who was a member of this important family, was for a while Michelangelo's patron). It dominates the little town spread out beneath it as well as the countryside for miles around. The palace, more like a vast pentagonal fortress, was built by Giacomo Barozzi da Vignola, the influential 16th-century architect, on the foundations of an

BACK TO NATURE

Lying to the north of Lago di Vico, the Riserva Naturale del Lago di Vico comprises wooded hills and mountains. In this region to the west of Caprarola, birds of prey soar overhead and wild boar and other forest animals haunt the slopes. Most of the reserve's creatures are rather shy of people, and patience and luck are needed to get good views.

Villa Farnese, status symbol of Cardinal Alessandro Farnese

earlier fortress. Inside there is a massive circular staircase that spirals up to the centre of the building, and all around it are frescos glorifying aspects of the Farnese family's sudden rise to power. The sheer vulgarity of these is the early equivalent of a modern billionaire's tendency to display his new-found wealth.

you stand in the forecourt of the palace and look to the right you can see the 17th-century Church of Santa Teresa, designed by the important baroque architect Girolamo Rainaldi.

▶ *From Caprarola, return to Viterbo by the same route.*

13th-century Palazzo dei Papi (Papal Palace), a battlemented pile more like a city hall than a palace, was where the Viterbo popes were elected. These elections were never easy and on one occasion, after the death of Clement IV, the cardinals were locked into the building and not allowed out until they had done

The main rooms are no longer furnished, decoration being provided by the frescos. The gardens behind the palace are still well kept (by the state – the family is now extinct), and they make much use of water, with fountains and a 'water chain'. There is also an elegant little summer house, the Palazzina. If

⑥ Viterbo, Lazio
The biggest town in this northern corner of Lazio, Viterbo is an impressive walled city, full of medieval buildings and fountains and with a lovely Romanesque cathedral with Gothic campanile. Viterbo once rivalled Rome as the place of residence of the popes. The

Grotesquerie in the extraordinary Monster Park at Bomarzo

their duty and elected a new pope. It took two years, during which the people of Viterbo tried to hurry the unfortunate cardinals by starving them out and then taking the roof off the building.

The pleasant beach resort of Santa Marinella

There is a variety of churches, including the rebuilt Santa Rosa, where you can see the remains of Viterbo's patron saint. Santa Rosa's preaching is supposed to have helped the people of Viterbo defeat Emperor Frederick II in 1243 when he laid siege to the town. Santa Maria Nuova, the cathedral, is a good example of the local Romanesque style, altered during the Renaissance. The Church of San Sisto dates in part from the 9th century. Throughout the old centre of Viterbo, there are little medieval alleys, flights of steps and carved balconies hanging on to the ancient buildings. Some of the houses have little stone towers.

RECOMMENDED TRIPS

Instead of driving or walking, why not take a boat trip? On the lake of Bolsena, in the crater of a volcano just north of Viterbo, boat trips are organised from the towns of Bolsena or Capodimonte. Trips are to Martana, a rocky island covered in woodland, and to Bisentina, another island which has a lovely church, SS Giacomo e Cristoforo. There is also the Chapel of Santa Caterina with, below it, an artificial grotto and gardens created by the Farnese family. This island is a must.

i *Piazza S Carlucci*

▶ *Bagnaia lies on the eastern outskirts of Viterbo, about 5km (3 miles) from the centre.*

7 Bagnaia, Lazio
This hill village juts out on a spur overlooking the surrounding countryside. It is part medieval and part Renaissance. In the older section, crammed behind the old walls and overlooked by a watchtower, the houses line dark stone alleys and there are splendid views out to the surrounding countryside. In the newer part of town, built around the square that faces the watchtower and the old town gate, the streets are more regular. In this quarter is one of the most beautiful gardens to have emerged from the Italian Renaissance, and what it more, it is mostly still intact.

The Villa Lante was built by Giacomo Barozzi da Vignola, in the late 1560s, for Cardinal Gambera, whose family emblem, the crayfish (in Italian *gambero*), is scattered around the garden carved in stone. The gardens are more important than the buildings: there are fountains linked by an underground stream, a water chain, formal parterres and a series of

Etruscan tombs in Cerveteri's 'city of the dead'

Tarquinia's Roman aqueduct

giocchi d'acqua, water jokes. The Cardinal enjoyed entertaining his guests (and himself) with these mechanical practical jokes. A servant would trigger a secret mechanism somewhere behind the fountain, and the guests would be sprayed with water from some hidden source. The keeper of the garden might be persuaded to show you these – some of them still work.

▶ *Take the cross-country route that leaves the main square in the centre of Bagnaia. Vitorchiano is only 7km (4 miles) away.*

SPECIAL TO...

The menus of this area include great plates of wild boar, dishes using offal, and lamb scented with rosemary. Try *Saltimbocca alla Romana*, which is slices of veal cooked with *prosciutto*, *mozzarella* cheese and sage. The whole lot is dunked in Marsala. Its name means 'jump in the mouth'. Most of the wines from this region are white, and by far the most common is one called *Est Est Est* from Montefiascone.

---

8 Vitorchiano, Lazio
Vitorchiano is very similar to Bagnaia. Both are built of *peperino*, the local volcanic stone, purplish in colour. They also have the same medieval aspect. Vitorchiano is fortified

only on one side. The rest of the town sits on a huge impregnable rock that provided a natural defence. Walking through the little dark streets, look out for the SPQR ('Senatus Populusque Romanus') symbol of Vitorchiano's allegiance to Rome. Traditionally this goes back to when an ancient Roman is said to have run from Vitorchiano to Rome to warn the city that it was about to be attacked by the Etruscans. The man died soon afterwards but the City of Rome rewarded the people of Vitorchiano calling it the 'faithful city', and giving it special powers. This relationship persisted, hence the little medieval wall plaques showing the wolf suckling Romulus and Remus, symbol of Rome.

Have lunch at Vitorchiano and wander slowly around the town. It has no special art treasures or monuments. Quite simply it is an enchanting, if strange, place, full of young people restoring their old family houses.

▶ *From Vitorchiano, follow the signs to Bomarzo via the SS204.*

9 Bomarzo, Lazio
Bomarzo is another town built out of *peperino* stone. Very small, it has a forbidding military look about it. Most of its houses are crammed around a large fortress traditionally belonging to the Orsini family, though now partially divided into flats. After

wandering through the slightly damp streets, and paying a quick visit to the brightly painted but tiny main church, you should spend some time at the Parco dei Mostri (Monster Park) on the edge of town.

FOR CHILDREN

The Parco dei Mostri (Monster Park) at Bomarzo is an extraordinary park filled with enormous fantastical creatures, beasts, grotesques and monsters hewn from the local rock by Turkish prisoners of war in the 16th century. Among these is a huge elephant squeezing a helpless Roman soldier in its trunk and a figure tearing its adversary in half. The sheer madness exhibited could frighten children and can only be fully appreciated by adults. Children would enjoy another grotesquerie – a little house with a steeply inclined floor, which gives the impression of walking across the deck of a ship at very rough sea. There is a small park adjacent offering tamer delights – swings and a herd of deer, as well as a café and shop.

▶ *Return to the SS204. Turn left and take this road to the A1 autostrada which leads to Roma (from the nearby Orte junction). Follow the signs.*

In the **Shadow**
of Vesuvius

Campania divides neatly into two areas – a coastal region and an inland landscape of mountains and valleys. This tour covers the coast which, after Liguria, is one of the most popular in Italy. The difference between the two rivieras is that, in addition to the idyllic seaside resorts, Campania's coast also has a series of rich historical sites to be visited, such as Pompeii and Ercolano.

5 DAYS •323KM • 199 MILES

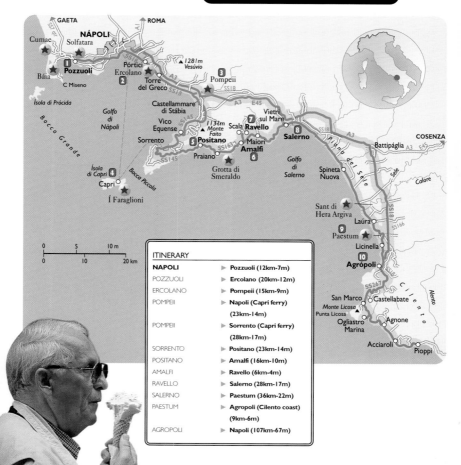

i   *Piazza dei Martiri 58*

▶ *From Napoli, take the autostrada or the coastal road to Pozzuoli – it is only 12km (7 miles) from the centre of Naples going in the direction of Gaeta.*

FOR HISTORY BUFFS

Near Pozzuoli are the ancient sites of *Cumae* (about 5km/3 miles) and Baia (about 4km/2½ miles). At *Cumae*, thought to be the oldest Greek colony in Italy, visit the Antro della Sibilla (Cave of the Cumaean Sibyl) just below the summit of the Acropolis. The hero Aeneas consults the Sybil in Virgil's great poem the *Aeneid*. At Baia, there are the remains of an imperial villa and at Capo (Cape) Miseno, 5km (3 miles) further on, are the tumbledown remains of what was the greatest naval base of the Roman Empire.

❶ Pozzuoli, Campania
Pozzuoli was once a city in its own right, though nowadays it seems more like an extension of Napoli itself. Its claim to fame is that from among its aged villas and the clutter of houses around the Roman ruins, emerged the sultry film actress Sophia Loren. This, her birthplace, was once a Roman city, named *Puteoli*. It has the remains of the third largest amphitheatre in Italy – the Anfiteatro Flavio. You can see the well-preserved dens for wild animals beneath it, but earthquakes as well as intermittent eruptions of Mount Vesuvius have otherwise destroyed much of its ancient character. What was once thought to be a Serapeum (Temple of Serapis – an Egyptian god), survives from the 1st century AD, though it is partially submerged beneath the water near the harbour. It is now believed to be the remains of a market building. You can visit other parts of the archaeo-

logical park in which it is situated. Back in the centre of town is the Duomo (cathedral) dedicated to St Procolo. Nowadays it is a rather tumbledown building, most of it destroyed in 1964 in a fire; after the fire, its baroque additions were removed revealing a Roman structure in marble beneath.

i   *Via Campi Flegrei 3*

▶ *Go back through the centre of Naples and follow the signs to Ercolano (Herculaneum) which lies on the other side of the city beyond Portici.*

❷ Ercolano, Campania
Ercolano is an important Roman site. Not as big or important as Pompeii, the city was once a residential enclave for wealthy Romans. A great many villas have survived, some with their furnishings, the whole lot having been buried beneath the mud and lava from the eruption of Vesuvius in AD 79. You can see the excavations in just a couple of hours, time enough to appreciate this fossil of everyday Roman life, eerily

Amalfi's striking duomo – an exotic blend of styles

preserved by the catastrophe of nearly 2,000 years ago. The Casa del Tramezzo Carbonizzato (House of the Wooden Partition) gives some

volcanic ash rather than mud. The site is huge and would take at least a morning to complete successfully. Buy a map or a guide before you enter: villas,

the ruins. Pompeii is an extraordinary and evocative place. To see many of the movable treasures found here you will have to visit the museum in Naples.

idea of an early double-storeyed house, while in the Casa del Mobilio Carbonizzato (House of the Carbonised Furniture) you can examine ancient furniture left in the position in which it was found. In the Casa dell'Atrio a Mosaico (House of the Mosaic Atrium) are some splendid mosaic floors, while the House of the Gem still preserves an ancient kettle in its kitchen. Public places such as the *palaestra* (the gym) and the baths survive; access around the town is by way of streets paved with original limestone slabs.

▶ *From Ercolano, the* **SS18** *continues to Pompeii, about 15km (9 miles) – follow the signs.*

3 Pompeii, Campania
Pompeii was a large commercial city also destroyed by the eruption of Vesuvius in AD 79, but, in this case, covered by layers of

shops, temples – there is much to see and the extent of it is confusing without some kind of guide. There are human ones only too willing to offer their services; agree a price in advance. One of the most sumptuous villas is the Casa dei Vettii (House of the Vettii), a large house with a decorated interior. Much of it has been reconstructed and in addition to the lavish frescos there are fountains and statues.

In the Via di Nola is a tavern in which were found three trumpets dumped by gladiators as they fled from the nearby amphitheatre and in the shop of Verus the Blacksmith you will see a lamp and other objects either under repair or being made at the time of the eruption. Of the public buildings, the basilica (law courts) was the most monumental; in the Antiquarium you will see casts taken from the impressions left by original bodies found among

Pompeii's amphitheatre could accommodate 12,000 spectators

i *Via Sacra 1*

▶ *To get to the island of Capri, you could either go back to the port of Naples or go to Sorrento via the* **SS145,** *28km (17 miles) further along the coast. If you choose the latter it will add about 5km (3 miles) to the total road mileage of the tour. Either way, both ports have regular island ferry services. From Naples the trip takes one hour and 10 minutes; from Sorrento 35 minutes.*

4 Capri, Campania
Capri is a good place to avoid in the middle of the summer when it is absolutely packed with tourists. Just before or just after the season you will have the benefit of pleasant rocky coves in which to swim and tan unmolested by the hordes. There is

plenty to see and do on the island. Capri town is bursting with designer shops but if you are not interested in these, you can visit the Duomo built in the 17th century and the Giardini di Augusto (Gardens of Augustus), founded by Augustus himself. The Villa Jovis, a 45-minute walk from the town, was the home of the Emperor Tiberius towards the end of his reign. Combine a visit to the ruins with the grim Salto di Tiberio, the cliffs from which the emperor was supposed to have flung his enemies.

The little town of Anacapri is known for the Villa San Michele, immortalised by Axel Munthe in *The Story of San Michele*. Near by are the remains of the Villa Imperiale, Augustus' villa (not as well preserved as the Villa Jovis). You could walk to here as well as to the ruined Castello di Barbarossa, but buses do the rounds and there are a great many other places to visit. Of great natural beauty are the Grotta Azzurra (Blue Grotto) – take a boat from Capri port – and the Grotta Verde (Green Grotto), reached from Anacapri.

i   *Piazza Cerio II*

▶ *From Capri, the quickest way to Positano is to take the boat back to Sorrento. From*

Sorrento take the SS145 (which joins and becomes the SS163) to Positano, about 23km (14 miles).

5 Positano, Campania
The town of Positano falls almost vertically into the sea. From the high cliff road above it, it seems as though the characteristic whitewashed houses have been tipped over the edge to the water. There are no great monuments to be seen in Positano; the little town is simply a picturesque coastal resort, full of restaurants and cafés in which to while away the days.

Within easy reach of Positano are a number of other tiny ports. One of these, Praiano, has a fine beach while at Conca dei Marini are the remains of a Norman watchtower. Just before Conca dei Marini is the Grotta dello Smeraldo (Emerald Cave), a large cavern to which you can descend in a lift from the roadside. It gets its name from the colour of the light filling its interior. If you look carefully, you can see, now under water, stalagmites formed when the cave was above sea-level.

i   *Via del Saracino 4*

▶ *The SS163 continues to Amalfi, 16km (10 miles).*

6 Amalfi, Campania
In the early Middle Ages, Amalfi was an important trading post, possibly the most important in Italy. This seems surprising at first glance, because the

Ancient Pompeii started life in the 6th century BC as a Greek trading post

town today is so small. But its monuments reveal the truth. The Duomo (cathedral), in a mixture of styles, is one of the loveliest south of Naples. You approach it up a long, steep flight of steps and enter via a set of bronze doors made in Constantinople in 1066.

Next door to the cathedral is the 13th-century Chiostro del Paradiso (Cloisters of Paradise), with beautiful double columns, the pair intertwining voluptuously. This cloister would perhaps be more at home in Sicily where this style of Saracenic (oriental) decoration is more common. Climbing up the steep hillside outside Amalfi are villas and small hotels. One of the latter – the biggest – was at one time a Capuchin convent. Access is via a lift that rushes up the side of the mountain; the views from

its terrace are spectacular, while the characterful interior is filled with antique furnishings.

[i] *Corso delle Repubbliche Marinare 19–21*

▶ *From Amalfi, branch off the SS163 on to a minor road which winds up the hillside to Ravello, about 6km (4 miles).*

7 Ravello, Campania
The beautiful village of Ravello is isolated at the top of the hill directly above Amalfi at about 350m (1,150 feet) above sea-level. It has two historic villas, Villa Cimbrone and Villa Rufolo, both of which have splendid gardens.

The Villa Rufolo was begun in the 11th century and its remarkable Saracenic-Norman character has survived. The composer Richard Wagner was its most illustrious guest; in fact its gardens were the inspiration for the magic garden of Klingsor in

There is a Moorish look to Positano, clinging to the cliffs

The enchanting town of Ravello is set high above the Amalfi Coast

those of the other more popular towns along the coast, but it has a Duomo (Cathedral of St Matthew), consecrated in 1085, but much altered. This cathedral follows the local fashion in having a pair of bronze doors (from Constantinople) and another set of 12th-century mosaic-inlaid pulpits of the kind found in Ravello. Leading off the cathedral's sacristy is the Museo del Duomo, containing various fragments from the cathedral building as well as some of its greatest treasures. Of the latter, the early medieval altar front, with 54 ivory panels showing biblical scenes, is the most interesting. Try to get to the Provincial Museum, which contains finds from excavations from all over the province of Salerno.

i *Via Velia 15*

SCENIC ROUTES

The most scenic route on this tour is the journey from Positano to Salerno on the SS163. On the way look out for the ceramic-covered domes of the churches in the midst of the hamlets that cling to the side of the steep hillsides just above the sea.

► *From Salerno, follow the long straight coastal road for about 36km (22 miles) to Paestum.*

9 Paestum, Campania
There was once a great city at Paestum. All that remains is a handful of ancient buildings in a remarkable state of preservation – the Basilica (dedicated to the queen goddess Hera), the Tempio di Nettuno (the Temple of Neptune), the Tempio di Cerere (Temple of Ceres) and about 4km (2½ miles) of walls that once surrounded the old city.

Paestum was abandoned around the 9th century because of the threat of malaria from

the opera *Parsifal*. The villa, once the residence of popes, has a fine view of the coastline from its terrace. But the gardens of the Villa Cimbrone are more spectacular. These rather wild and surprisingly lush gardens with their arbours and old lichen-covered terraces, end in a long terrace from which you have an unrivalled view of the Amalfi coastline. Ravello's Duomo (cathedral) contains some very early art: 12th- and 13th-century pulpits, with inlaid marble and mosaic, and fine bronze doors, dating from 1179 and modelled on the more famous Amalfi cathedral doors. There is a small museum in the cathedral.

i *Piazza Duomo 10*

RECOMMENDED WALKS

A good walk to take is from Ravello to the little village of Scala, about 1.5km (1 mile) away. It has a pretty miniature cathedral.

► *From Ravello, go back to the SS163, then continue eastwards along it for 24km (15 miles) to Salerno.*

8 Salerno, Campania
The name of Salerno is familiar as the site of the Allied invasion of Italy in September 1943. Today it is a town that people tend to ignore on a tour of Campania. It is a working town with a busy port and industries. Its treasures are eclipsed by

surrounding marshes and attacks by invading Saracens, and the temples lay hidden for centuries in a kind of subtropical forest, now converted, into a dry plain.

The Temple of Neptune, dating from about 450 BC, is the best preserved building here. Huge and solid, it is in the unadorned, Doric style. The museum contains some of the sculptural fragments from the temples here as well as finds from the Sanctuary of Hera, about 10km (6 miles) to the north of Paestum. But the prize exhibits in the museum are the tomb paintings – in particular those from the Tomba del Tuffatore (Tomb of the Diver), thought to be the only surviving examples of Greek funerary mural painting anywhere.

☐ *Via Magna Grecia 151*

▷ *From Paestum, it is only a short run to the beginning of the Cilento Coast. Go south for about 9km (6 miles) and begin at Agropoli.*

🔟 **Agropoli,** Campania
The coastline changes completely after Paestum; if you follow the sea all the way to Pioppi you encounter miniature bays, long white beaches and a series of small ports with nothing more than a fine position to recommend them. Agropoli is perhaps the most popular. Its core is medieval and you can visit the Convent of San Francesco.

Further along at San Marco there are ancient Roman remains including the breakwater carved out of the rock. From here the road leads to Agnone, bypassing Monte Licosa which drops down into

the sea. You should not miss this part of the coast, so take the smaller road – or track – to Ogliastro Marina, park the car, then walk around to the Punta Licosa (Licosa Point), named after a siren, Leucosia, who is said to have jumped into the sea from the promontory after failing to enchant Odysseus as he sailed past.

▷ *From Agropoli, make for the SS18 going north across the Sele Plain to Battipaglia, 31km (19 miles), at which join the A3 going back to Naples, a further 76km (47 miles).*

BACK TO NATURE

Because it is effectively land-locked, the Mediterranean has a small tidal range and so relatively few marine creatures can be seen on its shores. However, the coastal vegetation is impressive in unspoilt areas. For bird-watchers, colourful *macchia* vegetation may grow almost to the shore-line and this harbours a wide variety of warblers. Blue rock thrushes sing from exposed rocky outcrops.

FOR CHILDREN

If you are here towards the end of the year, the children will be fascinated by the *presepi* (Christmas cribs). Churches and private homes begin preparing to display their *presepi* in November. You find the best ones in Naples itself, but all over Campania – even in little country churches – you will find the tradition adhered to. They usually have miniature Roman ruins, animals, beggars, musicians and many other figures, quite apart from the Holy Family.

The superb Temple of Neptune at Paestum

Small Cities
of Campania

Away from the coastal resort, Campania is a quiet rural region. Great tracts of countryside are empty but even the loneliest parts are within reach of Napoli (Naples). Here you will find good restaurants representative of the great variety of cooking from the provinces. Napoli is Campania's melting pot. As in the provincial towns surrounding it you will find Roman and Greek remains as well as buildings with Byzantine or Spanish influences.

4 DAYS • 176KM • 110 MILES

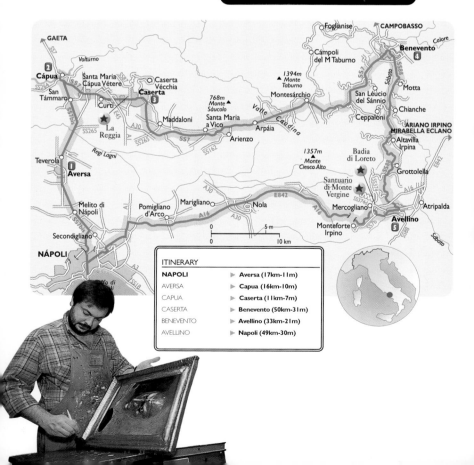

ITINERARY		
NAPOLI	▶	**Aversa** (17km-11m)
AVERSA	▶	**Capua** (16km-10m)
CAPUA	▶	**Caserta** (11km-7m)
CASERTA	▶	**Benevento** (50km-31m)
BENEVENTO	▶	**Avellino** (33km-21m)
AVELLINO	▶	**Napoli** (49km-30m)

BACK TO NATURE

Although built up to a large extent, the outskirts of Naples still support areas of woodland, with associated wildlife. Look and listen for firecrest, golden orioles and spotted flycatchers in the trees. It can also be rewarding to look down, as orchids often grow in the leaf litter on the ground below in early spring.

i *Piazza dei Martiri 58, Naples*

▶ *From Naples, take the **SS7bis** north to Aversa for 17km (11 miles).*

❶ **Aversa,** Campania
This small town was founded by the Normans in 1029 – in fact it was their very first settlement in this part of Italy. Although the castle was originally their work, it was rebuilt in the 18th century and later turned into a hospital. King Andrew of Hungary was murdered here in 1345 and here, too, his death was avenged by his brother Louis

of Hungary. The Duomo (cathedral of San Paolo) was also founded by the Normans. Though it was altered later, you can see some original Norman work inside. If you are not reeling from the effects of the potent local brew, a white wine called *Asprinio* which is generally considered a 'thirst-quenching' wine for hot summer days, then be sure to visit the Church of San Lorenzo which has a beautiful cloister.

Galleria Umberto I, Naples' elegant glass and iron arcade

Caserta is famous for its
18th-century palace and gardens

2nd century AD and is probably
the best example of a rectangu-
lar underground area with a
vault painted with stars. The
rites of the cult included the
slaying of a bull and here there
is a fresco of Mithras killing a
large white bull – a very rare
survival.

New Capua contains the most
interesting finds from these
ancient sites in the Museo
Campano, including an array of
ancient sculpture. The Duomo
(cathedral), founded in AD 835,
was destroyed in 1942 and
completely rebuilt, though its
beautiful campanile (bell tower)
dates from 861.

▶ *From Capua, follow the signs
to Caserta, only 11km (7
miles) away.*

3 **Caserta,** Campania
The only reason to come to
Caserta is to see the biggest
palace in Italy, started in 1752
by Vanvitelli for the Bourbon
King of Naples, Charles III, and
intended to rival Versailles.
Known as La Reggia, or the
Palazzo Reale, its interior, in
which there are some 1,200
rooms, is extremely richly decorated (in particular the State
Apartments) with gilding,
different types of marble, tapestries, paintings and frescos. The
park and the gardens, famous
for their water gardens, cascades
and fountains, are as elaborate
as the interior is extravagant.
They are also huge. One of the
focal points, the statue group of
Diana and Actaeon, is about 3km
(2 miles) from the palace itself.
If, for some reason, you cannot
get into the building, there is
plenty to see and do in the
garden. Look out for the 18th-
century English Garden. King
Vittorio Emanuele III
presented the palace to the
State in 1921.

Not far from the palace,
which is situated in the newer
town, is Caserta Vecchia, a
medieval town which was all

▶ *The **SS7bis** continues for
16km (10 miles) to Capua.*

SCENIC ROUTES

The most scenic parts of
this particular tour are the
following:
the last 20km (12½ miles) on
the SS88 from Benevento to
Avellino, which wind through
the mountains past Altavilla
Irpina and a scattering of small
hilltowns. There is nothing in
particular to look out for; it is
simply a lovely scenic route;
the trip to the Sanctuary of
Monte Vergine from Avellino
looks back over the valley to
Altavilla Irpina.

2 **Capua,** Campania
Capua was the greatest town in
Campania during the Roman
period. Its small size today

makes this hard to believe, but
enough survives from its
heyday to give some idea of its
early importance. At Santa
Maria di Capua Vetere, the old
city that was utterly destroyed
in about AD 830 by the Arabs,
and about 2km (1 mile) from
newer Capua, are the remains
of a large amphitheatre, second
in size only to the Colosseum in
Rome. Great blocks of stone
and a hefty arched construction
survive among the cypresses.
Here, too, is the Arco di Adriano
(Hadrian's Arch – also called the
Arch of Capua) built in honour
of the emperor who restored the
amphitheatre in AD 119. One of
the best preserved ancient
monuments here is the
Mithraeum, an underground
hall dedicated to the worship of
the Persian Sun-god Mithras – a
cult very popular with Roman
soldiers. It dates from about the

but abandoned when the newer one was built along with the palace. There is an interesting Norman and Sicilian-style cathedral. Its interior is a hotch-potch of fascinating details: particularly noteworthy are the 18 antique columns and the early mosaic details.

[i] *Piazza Dante 35*

RECOMMENDED WALKS

The best walks on this tour would, perhaps surprisingly, be in the vast grounds of La Reggia, the royal palace at Caserta. They are amazingly big and full of little surprises, such as hidden fountains among the undergrowth.

▶ *The SS7 leads to Benevento, 50km (31 miles).*

4 Benevento, Campania
Benevento is possibly the most interesting town on the tour of Campania's hinterland. The old streets in its centre preserve monuments ranging from a Roman theatre to an early medieval gate, the Port'Arsa. Benevento was badly bombed in World War II, with the near total loss of its cathedral, a 13th-century Romanesque building of which only the richly sculpted façade and campanile (bell tower) are original. The rest has been rebuilt. The Roman theatre was begun in the 2nd century AD, in the reign of Hadrian; its most remarkable features are three monumental gates.

The *triggio* quarter of town contains more visible remains of Benevento's Roman past. You will see bits of ancient stonework built into the walls of the houses, and on the outskirts of town is the Ponte Leproso (Leproso Bridge), a Roman construction carrying the Via Appia (Appian Way) over the Sabato river. A particularly fine Roman monument is the Porta

Aurea (Arch of Trajan), a marble triumphal arch 15m (50 feet) high, excellently preserved, with bas-reliefs of the life of Trajan and a variety of mytho-logical subjects.

[i] *Piazza Roma*

SPECIAL TO...

Special to Benevento is *Strega*, a sweet liqueur made from a variety of herbs. Bright yellow in colour, it is named after the witches of Benevento (*strega* means witch).

▶ *From Benevento, take the SS88 to Avellino, a cross-country route of 33km (21 miles).*

FOR CHILDREN

Just outside Benevento (about 16km/10 miles to the east) is the town of Foglianise where every year, on 16 August, the villagers celebrate with a wheat festival. Children would proba-bly like to see this: tractors decorated with straw are paraded through the streets followed by young girls in tradi-tional costume with baskets of wheat on their heads. In the evening there is a display of coloured lights.

5 Avellino, Campania
Like many of the cities in this region, 'modern' Avellino occu-pies a site just a few kilometres from its original position. In this case, ancient *Abellinum* was situ-ated near to the present-day village of Atripalda, just 4km (2½ miles) to the east of Avellino. The Museo Provinciale in Avellino (Corso Europa) houses the finds from the old town as well as archaeo-logical collections from the necropolises of Mirabella Eclano (take the A16 going north from Avellino for 40km/25 miles) and Ariano Irpino (about 12km/7½ miles further on, just

off the A16 on the SS90). Also in the town are a medieval castle and a 17th-century customs house, the Palazzo della Dogana, with a sculpted façade. Avellino's art gallery displays a magnificent 18th-century crib (*presepio*), a very popular element of southern Italian religious culture.

▶ *From Avellino, take the A16 going west for 41km (25 miles) to the junction with the A1. Take the latter back to Naples (south), 8km (5 miles).*

SPECIAL TO...

The province of Avellino has a wide variety of arts and crafts including inlaid and carved woodwork. In Avellino you will also find lots of shops selling the local brands of *mozzarella*, *pecorino* and *treccia* cheeses — *mozzarella* is made from buffa-lo's milk, *pecorino* from the local ewe's milk, while *treccia* (which means 'plait') is a mixture of cheese from cow's milk and *mozzarella*.

FOR HISTORY BUFFS

About 22km (15 miles) from Avellino up in the heart of the Partenio massif is the Santuario di Monte Vergine (Sanctuary of Monte Vergine), a church dedicated to the Mother of God, founded in the 12th century. Preserved here, in this very beautiful spot on the mountainside, is a painting of a head of the Virgin, supposed to have been done by St Luke. Visit the museum and the basilica.
If this is not enough, further down the hill is the Convent of Loreto which was built on the site of a pagan laurel grove. Here you will find an 18th-century pharmacy with a collection of majolica apothe-cary's jars, important 16th-century Flemish tapestries and a vast archive.

CALABRIA, BASILICATA, PUGLIA

The far south is perhaps the most intriguing and dramatic part of Italy. Wild, uncontrollable territory alternates with dense woodland and gentle, cultivated plains. For many people, Italy stops at Rome or, at a push, Naples. Beyond, there is nothing but an unfamiliar, mountainous land mass, full of strange rustics with peculiar customs and leading backward lives. Nothing could be further from the truth; the attractions of the south are merely less obvious and altogether extraordinary. Who would have thought that some of the strangest customs and dialects in Calabria had their origins in 15th-century Albania; or that some of the inhabitants of Matera in Basilicata are quite happy to live underground; or even stranger – that people in parts of Puglia live in prehistoric-type houses that look like beehives?

Most of Calabria and Basilicata is mountainous, with craggy outcrops of rock blanketed with thick forests. Shut away in the hinterland of both regions are remote whitewashed hill villages, cities and castles. Ancient buildings, medieval city centres, and traditional customs, dress and dialect have survived in Calabria and Basilicata as a result of the lie of the land and its inaccessibility.

But these areas are fascinating, especially to anyone interested in archaeology and history. Much of the south was once a part of Magna Graecia – the name given to the ancient Greek colonies founded in southern Italy and Sicily from the 8th century BC – and the archaeological sites of the region have yielded important finds from that period, the time of their greatest prosperity. In these areas, and in Puglia too, there are Roman remains as well as Byzantine and Norman architecture and a variety of other evidence of the trail left behind by the conquerors of the south over the centuries.

In Puglia, which forms the spur and heel of the boot of Italy, the terrain is mostly gentler – flatter, with greater areas of cultivation. Some of the region's ports are the busiest in Italy, with regular ferries to Greece and Croatia. It bustles with life, where Calabria and Basilicata seem to brood on their past.

The lovely hilltop town of Rivello, Basilicata

Catanzaro

Catanzaro is a lively town. It sits on a stony peak with deep gorges on either side, surrounded by a wonderful panorama. Just a few kilometres away is the sea. Although it might not be obvious behind the results of Catanzaro's rapid modern development, the city has ancient Byzantine origins and a rich cultural tradition, some traces of which can be seen in the fine Museo Provinciale (Provincial Museum).

Cosenza

Cosenza had an eventful history giving it a varied cultural background – at different times it fell under the sway of the Romans, Normans, Swabians, Angevins and Aragonese. All these have left their mark, though the old city has a predominantly medieval aspect, dominated by a huge Norman castle. Cosenza is a thriving market town, and can boast some of Calabria's best restaurants.

and labyrinthine grottoes; there are also rock chapels, some of whose walls are covered with frescos. Just outside town there are many more small churches cut into the hills. But more normal buildings are in plentiful supply – the Duomo is 13th-century Romanesque, with much of interest to be seen both inside and out.

Bari

Bari, Puglia's capital, consists of an old quarter – the Città Vecchia – which lies nearest the sea and has medieval buildings in its streets; the newer Città Nuova, with a neat grid-plan of streets; and the industrial area further inland. The city contains some of the most magnificent buildings in the region: the Romanesque cathedral, the castle and the great Basilica of San Nicola, founded in the 11th century by the Normans – their first major church in Puglia. The Museo Archeologico, with its fine

between two arms of land, at the head of a wide inlet, forming a natural harbour. Strangely, for a city whose claim to fame is as the major point of embarkation for Greece, the centre of Brindisi has the air of a small provincial town. Cafés line the main street and there is a pretty promenade at the town centre overlooking the water. Brindisi's archaeological museum (Museo Archeologico Provinciale) preserves the best of the finds from nearby Roman sites. Be sure to visit the colourful Church of Santa Maria del Casale with its impressive Byzantine *Last Judgement*, a few kilometres north, near the airport.

Foggia

Foggia, once known as 'Capitanata', is Puglia's third city. Not much of its ancient aspect survives. Today it is a city of wide avenues and mostly low-rise, modern buildings. However, the

Matera

The different periods of Matera's history are clearly defined as you walk through the city centre and around its outskirts. The town's main attraction is the fascinating Sassi, with rockcut dwellings gouged from the city's foundations along with tunnels

ceramics, and the Pinacoteca Provinciale, full of southern Italian art from the 11th to the 18th centuries, are also worth seeing.

Brindisi

Both Bari and Brindisi are important Adriatic ports. The latter sits on a peninsula

Green and rolling Apulian countryside near Bovino

cathedral survives, a strange mixture of Romanesque and baroque. The Museo Civico (Civic Museum) contains archaeological finds from the area as well as an exhibition of Puglian traditional crafts.

The Toe of
the Boot

Southern Calabria consists mostly of the Aspromonte mountain range. While its coastline is largely built up, the interior, being more difficult to access, has been left relatively untouched. Catanzaro is the exception. Big, lively and modern, it engulfs the outcrop on which it stands.

5 DAYS • 478KM • 296 MILES

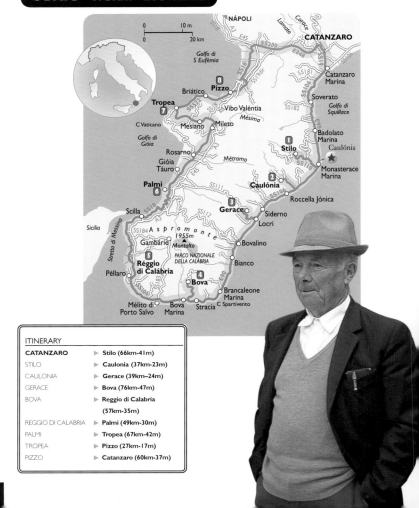

ITINERARY		
CATANZARO	▶	**Stilo (66km-41m)**
STILO	▶	**Caulonia (37km-23m)**
CAULONIA	▶	**Gerace (39km–24m)**
GERACE	▶	**Bova (76km-47m)**
BOVA	▶	**Reggio di Calabria (57km-35m)**
REGGIO DI CALABRIA	▶	**Palmi (49km-30m)**
PALMI	▶	**Tropea (67km-42m)**
TROPEA	▶	**Pizzo (27km-17m)**
PIZZO	▶	**Catanzaro (60km-37m)**

SCENIC ROUTES

To get to the sea at Copanello, about 6km (3½ miles) on the SS106 south of Catanzaro, you drive through the flat lands between the sea and the mountains, an area characterised by clumps of umbrella pines and 2m (6-foot) high reeds. From here, right down the coast of Calabria, the scenery is the same.
The whole of the SS18 going north is a panoramic route: to one side are the famous white Palmi sands and the beautiful beaches right up to Nicotera (2km/13 miles from Tropea), and on the other high mountains which drop sharply down to sea-level.

▶ *Take the SS19 south to the coast, then branch southwest on the coastal SS106 for 48km (30 miles) until Monsterace Marina. Follow the SS110 to Stilo.*

❶ Stilo, Calabria

Stilo, halfway down the Monte Consolino, contains one of the most exquisite buildings in Calabria. Called La Cattolica, it is a terracotta-coloured Byzantine chapel. Inside, one of its antique columns has been placed upside down as a symbol of the defeat of paganism by Christianity. On a ledge above the town, La Cattolica looks out over the rocky valley at the head of which Stilo stands. The best time to come to Stilo would be at Easter, when Holy Week is celebrated with religious processions which meander through the town from church to church. In one of these the inhabitants start at the parish church, the Chiesa Madre, following the statue of the Madonna Addolorata, weaving through the ancient and narrow stone-walled streets, on their way to the Church of San Giovanni Jeresti where, before a large cross they pray, listen

to music and sing hymns in dialect. Special cakes with names like *nzulle* and *cuzzepe* are prepared for the casion. Shaped like hearts fishes, they are made of nuts, eggs, dried figs and sugar. In addition to this all the town's churches (there are five) are open for the event. Try to see the Church of San Francesco, founded in 1400, with its ornately carved wooden altar. On the edge of town the Porta Stefanina, one of Stilo's ancient gateways, still has an intact defensive tower.

▶ *Go back to Monsterace Marina and continue south on the SS106 for 14km (9 miles) until the turning west for Caulonia, 8km (5 miles).*

❷ Caulonia, Calabria

This little clay-coloured town, situated between the rivers Assi and Amusa, was founded by refugees from the ancient city of Caulonia which was destroyed by Dionysius I of Syracuse in 389 BC. There is little to be seen here except for a notable tomb in the Chiesa Madre (parish church). By a Tuscan sculptor, it belongs to one of the members of the Carafa family and is dated 1488. There is also the Chiesetta Zaccaria, a little church filled with Byzantine frescos. None the less, Caulonia is interesting as a country town where not much has changed for centuries.

The little Church of Santa Maria dell'Isola in Tropea

▶ *Returning to the SS106, continue south for 23km (14 miles) as far as Locri at which follow the signs west to Gerace on the SS111.*

FOR HISTORY BUFFS

For those interested in clambering over the ruins of ancient Calabria, Locri (near Gerace) has the most visible remains – temples, a theatre, and both Greek and Roman tombs. Though most of the artefacts from the site are now in the museum at Reggio di Calabria, on site is an Antiquarium with a small collection of vases, votive statues and sculpture as well as a diagram of the site which, for the uninitiated, is a must. The ruins of old Caulonia (on the coast near Stilo) are more fragmentary. If you haven't time for both, go to Locri.

❸ Gerace, Calabria

You could spend hours in Gerace simply sitting in the sun in the piazza in front of the cathedral. Wild flowers poke up between the old battered cobbles; goats wander by; widows in black and old men in grey peaked hats slowly pass; while the odd tiny Fiat 500 might squeeze into sight from

The market in Scilla, between Reggio di Calabria and Palmi

some narrow adjacent alley. Gerace, sitting on an impregnable crag above the Gerace river on one side and the great dried-up bed of the Novita river on the other, is an ancient place, originally founded by refugees from Locri who fled there in the 10th century to escape the continual stream of Saracen attacks. It is full of little churches and houses ranging from the Norman period to the baroque. The Cattedrale, the largest cathedral in Calabria, dominates the town. It is a strange building containing additions from a variety of centuries. Consecrated in 1045, it was rebuilt in the 13th century and restored in the 18th. Worth studying are the columns supporting the vault of the crypt – which you will not want to leave in summer because it is cool and dark – and those dividing the nave from the aisle in the upper church. Some of red and white marble, others of granite, they are believed to have come from ancient Locri down on the coast where they would have adorned an antique temple. Do not miss the cathedral treasury with its exquisite Renaissance ivory crucifix.

Picking your way over the cobbles to the right of the cathedral, through the elaborate

baroque archway you come to the Church of San Giovanello, part Byzantine and part Norman in style. At the back of the town is the old ruined fortress of Gerace, which still bears traces of its Roman origins. Before leaving Gerace you should consider buying some of the local ceramic vases and jugs. The origins of their decoration can often be traced back to the period when southern Italy was part of Magna Graecia (ancient Greek colonies in the west) – long before the Romans. You will see the ceramics spilling out of shops in the piazza by the cathedral.

SPECIAL TO...

The district around Gerace is noted for *Kalipea*, another local red wine, best drunk with piquant dishes and with roast meat, and for the locally produced ceramics.

▶ *Returning once again to the coastal SS106, continue still further south for 53km (33 miles) until Bova Marina at which branch inland for 14km (9 miles) to Bova.*

4 Bova, Calabria

The most extraordinary thing about Bova is that the dialect spoken by its inhabitants is a version of ancient Greek. The little mountain town is of great antiquity, shut away at a height of 820m (2,690 feet) on a remote peak of the Aspromonte. But the oldest visible remains – part of the cathedral and the ruins of the castle – date only from the Norman period, and the cathedral was rebuilt in 1783 after a tremendous earthquake. Also worthy of a visit is the Church of San Leo which, along with the cathedral, is the town's most prominent building. It dates from the 16th century, and is a later reconstruction of a much earlier church.

The countryside around Bova, which you can observe from the

ramparts of the town, gives a wild, rugged and desolate impression. However, it is also full of gnarled old olive trees and in spring glows with masses of wild flowers. You might perhaps be tempted to go for a walk along the rocky, dried-up bed of the Palizzi river.

▶ *Back to the coast, the SS106 continues to Reggio di Calabria, 43km (27 miles) further on.*

5 Reggio di Calabria, Calabria

From Reggio di Calabria, the regional capital, you can see across the Straits of Messina to Sicily – one of the most stunning views in southern Italy. This city is a big, lively town, straddling the coastline beneath the great peaks of the Aspromonte. It was shattered by an earthquake in 1908 and subsequently rebuilt, mostly of concrete. However, older fragments of its past have survived and, apart from viewing them in the important Museo Nazionale della Magna Grecia (see below), you can see one or two of them still *in situ* in the town. Apart from the mid-15th-century Castello Aragonese (Aragonese fortress), of which two massive circular bastions remain, there are the remains of the old Greek city walls and the Roman baths – both near the cathedral.

But not to be missed on a visit to Reggio di Calabria is the Museo Nazionale (National Museum). It contains a fascinating array of treasures – statuary, jewellery, sarcophagi, vases, glassware and mosaics – from classical sites like Locri and ancient Caulonia, but its most celebrated exhibits are the Bronzi di Riace (the Riace Warriors), two sculptures dredged from the sea in 1972. Of ancient Greek origin, one dates from about 460 BC., the other from about 430 BC. The later figure is thought to be by the greatest of ancient Greek sculptors, Phidias, and to have come from the temple at

Delphi in Greece. What they were doing at the bottom of the sea off the coast of Italy is anyone's guess.

☐ *Via D Tripepi 72*

RECOMMENDED WALKS

Above Reggio di Calabria is the little town of Gambarie, on the side of the Aspromonte mountain. Here you can walk among the pinewoods and admire the views out over the Straits of Messina to Sicily.

▶ *The route continues out the other side of Reggio di Calabria and is now called the SS18. After 49km (30 miles) it comes to Palmi.*

BACK TO NATURE

Nature-lovers should not miss the Parco Nazionale della Calabria. To the east of Reggio di Calabria lies the southernmost of the 10 zones of this fragmented national park, an area of granite mountains with forests, rivers and meadows. The wildlife includes birds of prey, wild cats and deer.

---

❻ Palmi, Calabria
Palmi is the best place in which to examine the minutiae of rural Calabrian life. Its Museo Calabrese di Etnografia e Folclore (Ethnographic and Folklore Museum of Calabria) displays all kinds of everyday tools and household equipment that went out of use long ago in the mountains and valleys of the region. It also has an exhibition of ritual sweets handed out on religious occasions (some of which you might still find in the remoter areas of Calabria), allegorical masks relating to popular superstitions and legends, fascinating in an area noted in the past for Saracen raids and brigands, and traditional costumes.

Palmi is also the first place after Reggio di Calabria where the coastline is pleasant enough to swim.

Palmi was first developed in the 10th century by the inhabitants of ancient *Taurianum*. Of this old settlement, there are only the barest remains 4km (2½ miles) further up the coast. Palmi was devastated in the 18th century and again in 1908 by violent earthquakes. Today, while its wide streets are pleasant enough to stroll through, the attractions of the coastline are greater. Just off the coast there is an odd clump of rock with a single olive tree, known as Isola d'Olive (Isle of the Olive), to which you can swim (if you have the energy on one of Calabria's scorching summer days).

▶ *From Palmi continue north on the SS18 to Mileto. After 6km (4 miles) branch left and take the small country road towards the sea to Tropea.*

❼ Tropea Calabria
Tropea is a fishing town with the prettiest stretch of beach on Calabria's western coastline. The town, clamped to the cliff above the sea, is faced by a great lump of rock out in the sea, joined to the mainland by a stretch of sand. The islet is known as Santa Maria dell'Isola, after the old Benedictine sanctuary there. Since everything closes in the afternoon in Italy – churches, shops and most museums – you should spend the morning in the old town, whose most impressive monument, the Duomo (cathedral), is of pre-Norman origin. Try not to miss the *Madonna of Romania*, in a silver frame, supposed to have been painted by St Luke himself, and the even stranger 15th-century black crucifix with wood inlay.

There are numerous little old palaces scattered about the town: Casa Trampo, in Vicolo Manco has an elaborate doorway; and further down the same alley you will find the Palazzo

Cesareo, whose balcony has lovely carved corbels. Further on there are others – some with carved doorways, others sporting the occupants' defence against the evil eye. Most often this takes the form of a grotesque face but sometimes it is a single eye in a circle. Other sights include the 18th-century Church of San Giuseppe and, of course, the startling views out over the sea that suddenly meet you as you turn a corner in one of the town's alleys. You can sometimes see as far as the Lipari Islands, out over the bright roofs of the fishermen's cottages.

▶ *Continue northwards along the SS522 to Pizzo.*

❽ Pizzo, Calabria
While Tropea has generous expanses of white sandy beaches, the country around Pizzo plunges dramatically into the sea. The medieval origins of this little fishing town are obvious when you wander through its narrow streets full of ancient houses crammed into the confined space. Ferdinand of Aragon's stout, impregnable Castello di Pizzo greets your arrival at one side of the town. Built in 1486, and since restored, it is famous for having been the scene of the execution in 1815 of Joachim Murat (or Il Re Gioacchino, as locals called him), ex-king of Naples. Not far from this unhappy place you can visit the Collegiata di San Giorgio with a lovely baroque façade and, inside, some 16th-century sculpture.

▶ *Take the SS18 north until it joins the SS280 and follow to Catanzaro.*

FOR CHILDREN

Apart from private facilities at individual hotels around the Calabrian coast, this region is not noted for facilities provided for the amusement of children.

The Highlands
of Calabria

Little-known, unexplored towns where some of the inhabitants
speak ancient Albanian are common in this more northerly part
of Calabria. Known as La Sila, it is only slightly less mountainous
than its southern counterpart.

4 DAYS • 556KM • 345 MILES

ITINERARY		
COSENZA	▶	**Morano Calabro** (81km-50m)
MORANO CALABRO	▶	**Spezzano Albanese** (42km-26m)
SPEZZANO ALBANESE	▶	**San Demetrio Corone** (37km-23m)
SAN DEMETRIO CORONE	▶	**Rossano** (41km-25m)
ROSSANO	▶	**Santa Severina** (120km-75m)
SANTA SEVERINA	▶	**San Giovanni in Fiore** (34km-21m)
SAN GIOVANNI IN FIORE	▶	**Tiriolo** (96km-60m)
TIRIOLO	▶	**Nicastro** (28km-17m)
NICASTRO	▶	**Rogliano** (59km-37m)
ROGLIANO	▶	**Cosenza** (18km-11m)

ⓘ *Corso Mazzini 92, Cosenza*

▶ *Take the Autostrada A3 north from Cosenza until the Morano Calabro turning. Then follow the signposted country road.*

❶ Morano Calabro, Calabria
From afar Morano Calabro looks like a part of the rock on which it was built. Although constructed on the pinnacle of a conical mountain 694m (2,277 feet) above sea-level, it is dwarfed by the huge Pollino mountain range all around it. The approach from the autostrada is enchanting: as you wind through the valleys at its feet, the town appears and vanishes with equal consistency as the car dips and turns. At dawn it is shrouded in mist, only the tips of the highest buildings visible from below. At dusk it is a murky silhouette enlivened by flickering lights and the sound of hooters and radios which echo across the valley in front of it. Close inspection reveals little square houses piled one on top of the other beneath the gaze of the Church of Santi Pietro e Paolo and the derelict remains of a Norman castle, partly rebuilt in the 16th century. The town was once an important centre of the local rural economy and some of the houses lining the steep streets have a prosperous air about them. Some have carved doorways. Many still have barns for livestock in use on the ground floors; while cattle were taken to the fields during the day to graze, they were brought home for the night for their own protection against thieves.

A steep walk to the top of the town's hill will be rewarded in Santi Pietro e Paolo by statues of Santa Caterina and Santa Lucia thought to be by Pietro Bernini, father of the more famous Gianlorenzo Bernini, architect of St Peter's in Rome. Others in the church are by

Bernini Senior's followers. Other churches include the 15th-century San Bernardino, with a fine portal and the baroque Collegiata della Maddalena which has a very pretty cupola. The little town is an excellent base for excursions into the Pollino massif, in particular the Serra del Prete and the Serra Dolcedorme which, at its highest point, is 2,271m (7,451 feet) above sea-level.

▶ *Back to the A3, return southwards for 23km (14 miles) until the Spezzano Albanese turning. Follow the SS534 eastwards for 4km (2½ miles), then branch right along the SS19 until Spezzano Albanese.*

SCENIC ROUTES

Stretches of this tour that are particularly scenic are the countryside around Morano Calabro, excellent for walks and drives, and the views from Tiriolo to the sea on either side of the Calabrian peninsula. The approach roads to the town (SS109 and SS19) are spectacular.

A quiet corner of Cosenza, flourishing provincial capital

Vineyard in the Santa Severina
region – home of fine wines

❷ Spezzano Albanese,
Calabria

This little town has a very un-
Italian aspect. In the height of
summer, as the bleached, whitewashed walls of the buildings
hurt your eyes in the glare of
sunlight, visions of Greece are
never far from the mind's eye.
The flat-roofed houses in the
old quarter, with their small,
square windows and their
outside staircases, abut a warren
of old passages and alleyways
stacked with firewood. Adding
to the strangely foreign character is the fact that most of the
inhabitants of Spezzano speak
Albanian – not the modern
version but a dialect going back
to the 15th century when their
ancestors fled here from the
Turks. You hear it in the bars, in
the market, in the pastry shops,
in the streets – everywhere.
Some older women wear
antique-looking costume; the
everyday version is simple and
rustic with floral-printed long
skirts and wide lace collars. A
more elaborate outfit is kept for
festive occasions such as the
Easter celebrations during Holy
Week. For these events the
women often wear costumes of
great antiquity and deck themselves with gold jewellery.

The Sanctuary of the
Madonna delle Grazie on the
outskirts of town is the focal
point of the Easter celebrations
during which its resident
Madonna is covered in
jewellery matching that of the
local girls. Perhaps this is the
best time to come to Spezzano
Albanese. Everyone flocks here
from the surrounding countryside; cakes and drinks are sold
and most people make an effort
to wear their traditional
costumes. Spezzano is also a spa
town, its installations dating
from the 1920s and 1930s.

▶ *Leave by the SS19 travelling
south, branching left within
2km (1 mile) on to the
SS106bis, passing through*

*Terranova da Sibari, and
continue until you join the
SS106, turning right. One kilometre (½ mile) further is the
turning for San Demetrio
Corone, just by the River
Mizofato. Continue along this
small country road for 15km
(9 miles) until San Demetrio
Corone.*

❸ San Demetrio Corone,
Calabria

While Spezzano Albanese is
sometimes called the capital of
'Little Albania', as this district is
known, San Demetrio Corone is
perhaps its most picturesque
town – and its most uncompro-
misingly Albanian one. Here
the street signs are in two
languages and there is an Italo-
Albanian college which trains
young men as priests for the
Orthodox church. The college
stands next to the 12th-century
Church of Sant'Adriano where
you will see antique columns
incorporated into the building
work and a Byzantine tessel-
lated pavement decorated with
pictures of leopards, birds and
snakes.

In the main square is a statue
of Skanderbeg, the Albanian

hero who died in the fight
against the Turks in the 15th
century.

▶ *Return to the SS106. Turn
right and continue along it for
7km (4 miles), then turn left
at Corigliano station. After
2km (1 mile) you reach the
SS106r. Join this and continue
south for 10km (6 miles)
until the turning for Rossano,
7km (4 miles) further.*

❹ Rossano, Calabria

This is one of the most important and picturesque hilltowns
in the Sila Greca (so called
because the Albanians were
formerly thought of as Greeks
by the locals). It has had a
colourful history and was an
important settlement during the
Roman period and again during
the 9th and 10th centuries. The
single most important monument to its great past is the
Codex Purpureus, the 6th-century
Greek 'Rossano Gospels', in the
cathedral's treasury, the Museo
Diocesano. This early Christian
illuminated manuscript is
extremely rare. Scenes from the
New Testament are jewel-like
with brilliant colour and fine

FOR HISTORY BUFFS

The site of the ancient Greek city of *Sybaris*, once with a population of nearly 300,000 people, lies on the plain about 20km (12½ miles) along the SS106 northwest of Rossano. Destroyed in 510 BC, it disappeared for millennia under the swamps of the Crati river and its ruins have been excavated only in the past 30 years. There are the remains of houses, some of which have surviving mosaic floors. Some of the artefacts found here have been deposited in a museum on the site. Otherwise you have to go to Crotone (on the way to Santa Severina) to see items from *Sybaris* in the museum there. It was once the richest city in Magna Graecia, and its luxury and decadence – as well as its corruption – were legendary (giving rise to the word 'sybaritic').

Don't miss the site of the Tempio (Sanctuary) di Hera Lacinia at Capo Colonna, 11km (7 miles) south of Crotone. It has a single huge remaining column near the beach.

detailed drawing. There is more to see in the town. A walk around the upper part will take in the Church of San Bernardino and the cathedral, which contains early sculpture. Perhaps more worthwhile are the small Byzantine churches of Santa Maria del Pilerio and the Panaghia, the latter with pretty frescos, while San Marco is not to be missed. Standing on high above the Celati river, this Byzantine church is not unlike the Cattolica at Stilo, with five little domes covered in terracotta tiles.

▶ *Return to and continue along the coastal **SS106r** (which becomes the **SS106**) for 84km (52 miles) until the junction with the **SS107**, approximately 5km (3 miles) before Crotone. Take the **SS107** to Santa Severina, about 28km (17 miles) further on.*

RECOMMENDED WALKS

Continue from Rossano to Longobucco (take the SS177 via Cropalati – 23km/14 miles to Longobucco – 18km/11 miles) at the edge of a section of Parco Nazionale della Calabria. In the national park there are walks, wonderful scenery, rivers and places for picnics.

Cascading down the hillside, the town of Morana Calabro

Santa Severina now dreams peacefully of its days of glory

5 Santa Severina, Calabria
From its much eroded rocky pinnacle, Santa Severina dominates a now deforested, hot, dry landscape. It was denuded of its trees by the ancient Greeks and the Normans, who needed wood for their ships. This particular area of the Sila is called the Marchesato and is characterised by *calanchi* – strange other-worldly rock formations scattered about among the huge old, gnarled olive trees – and by *timpe*, other strange conical formations of clay. Santa Severina's situation on its table-like rock means that it has always been provided with natural defences, made use of first by the Byzantines then by the Normans.

Part of the town was abandoned after an earthquake in 1783. This is the Grecia quarter, in which you can still wander and see the remains of buildings which cannot have changed much since the first Byzantine settlement of the town. Do not

miss the adjacent Iudea (Jewish) quarter either – this is still inhabited. There is enough up here to keep you busy for a good few hours. As so often, it is the churches that are full of the more interesting items of the town's history, in particular the Addolorata, the Norman cathedral with its 13th-century entrance portal. While the cathedral has largely been rebuilt, the adjacent Battistero (Baptistery) is still very largely Byzantine, dating mostly from the 8th century. Its construction is reminiscent of the buildings of Ravenna.

The little 11th-century Church of Santa Filomena, with the Church of the Pozzolio underneath, looks like something from Armenia or Anatolia, its construction very un-Italian. It is a remarkable survivor in this part of the world. The old Castello may have been rebuilt by Robert Guiscard on top of an earlier Byzantine one. In its present form it dates from the Norman period; from here there are incredible views out over the Neto valley.

▶ Continue on the **SS107** in a northwesterly direction for about 34km (21 miles) until you reach the turning for the town of San Giovanni in Fiore.

SPECIAL TO...

In certain areas of this region are individual wines which you will not find outside Italy. *Val di Neto Bianco* (best with antipasti and fish), *Rosso* (good with local cheese) and *Rosato* (drunk with any local dishes), are wines from the Santa Severina district.
Melissa Bianco (best with antipasti and fish) and *Rosato* (best with soups, dishes using offal and light sweet cheese), originate from around Santa Severina and Crotone.
Ciro Bianco DOC (best with antipasti and fish) and *Rosso DOC* (best with any sort of local dish) are both excellent and well known wines from Ciro, just off the SS106 about 32km (20 miles) from Crotone.

6 San Giovanni in Fiore, Calabria

From San Giovanni in Fiore, 1,049m (3,442 feet) above sea-level, there are fine views of the surrounding countryside. This hilltown, in the heart of the Sila, grew up around the old *Badia Florense*; in fact, the town's community land today corresponds to the former territories of the *Badia* (abbey), which was founded by the Abbot Gioacchino in 1189. The abbey itself was suppressed at the beginning of the 19th century and its buildings are currently being restored. You can see its original buildings near the base of the town.

The older townswomen still wear the traditional costume (the *rituartu*) of black velvet skirt, bodice, white lacy blouse and jewellery. All the town's traditional crafts continue to flourish, including its wrought-iron workshops. It is also an important textile centre, as well as one of the few places where you will find craftsmen working with inlaid wood.

▶ *Go directly south from San Giovanni in Fiore for about 15km (9 miles) until you reach the **SS179**. Turn right and follow this west for a further 15km (9 miles) at which point turn left on to the **SS179dir** heading south. On reaching the **SS109** after a further 27km (16½ miles) turn right and follow this road through Taverna and (remaining on the **SS109** where the **SS109bis** branches off to Catanzaro) follow the signs to Gimigliano to Tiriolo.*

----------- FOR CHILDREN -----------

The hilly interior of Calabria is not particularly suitable for families travelling with young children. Local colour, particularly during religious festivals, would interest older children, and their are special sweetmeats made from nougat, chocolate and walnuts or dried figs for festivals.

7 Tiriolo, Calabria

The views of the surrounding countryside from Tiriolo are legendary. It stands high above the narrow ridge of mountains that divides the Tyrrhenian Sea from the Ionian Sea. If you venture about 200m (650 feet) further up the mountain from Tiriolo, you can see both seas – one of the great views of Calabria. In summer it is far cooler up in Tiriolo than at the bottom of the valleys – a good place to stop for lunch. Some of the women, usually the older ones, still wear their antique traditional costumes.

▶ *Take the **SS19** from Tiriolo going south but almost immediately turn right on to the **SS19dir** for 17km (11 miles) until the **SS18dir** turning for Nicastro.*

8 Nicastro, Calabria

Nicastro is another Calabrian town of Byzantine origin.

Red-roofed Rogliano in its green setting is largely 17th-century

Hanging precariously from the side of Monte Reventino, it is dominated by what remains of the Norman castle, mostly demolished in an earthquake in 1638. The Emperor Frederick II rebuilt the fortress and imprisoned his son Henry there. Scattered up and down the precipitous streets of this little town are a number of churches worth looking at.

Apart from the 18th-century cathedral and Church of San Domenico, there is the Church of Santa Caterina and the even more interesting Church of the Cappuccini dedicated to Sant'Antonio.

▶ *The **SS109** wends its way north to Rogliano, becoming the **SS19** at Soveria Mannelli after 27km (16½ miles).*

9 Rogliano, Calabria
A town has existed on this site since before the Romans ever came here. An earthquake

destroyed the medieval town in 1638 so that much of what survives today dates from the later 17th century.

The Church of San Giorgio, built from the local tufa stone and dating from 1544, has a mixed interior with items from various periods. It was restored in 1924. Other churches include the Cappuccini with a good wooden altar, and the Church of Santa Maria delle Grazie with a wonderful inlaid and gilded wooden ceiling. Wooden artefacts in the churches seem to be a speciality of this town – you

SPECIAL TO...

Savuto DOC, a robust red wine best with more piquant dishes and with roast meat, comes from the province of Cosenza, in particular from the countryside near Rogliano.

---

will see more in the little Chiesetta dell'Annunziata.

▶ *Continue north on the **SS19** to Cosenza, a distance of 18km (11 miles).*

BACK TO NATURE

In the northern part of the Sila, in the Sila Greca, is another part of the Parco Nazionale della Calabria. Easy to reach from either Cosenza, Rossano or San Giovanni in Fiore, the national park comprises mostly forest of ancient larch, beech, chestnut and Hungarian oak. In the spring there are clearings of asphodels and wild violets. The greatest wild population of wolves left in Italy survives in this park and in another just south of San Giovanni in Fiore. There are also wild cats and fallow deer, kept in enclosures which can be visited. Walks in the parks are recommended – the best way to see the goshawks, buzzards and eagle owls of the region.

The delightful town of Cosenza, set on the River Crati

Forgotten
Basilicata

The towns of this region are the least discovered in southern Italy. The countryside is possibly also the most unspoilt in the south. From the troglodytic old city of Matera to the great castle of Melfi, the Norman tombs at Venosa and the Greek-looking, white-washed town of Pisticci, Basilicata is a world all on its own.

4/5 DAYS • 710KM • 442 MILES

ITINERARY		
MATERA	►	**Metaponto (50km-31m)**
METAPONTO	►	**Pisticci (31km-19m)**
PISTICCI	►	**Maratea (169km-105m)**
MARATEA	►	**Rivello (24km-15m)**
RIVELLO	►	**Melfi (192km-120m)**
MELFI	►	**Venosa (25km-16m)**
VENOSA	►	**Pietrapertosa**
		(110km-68m)
PIETRAPERTOSA	►	**Tricarico (45km-28m)**
TRICARICO	►	**Miglionico (42km-26m)**
MIGLIONICO	►	**Matera (22km-14m)**

Matera holds its Festa della Bruna on 2 July, an event linked to the fertility of the earth and an abundant harvest. It involves a procession in which a large wagon containing the Madonna is dragged around the town by eight mules. Although the wagon, constructed by the same family each year, takes a laborious four months to complete, it is destroyed during the procession each year (as a part of the rite and not the work of vandals), everybody hoping to grab a piece of it as a relic. This is a strange festival in which the whole town takes part.

[i]   *Via De Viti de Marco 9, Matera*

▶ *Leave Matera going south on the main road to Ferrandina, the SS7, and after 12km (7½ miles) branch left on the SS380 (which, after about 12km/7½ miles becomes the SS175) and continue for 38km (23½ miles) to Metaponto.*

❶ **Metaponto,** Basilicata
The countryside on the way to Metaponto has a North African look. The eucalyptus and the maritime pines lining the route are strangely out of place. The ancient city of *Metapontum* was founded in the 7th century BC by Greek colonists and today is one of the better known sites of Magna Graecia (the Greek colonies in southern Italy). By contrast, the modern town is no more than a small resort by the sea. Beaches, hotels and restaurants make it a good place to stay and a convenient base from which to explore the ruins of the old city. Much of the latter survives including the remains of four large temples, a theatre, a forum and a Roman camp. *Metapontum* is famous for having been the town in which the mathematician and philosopher Pythagoras chose to live (at the end of the 6th century BC). He taught here and you can still see the 15 surviving columns (out of a total of 30 plus) of the Tavole Palatine, once his home and school, later transformed into the Temple of Hera. The antiquarium on the site provides

The glory that was Greece: the Temple of Hera at *Metapontum*

welcome relief in its cool dark rooms from the hot sun. Look out for the ancient fertility statues.

FOR HISTORY BUFFS

At Policoro, 19km (12 miles) south of Metaponto on the SS106, are the remains of the ancient colony of *Siris-Heradeia*. It has the remains of living quarters and a Temple of Demeter. An outstanding museum of antiquities from the area – Museo Nazionale della Siritide – contains sculpture, metalware and some fine Greek painted pottery.

▶ *From Metaponto, take the SS407 west, turning left on to the SS176 after 22km (14 miles). A further 2km (1 mile) along this road, a minor road leads off to Pisticci.*

2 Pisticci, Basilicata

The country town of Pisticci, built on an incline, has a colourful daily market. Go in the morning, because that is when you will see the women of the town shopping in their traditional costumes, with huge wide skirts and strange headgear. The streets are lined with houses, linked together with whitewashed walls and dusty brown terracotta roofs. The Chiesa Madre, the parish church (1542),

was built on the ruins of a 13th-century building and there is also a ruined medieval castle.

BACK TO NATURE

Basilicata is predominantly a mountainous region. The most peculiar rock formations found in the area are the *calanchi* around Pisticci, strange dry hillocks of rock.

▶ *From Pisticci, return to and take the SS176 going south. Turn left at the junction with the SS103 and continue for 19km (12 miles) until you hit the SS598. Go east along this for 16km (10 miles) until you reach the coastal SS106. Follow this for about 9km (6 miles), going south, until you reach the SS653. This latter goes inland again – follow it for 85km (53 miles) until you reach the autostrada A3. Go under this and turn left on to the SS19. After 5km (3 miles), turn right and follow the country road through Lauria to the SS585. Turn right on to this and very shortly left on to the minor road which leads, via Trecchina, to Maratea.*

3 Maratea, Basilicata

This is perhaps the best known part of Basilicata. The coastline is unspoilt and is studded with little rocky coves where you can swim in complete privacy. The Marina di Maratea and the old port have a number of restaurants and little hotels. The old town, climbing up a hill, is still mostly intact. You can visit the picturesque medieval quarter with its loggias and small doorways. Maratea is the kind of place to explore on your own, discovering the odd café for a quick drink or *cappuccino*. you can also visit the 17th-century former Convento di San Francesco with its two-storeyed cloister of pointed arches. On a peak just above Maratea you cannot fail to notice the enor-

Fine local cheeses for sale near Rivello

mous statue of the Redeemer – 22m (72 feet) high.

ℹ *Piazza del Gesù 40*

SCENIC ROUTES

Monte Biagio, way above Maratea, affords magnificent views of the Gulf of Policastro. The drive to the top of the mountain is worth every crippling hairpin bend. Bagni, on the western slopes of Monte Vúlture, gives you some stunning views of the extinct volcano.

▶ *From Maratea, retrace the route of the SS585. Turn left and after a short distance you come to the minor road off to Rivello.*

4 Rivello, Basilicata

This must be one of the prettiest towns in southern Italy. It straddles the spine of two hills and, because of its shape, is thought to look like a dragon. Rivello coils itself around the top of the hill, each little street thick with outside staircases and small galleries and overhung with wrought-iron balconies. At each end of the town is a – mainly Byzantine – church. Santa Barbara has a very pretty apse decorated with tiny hanging arches, while San Nicola dei Greci seems more like a fortress than anything else. The lovely, frescoed 15th-century Convento dei Minori has a wooden choir carved by local monks, and depicting various trades.

▶ *Take the SS585 to its junction with the autostrada A3, then follow the latter for 70km (44 miles) until you hit the autostrada going east to Potenza from the Sicignano junction. At Potenza, go north*

on the SS93 for 50km (31 miles) towards Melfi before branching off on the SS303 for the final 6km (4 miles) of the journey.

BACK TO NATURE

Sirino Range, the highest peak of which is Monte del Papa (Mount Papa) 2,005m (6,578 feet), is visible as you leave Rivello and join the A3. It is densely wooded with hazelnut, oak, chestnut, alder and beech and it harbours forest birds, foxes and wolves.

5 Melfi, Basilicata

Dark and medieval Melfi is crammed with the remains of its illustrious past, in particular those from the Norman and

Hohenstaufen periods. You can see part of the old perimeter wall, the Norman castle with its eight towers, each one different, and the cathedral of 1155, with its Norman Sicilian bell tower. The castle contains a museum of antiquities whose prize exhibit is a 1st-century Roman sarcophagus, the *Sarcofago di Rapallo*. The old city gate, the Porta Venosina, is Norman, though Frederick II (Hohenstaufen) tampered with it. A walk around the town would include a handful of little churches including the very much restored 17th-century San Lorenzo.

▶ *Return via the **SS303** to the **SS93** at Rapolla. Turn left and proceed for 8km (5 miles) before turning right on to the **SS168** for Venosa, a total of 25km (16 miles).*

RECOMMENDED
WALKS

Just south of Melfi, around the base of the extinct volcano, Monte Vúlture, are some good walks that follow the paths used by brigands in the past. However, there is nothing to fear today: the paths are quite safe, and the only thing that will cross your path will be wild game and maybe shepherds and their flocks. Walks in this area take you around the beautiful Laghi (Lakes) di Monticchio. You can also use horses on the longer routes and local people sometimes act as guides.

larly favoured by the Romans, whose *Via Appia* passed through it, and it was the birthplace of

while the cathedral, which shows Catalan influence, is early 16th-century.

Wander around the medieval centre with its huge old paving slabs and carved doorways. Behind the Church of San Rocco you can see the even older remains of Roman houses and baths, while further on appear some fragments of an early Christian baptistery and a Roman amphitheatre. Perhaps the most interesting of all is the Abbey of La Trinità. Begun around 1050, it is in three parts, having an old church, an abbey and a later (1135), but unfinished, 'new' church. It became the final resting place of the five De Hauteville brothers who were responsible for conquering southern Italy for the Normans (while William the Conqueror was doing the same to England).

6 Venosa, Basilicata
Venosa belongs, visually, more to the nearby region of Puglia than to Basilicata. As in Melfi, you can trace the town's history in the streets, but here the various periods are more easily distinguishable. It was particu-

Quintus Horatius Flaccus, the poet Horace (65–8 BC). Others who came here include Byzantines, Saracens, Normans, Hohenstaufens, Angevins and the Spanish. The formidable castle, dominating Piazza Umberto, dates from 1470,

The pretty hilltown of Rivello

▶ *Return to the **SS93** and then to Potenza. Then take the **SS407** going east for 30km (19 miles), branching inland for about 11km (7 miles) to Pietrapertosa.*

7 Pietrapertosa, Basilicata
This rock town, poised way above deep surrounding valleys, is, at 1,088m (3,570 feet), the highest town in Basilicata. The road climbs up to it in a series of hair-raising bends. It is surrounded by strange irregular rock formations with names like Áquila Reale (Golden Eagle), Rocca Saracena (Saracen's Rock) and Grande Madre (Big Mother).

Like many of the other towns of the region, Pietrapertosa is full of little wrought-iron balconies and tiny houses with carved doorways of great antiquity. If you do not want to visit the town's several little churches, you can just sit on a wall and gaze out over the surrounding hills and the woods. However, the Church of the Minori Osservanti is well worth a visit with its 15th- and 16th-century art, and also San Cataldo, which has a fine 16th-century altarpiece and carved wooden choir.

▶ *Return towards the SS407. This time pass under it and take the minor road through Campomaggiore to the SS7. Turn right and drive to Tricarico.*

8 Tricarico, Basilicata
Tricarico has a strange Arab quarter, the Rabatana, which even today is more reminiscent of Morocco than the Italian mainland. You enter it via the Porta Saracena (Saracen Gate). The Rabatana is full of chickens running about and old women in black sitting in doorways. On the whole, however, Tricarico is a town of medieval houses with ancient sculpted doorways and old balconies. Many of these houses have the evil eye symbol embedded into their stonework. The cathedral is 11th-century, though much restored, and there is a variety of other churches, notably Sant'Antonio with its frescoed cloister.

Venosa – an attractive town with rich historical associations

Although much of the old centre is dilapidated, Tricarico has an air of faded grandeur, much of it owed to the wealthy Carafa family.

▶ *From Tricarico, take the SS7 for 42km (26 miles) to Miglionico.*

9 Miglionico, Basilicata
Miglionico is still a fortified town, its Norman defences and 11th-century castle partially intact. The castle dominates the town and was the scene of a notorious plot late in the 15th century, in which the local barons conspired to overthrow the king, Ferdinand of Aragon. It failed and the castle acquired the nickname 'Malconsiglio' – 'bad counsel'. If you are short of time, go straight to the Church of San Francesco and see the altarpiece painted by Cima di Conegliano, an important early 16th-century Venetian painter much influenced by Bellini. It has 18 sections and is Basilicata's most important painting.

▶ *From Miglionico it is only 22km (14 miles) back to Matera via the SS7.*

FOR CHILDREN

In a variety of places you can stay on a farm in self-contained accommodation. Most have farmyard animals, some have swimming pools. Ask the tourist office for the *Guide to Rural Hospitality (Guida dell'Ospitalità Rurale)* for details of locations.

Ancient Puglia

From towns with hefty, solid Norman cathedrals and castles, to villages with curious, prehistoric-looking, conical-roofed houses and farmsteads, central Puglia is packed with the evidence of a rich and diverse past. Bari is one of the biggest cities in Puglia, and the most cosmopolitan spot on this tour with a large variety of shops and restaurants as well as a medieval centre and a busy port.

3/4 DAYS • 314KM • 196 MILES

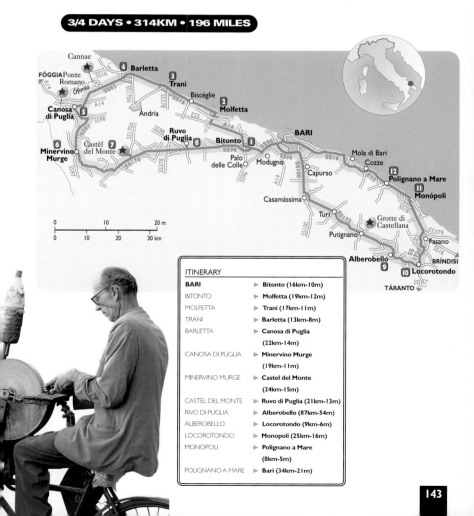

ITINERARY

BARI	▶ **Bitonto (16km–10m)**
BITONTO	▶ **Molfetta (19km–12m)**
MOLFETTA	▶ **Trani (17km–11m)**
TRANI	▶ **Barletta (13km–8m)**
BARLETTA	▶ **Canosa di Puglia (22km–14m)**
CANOSA DI PUGLIA	▶ **Minervino Murge (19km–11m)**
MINERVINO MURGE	▶ **Castel del Monte (24km–15m)**
CASTEL DEL MONTE	▶ **Ruvo di Puglia (21km–13m)**
RIVO DI PUGLIA	▶ **Alberobello (87km–54m)**
ALBEROBELLO	▶ **Locorotondo (9km–6m)**
LOCOROTONDO	▶ **Monopoli (25km–16m)**
MONOPOLI	▶ **Polignano a Mare (8km–5m)**
POLIGNANO A MARE	▶ **Bari (34km–21m)**

i   *Piazza Moro 32a, Bari*

▶ *Bitonto is 16km (10 miles)
from Bari. Take the **SS96** from
the city centre, then branch
along the **SS98**.*

❶ **Bitonto,** Puglia
Right in the centre of Bitonto is
the fine Puglian Romanesque
13th-century cathedral. Its best
features are the women's gallery,
the carvings of animals on the
entrance portals, and the pulpit
with its primitive bas-relief
portraits of Emperor Frederick
II and Isabella of England. Go
down into the crypt and see the
lovely column supports there.
Other interesting churches are
San Francesco with its late 13th-
century façade, and the Church
of the Purgatorio which has a
sculptured relief of human
skeletons just above the main
entrance portal. Most of the
centre of town is either
Renaissance or baroque. See in
particular the Palazzo Sylos-
Labini and its Renaissance
courtyard.

▶ *From Bitonto, travel north to
the **A14**. Take the autostrada
northwest for 11km (7 miles)
until the Molfetta exit.*

❷ **Molfetta,** Puglia
Molfetta is an active fishing
port – its fleet is one of the
larger ones on the Adriatic.
Predominantly medieval, it has

a lovely 12th- to 13th-century cathedral, the Duomo Vecchio, dominated by three domes – a Byzantine feature. There is also the Duomo Nuovo (new cathedral), though in this case 'new' means late 18th-century. This building has a baroque façade. The town has two museums. The Archaeological Museum contains the finds, including some Hellenistic ceramics, from local excavations. The Museo Diocesano (Diocesan Museum) is housed in the bishop's palace.

▶ *Take the coastal road SS16 going northwest via Bisceglie to Trani, about 17km (11 miles).*

❸ **Trani,** Puglia

Trani has always been an important port. Trade with the Orient in the 11th century drew into its orbit merchants from Genoa, Pisa and Amalfi and also created a large Jewish community. Still a large and prosperous port, it is full of little restaurants serving seafood.

The cathedral, which sits in an open-ended piazza facing the sea, is a fine building. Puglian Romanesque in style, it contains the remains of two other, earlier, structures on the same site. The oldest of these was an early Christian catacomb which you can still see with its marble columns and frescos: above that, though below the existing nave, are the remains of Santa Maria, the earlier Byzantine cathedral. The most noteworthy element of the present building is the pair of 12th-century bronze doors by a local master. Two other buildings that should not be missed are the Church of the Ognissanti, built by the Knights Templar as a hospice and, near the harbour, the Palazzo Caccetta, a 15th-century palace in the Gothic style – unusual in Puglia.

ℹ️ *Via Cavour 140*

Castel del Monte is one of the great medieval buildings of Europe

▶ *Continue up the coast on the SS16 to Barletta, 13km (8 miles).*

❹ **Barletta,** Puglia

In Barletta is the largest known bronze statue in existence. Called the Colosso, it is 5m (15 feet) high and represents a Roman emperor, possibly Valentinian, who died in AD 375. You can see it on its pedestal at the end of the Corso Vittorio Emanuele. In the Middle Ages Barletta was an important and prosperous port. Like Trani it still retains much of its prosperity and has a pretty, if somewhat dilapidated medieval centre. As usual, the cathedral is the town's most interesting building. Built in the 12th century, the Duomo has a lovely rose window and there is an inscription above the left entrance portal which records how the English king Richard Coeur de Lion was involved in its construction (he came here on his way to the Crusades). Visit the 13th-century Church of San Sepolcro, the design of which recalls the Church of the Holy Sepulchre in Jerusalem, and the former

Ruvo di Puglia's fine Romanesque cathedral

convent building of San Domenico which now houses the Museo Civico (Civic Museum) and picture gallery. The castle is a massive structure, originally built by Emperor Frederick II and enlarged by Charles of Anjou.

ℹ️ *c/o Comando Vigili Polizia Urbana*

▶ *The SS93 branches inland from Barletta and goes to*

Trani's cathedral is considered one of the best in Puglia

Canosa di Puglia, about 22km (14 miles).

5 Canosa di Puglia, Puglia
Standing in the Tavoliere Plain, this town was an important Roman centre, called *Canusium*. Remains of Roman baths, amphitheatres and basilicas can be seen, and there is a Roman bridge over the Ofanto river which only survives because its arches were rebuilt in the Middle Ages. There are two later items of interest in the town's Romanesque cathedral: the marble 11th-century bishop's throne, which rests on the backs of two elephants; and the Tomb of Bohemund, Prince of Antioch, who was the son of Robert Guiscard and who died in 1111. The tomb's doors were made from a single slab of bronze. Other relics of the town's past are kept in the Museo Civico (Civic Museum).

▶ *From Canosa di Puglia, take the SS98 towards Andria, turning off right after 7km (4 miles) on the SS97 to Minervino Murge, a further 12km (7 miles).*

6 Minervino Murge, Puglia
Minervino Murge is known as the 'Balcony of Puglia' because of its wonderful position at the edge of the Murgia Alta, the rolling hills on Puglia's southern border. 'Minervino' derives from an ancient temple dedicated to the worship of Minerva on whose remains rises the present-day Church of the Madonna del Crocifisso. Apart

from the church and the panoramas of the countryside, this little town has a 12th-century castle, a Palazzo Comunale built in local style and a Norman cathedral, re-embellished in the Renaissance.

SCENIC ROUTES

The views from Minervino Murge to the surrounding countryside show a landscape that is most typically Puglian – gently rolling, almost flat.

▶ Take the **SS170** eastwards for 22km (13½ miles) until the **SS170dir** branches off to the left. Follow the latter for 1km (½ mile) to the turning for Castel del Monte on the left.

7 Castel del Monte, Puglia
This huge isolated castle is one of the most impressive monuments surviving from the reign of Emperor Frederick II and is well worth a special excursion to visit it. With its eight Gothic corner towers, you can see it from miles away, crowning an isolated peak way above the surrounding countryside. It was built around 1240 and in plan is a perfect octagon – the number eight being the symbol of the crown. You can wander through huge rooms, eight on each floor, that were once decorated with reliefs in Greek marble, porphyry and precious stones, now mostly disappeared. The castle may have been used originally as a centre for astronomy as its proportions are supposed to relate to the movements of the planets. But it was also the very grim prison of Frederick II's grandsons, who were incarcerated here for 30 years. Notice the beautiful carved entrance portal and, among what is left of its decoration, the signs of classical, Gothic, Persian and Arabic influences.

▶ Return to the **SS170** and follow it eastwards. It joins the **SS98** 2km (1 mile) before Ruvo di Puglia.

RECOMMENDED WALKS

On a visit to the Castel del Monte, walk some way from the castle to appreciate the full impact of this extraordinary building.
All around is a pretty, agricultural and virtually empty landscape, called the Tavoliere, splendid for walks and also for picnics.

8 Ruvo di Puglia, Puglia
Ruvo di Puglia was a town celebrated in ancient times for its pottery. As long ago as the 5th century BC, its terracotta vases were highly sought after and some of these can be seen in the Palazzo Jatta. Here, too, is the magnificent red-figured Greek vase known as the 'Crater of Talos'. It is an important collection which you should not miss. Ruvo's cathedral is an important Puglian Romanesque building – one of the best in Puglia. Built in the 13th century, it has a richly decorated façade and a superb 16th-century rose window. In particular, notice the griffins surmounting the columns on either side of the main entrance. Around the sides of the building are little sculpted figures of ancient, pagan gods, which it is thought may have been copied from classical pottery.

▶ Return to Bari via the **SS98**. Skirt round the southern edge of the city on the **SS16** and turn right on to the **SS100**. Take the latter as far as Casamassima, 15km (9 miles), then branch left along the **SS172** to Alberobello, 35km (22 miles).

9 Alberobello, Puglia
Alberobello is a very curious town. Clustered together in its centre is a collection of the prehistoric-looking local buildings called *trulli*. These small, circular, single-storey, stone buildings with cone-shaped tiled roofs look a bit like upside-down ice-cream cornets. There is nothing quite like them in any other part of Italy. Once such houses were common in Mediterranean countries – the beehive-shaped prehistoric Sardinian *nuraghi* are not dissimilar – but in Puglia, for some reason, they are a living tradition. Wander through the narrow streets of the Rione Monti and Aia Piccola quarters of Alberobello, where most of the *trulli* (there are over 1,000) are whitewashed and still inhabited. Even the style of the

Conical-roofed *trulli*, the traditional houses of Puglia

Church of Sant'Antonio seems to have derived its looks from the *trulli*. Most of Alberobello is a national monument, so that what has survived of its strange appearance is in very good

Molfetta's domed 'old cathedral' gazes benignly over the harbour

condition. One or two of the *trulli* are open to the public or have been turned into shops and restaurants.

FOR CHILDREN

Puglia is really not an area to bring children. However, they might enjoy looking into the *trulli* – built, it seems, more for hobbtis than for humans. Everything in these igloo-like structures is in miniature. In both Alberobello and Locorotondo, one or two of them are open to the public. At Fasano, a developing holiday centre about 10km (6 miles) from both Alberobello and Locorotondo, there is a zoo/safari park, where animals of the African plains, such as giraffes, can be seen in the rough, dry terrain not far removed from their natural habitat.

▶ The **SS172** leads straight to Locorotondo.

10 Locorotondo, Puglia
Locorotondo was laid out in concentric circles around the pinnacle of a low hill, and takes its name ('round place') from this plan. From the town there are wonderful views out over the Itria Valley in which you can see clumps of *trulli* scattered about – generally farmhouses and barns. In Locorotondo everything is covered with whitewash and gleams in the scorching Puglian summer sun. Small Greek-looking houses cluster around secret courtyards. There are geraniums in pots on the balconies, and the cobbled alleys and passages make this one of the more picturesque towns of Puglia. If you want to get out of the sun for a while, visit the churches of San Giorgio and San Marco della Greca, the former neo-classical, the latter a much earlier, possibly late Gothic, building.

▶ The **SS172dir** leads via Fasano to the **SS16**. From Fasano, take the **SS16** to Monopoli, about 12km (7½ miles).

SCENIC ROUTES

The views from Locorotondo across the Trulli Zone of the Itria Valley make it easy to imagine yourself in a prehistoric landscape: the strange, *trulli* (beehive-like buildings) which dot the countryside are the kind of houses that the long-ago ancestors of present-day Puglians might have lived in. Nobody knows the real age or origins of these dwellings which are found solely in a small region round Alberobello and nowhere else in Europe.

11 Monopoli, Puglia
Monopoli is the most beautiful port on this strip of the Adriatic coastline. In the older quarter, tall medieval houses are built right up to the quay, overlooking the port and the little brightly painted fishing boats. The old centre is full of churches and other buildings which bear the traces of Byzantine and Venetian invaders. There is a castle, a Romanesque cathedral of 1107, with an impressive baroque façade and bell tower, and the Church of San Domenico, perhaps the most magnificent building in the town. The Renaissance façade of San Domenico is split into three parts by columns and decorated

with statues, and there is a fine rose window. At various points beneath Monopoli, there are underground chambers and places of worship. One such is the Chiesa-Grotta, a natural cave, decorated in Byzantine times.

▶ From Monopoli, take the coast road northwest to Polignano a Mare, about 8km (5 miles).

12 Polignano a Mare, Puglia
Polignano a Mare is a delightful old city with little alleyways and flights of stepss. In the old quarter is the parish church dedicated to Our Lady of the Assumption. Although Romanesque in style, it was added to during the Renaissance period. Ask to see the painting by the 15th-century Venetian artists Vivarini, in the sacristy. Just outside town are the Grotte Palazzese (Palazzese Caves), set into the cliffsides. These are two huge sea caves, reached by climbing down precarious steps set into the rock just below the town.

▶ The **SS16** leads back to Bari, 34km (21 miles).

SCENIC ROUTES

The coastline from Polignano a Mare to Mola di Bari, going along the SS16, is lovely unspoilt coastal scenery (though not suitable for swimming except from the rocks).

The Heel of
Italy

Scattered all over southern Puglia are monuments that seem more Greek than Italian, while others look as though they should be in northern Europe rather than in the hot sunny Puglian countryside. Greeks, Arabs, Normans – these were just some of the inhabitants of Puglia in the past.

3 DAYS • 352KM • 219 MILES

ITINERARY	
BRINDISI	► Ostuni (35km-22m)
OSTUNI	► Mesagne (28km-17m)
MESAGNE	► Grottaglie (38km-24m)
GROTTAGLIE	► Oria (20km-12m)
ORIA	► Lecce (50km-31m)
LECCE	► Otranto (48km-30m)
OTRANTO	► Gallipoli (30km-19m)
GALLIPOLI	► Manduria (60km-37m)
MANDURIA	► Brindisi (43km-27m)

SCENIC ROUTES

The approach road (either the
SS605, the SS16 or the narrow
country road that leads from
the coast) to Ostuni is
scenically outstanding,
principally for the stunning
views to the town itself. Rising
on to a little hill and bleached
white in the sun, it looks more
Greek than Italian.

[i] *Via C Colombo 88, Brindisi*

▶ *From Brindisi, the* **SS16** *leads
via San Vito dei Normanni to
Ostuni, 35km (22 miles).*

❶ **Ostuni,** Puglia
Ostuni is built on three hills
about 200m (600 feet) above
sea-level. The oldest part of the
town, also the highest, is the
most interesting, dominated by
the huge Gothic cathedral. This
building, which seems more
Spanish than anything else, has
three lovely rose windows in its
façade. Near by is the Palazzo
Vescovile (Bishop's Palace), the
two parts of which, on two sides
of the square in which it stands,
are connected by a little honey-
coloured stone bridge. Further
down the hill is the baroque
Church of Santa Maria
Maddalena, topped by a
patterned majolica cupola. All
around these three buildings,
and leading down to the huge
dusty Piazza Libertà in the
19th-century part of the town,

FOR CHILDREN

If you can make it to Ostuni
for La Cavalcata di
Sant'Oronzo (St Oronzo's
Cavalcade) – check with the
local tourist office for dates –
the children will be good for
the rest of the trip. Horses and
riders trundle through the
streets colourfully dressed in
Saracen attire – both animals
and riders decked out in
embroidered cloth and plumes.

Ostuni's whitewashed houses
climb steeply up its winding streets

are little alleys burrowing
through the gleaming whitewashed buildings of the old
quarter.

[i] *Via Continelli 47*

▶ *Take the* **SS16** *back to San
Vito, where you should turn on
to the* **SS605** *to Mesagne.*

❷ **Mesagne,** Puglia
Mesagne sits in the middle of
the Tavoliere di Lecce, a large,
flat plain heavily cultivated with
figs, olives and vineyards.
Nowadays, Mesagne prospers
from the fertility of the
surrounding landscape and its
market should be one of the
stopping points on this itinerary.
The castle is worth taking an
hour or two to look at. Built
originally in 1062 by the
Norman adventurer Robert
Guiscard, various attackers
destroyed it over the years and
the last time it was rebuilt was

in the 17th century. It is a spectacular construction with a
rather lovely Renaissance loggia
which runs along its north and
east sides. The parish church,
the Chiesa Madre, is baroque
and the Church of Sant'Anna is
rococo; both are worth a visit –
in fact the latter is the best
example of its style in the area.

▶ *Join the* **SS7** *on the north
edge of town which leads
west to Grottaglie, about
38km (24 miles).*

❸ **Grottaglie,** Puglia
This town is one of the most
renowned centres for ceramics
in southern Italy. Many of the
items for sale are traditional and
well-tried designs, long abandoned by more up-to-date
craftsmen elsewhere. The
ceramicists' quarters lie behind

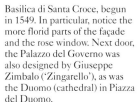

the massive castle. Here you can still see people making things in the traditional ways and their wares line practically every flat surface in sight – including roofs. This is an excellent – and inexpensive – place to buy ceramics. You can visit the Church of the Carmine which has a traditional Presepio (Christmas crib) of 1530. The early 12th-century Chiesa Matrice is a very decorative building. Its Chapel of the Rosary is topped by a cupola decorated with local coloured tiles, and the church also has an exotic Puglian Romanesque entrance portal.

▶ *Return along the SS7 branching off to Francavilla Fontana, 14km (8½ miles), at which head towards Oria, only 6km (3½ miles) – follow the signs in the south of the town.*

4 Oria, Puglia
Oria is yet another Puglian town dominated by a castle built by Emperor Frederick II. Although over the years it has been altered and enlarged, it still retains its basic triangular shape. In its vaulted hall is a small museum. Not far away is the Cripta dei Santi Crisante e

You can enjoy fresh seafood in the little port of Gallipoli

Daria, a small subterranean basilica dating from the 9th century topped by a series of shallow domes and decorated with frescos. Oria's cathedral was rebuilt in the 18th century following an earthquake; its most noteworthy element is its ceramic covered dome. In the old town, with its winding streets and whitewashed houses, search out the Jewish quarter – the Giudecca – which is still very much as it was in the Middle Ages when a large community of Jews lived here.

▶ *From Oria, continue along the country road for 20km (12 miles), via Torre Santa Susanna, to the SS7ter which runs to Lecce, 50km (31 miles), joining and becoming the SS16 shortly before the town.*

5 Lecce, Puglia
Lecce is to southern Italy what Florence is to central Italy. The city is an architectural gem and is filled with magnificently decorated, ebullient, baroque (mostly late 16th- and early 17th-century) buildings built from a soft, golden sandstone called 'Pietra di Lecce'. The most notable architects were Antonio and Giuseppe Zimbalo who, between them, were responsible for most of the

Basilica di Santa Croce, begun in 1549. In particular, notice the more florid parts of the façade and the rose window. Next door, the Palazzo del Governo was also designed by Giuseppe Zimbalo ('Zingarello'), as was the Duomo (cathedral) in Piazza del Duomo.

Not everything is baroque in Lecce. In Piazza Sant'Oronzio are the remains of a Roman amphitheatre which at one time could probably seat about 25,000 people, and a Roman column topped by a statue of St Oronsius. There is also a lovely example of Puglian Romanesque architecture in the Church of Santi Nicolò e Cataldo. Lecce is a busy, thriving town with good ceramic shops selling the more expensive end of Grottaglie's range of wares. There are antique shops, restaurants and an indoor market selling local produce.

ℹ *Via Monte San Michele 20*

▶ *Take the SS16 south as far as Maglie, 29km (18 miles). From the road bypassing Maglie, branch to the left along the SS16 to Otranto, 19km (12 miles).*

6 Otranto, Puglia
In the 11th century this little town was one of the leading Crusader ports. Nowadays it is better known as a port for ferries going to Greece. However, Otranto does have a good cathedral with one of the most stunning rose windows in Puglia. Founded by the Normans in 1080, it was added to and embellished over the years. This is the only medieval building in southern Italy to have preserved its entire original mosaic floor. There are scenes from the scriptures, depictions of animals and mythological subjects. In the oldest part of Otranto is the small Church of San Pietro, a delightful Byzantine building which may have been the town's old cathedral. There is also a castle here, built by

Ferdinand of Aragon at the end of the 15th century. Inside you can see the remains of Roman brickwork and some very early medieval masonry.

☐ *Lungomare Kennedy*

▶ *Retrace the route to Maglie, then continue on the SS497 as far as Neviano, about 17km (11 miles), then follow the signs for Gallipoli.*

7 Gallipoli, Puglia
Gallipoli is a remote place, on an island just off the west coast of the Salentine Peninsula. The oldest part of the town, with its narrow little streets, is joined to the mainland by a causeway. On the edge of it, and dominating it, is the Castello, the oldest part of which is Byzantine. There is also an elaborate baroque cathedral of 1630. The interior is

sprinkled with works by local artists – see in particular the *Madonna with Sant'Orontius* by Giovanni Coppola. If it is open, go into the Church of the Purità and see the richly decorated ceramic paving tiles of 18th-century majolica.

▶ *From Gallipoli, take the SS101 to Galatone, turning left on to the SS174 proceeding northwards via Nardo to Manduria, a further 47km (29 miles).*

8 Manduria, Puglia
Manduria was an important centre of the local Messapian civilisation which long predated

Jewish quarter, the confines of which are marked by three large tufa arches. The houses here have no windows. See also the impressive 1719 Palazzo Imperiale, in Piazza Garibaldi.

▶ *From Manduria, go across country to Oria, 11km (7 miles), then from there to the SS7 via Latiano, also about 11km (7 miles), then follow the SS7 to Brindisi, 21km (13 miles).*

The town of Grottaglie is noted for its fine pottery

the coming of the Greek colonists to the area. The Messapians here fiercely opposed the Greeks, and the ruins of their ancient settlement can be seen to the north of the 'new' town.

There is a necropolis and a stretch of ancient city walls. The oldest of the latter (there are three sets of walls concentrically sited around what was the old city) date from the 5th century BC and the latest from about the 3rd century BC. Carefully cut blocks of stone, a strange triple gate and 2,000 rock-cut tombs survive. In the middle of the excavations is the

famous Pozzo di Plinio (Well of Pliny – so called because Pliny himself mentions it), in which the water remains at a constant level however much you draw out of it. The most interesting part of the town itself is the

One of Puglia's many delightful hilltop towns

SPECIAL TO...

The western coast of the Salentine Peninsula, that is, between Gallipoli and Capo Santa Maria di Leuca, has some of Italy's best beaches. Gallipoli itself has good places for bathing, and there are other places at nearby Lido San Giovanni and Baia Verde, both within 10km (6 miles) of Gallipoli.

BACK TO NATURE

Wooded and shrub-covered hillsides in southern Italy are favoured by several species of birds of prey. They nest in the trees and use thermals generated off the land to gain lift. Species such as short-toed eagle, buzzard, sparrowhawk and goshawk are widespread and there is always a chance of seeing a golden eagle or Bonelli's eagle. Regrettably, birds of prey are much persecuted by Italian 'sportsmen'.

Puglia's harsh, dry landscape changes dramatically in spring

The Gargano
Peninsula

While most of Puglia is relatively flat, the Gargano Peninsula, a rocky, partially wooded outcrop, constitutes what is possibly the only really scenic stretch of Adriatic coastline since Venice. It is the spur of Italy's boot which rises unexpectedly from the sea, an area of saints and mystic legends.

3 DAYS • 366KM • 228 MILES

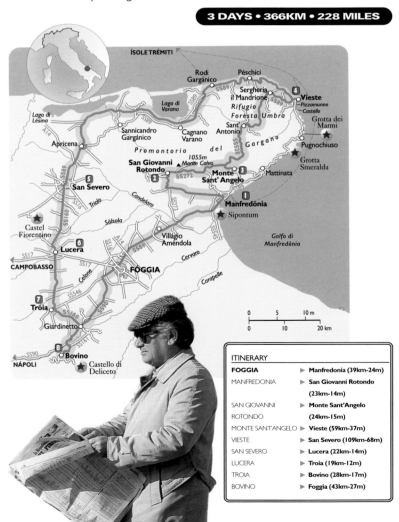

ITINERARY		
FOGGIA	▶	**Manfredonia (39km-24m)**
MANFREDONIA	▶	**San Giovanni Rotondo (23km-14m)**
SAN GIOVANNI ROTONDO	▶	**Monte Sant'Angelo (24km-15m)**
MONTE SANT'ANGELO	▶	**Vieste (59km-37m)**
VIESTE	▶	**San Severo (109km-68m)**
SAN SEVERO	▶	**Lucera (22km-14m)**
LUCERA	▶	**Troia (19km-12m)**
TROIA	▶	**Bovino (28km-17m)**
BOVINO	▶	**Foggia (43km-27m)**

i *Via Senatore E Perrone 17,*
Foggia

▶ *From Foggia, take the SS89*
to Manfredonia.

❶ Manfredonia, Puglia
This lively port takes its name
from Manfred, the son of
Emperor Frederick II and King
of Sicily and Naples. Not much
is left from that period in the
13th century, apart from the
hefty remains of Manfred's
castle, which now houses the
Museo Archeologico del
Gargano (National
Archaeological Museum of
Gargano), displaying artefacts
from the remains of nearby
ancient *Sipontum*. There is an
undistinguished cathedral, built
in 1680. More interesting is the
Church of San Domenico with
its Gothic doorway flanked by
two stone lions and, inside,
14th-century frescos.
Manfredonia is a base for ferries
to the Tremiti Islands on the
other side of the Gargano
Peninsula. These tiny resorts
are wonderful places to swim
and sunbathe and consequently
are extremely popular.

i *Corso Manfredi 26*

▶ *From Manfredonia, follow the*
signs inland to San Giovanni

Rotondo, about 23km (14
miles).

FOR HISTORY BUFFS

To the south of Manfredonia
are the remains of ancient
Sipontum, abandoned in the
Middle Ages because of
malaria. Hannibal conquered
it in the 3rd century BC, only
to lose it to the Romans. There
is a museum here as well as
the lovely Santa Maria Siponto,
an 11th-century church that
survives from the very last
period of the town. Near the
museum is a recently
discovered Christian catacomb
(for details of access, ask at the
museum).

SPECIAL TO...

Manfredonia is noted for its
delicious red wine called Orta
Nova. If you can stand up after
a lunch including this, then
good luck to you.

❷ San Giovanni Rotondo,
Puglia
The little town of San Giovanni
Rotondo drifts down the side of
Monte Calvo (Mount Calvo)

and is one of the principal
pilgrimage centres of Italy. Here
lived Padre Pio da Pietralcina, a
20th-century miracle-worker
who, like St Francis, received
the *stigmata* – the wounds of
Christ on his hands and feet and
in his side. This modern saint
(1887–1969) is buried in the
newish church near the 16th-
century Convent of Santa Maria
delle Grazie and his tomb is the
object of much veneration
today. The town takes its name
from a round temple, possibly
dedicated to Jupiter, which
became the Rotonda di San
Giovanni, a baptistery of uncer-
tain date. There are plenty of
hotels and restaurants, and
souvenir shops by the dozen.

SPECIAL TO...

In San Giovanni Rotondo, is the
Festa dell'Ospite (the Guest's
Festival). For a week there are
lively folklore celebrations,
exhibitions and displays, local
gastronomic treats and a great
deal of local – and very potent
– wine is consumed (usually
11–20 August, but check for
any changes to these dates).

i *Piazza Europa 104*

▶ *From San Giovanni Rotondo,
the SS272 winds eastwards
to Monte Sant'Angelo.*

❸ Monte Sant'Angelo,
Puglia

This is another of Italy's important pilgrimage sites. St Michael is supposed to have appeared, in the 5th century, in a cave set deep within the ground – the same Santuario di San Michele (Sanctuary of St Michael) that you can visit today. A church was built in front of the grotto in 1273 and its contemporary belltower copies the plan, though in miniature, of the Castel del Monte (see page 147). On your way down to the dark, damp cave, you will pass a set of beautiful bronze doors dating from 1076. Reputedly made in Constantinople, they depict scenes from the Old Testament. In the grotto itself is a statue of St Michael by Andrea Sansovino, a Renaissance Florentine sculptor much under the influence of Raphael. The oldest quarter of Monte Sant'Angelo is the medieval Junno district, which would have been known by illustrious visitors of the past, such as St Thomas Aquinas and St Francis.

In another part of town is the 'Tomb of Rothari', in fact a very early, and rather unusual, baptistery building. It stands next to the late medieval Church of San Pietro.

▶ *Retrace the route for 6km
(4 miles) before turning right
on the SS528 through the
centre of the Gargano for
24km (15 miles) to
Sant'Antonio. Here branch
right, following the signs to
Segheria il Mandrione, at
which take the SS89 to Vieste.*

❹ Vieste, Puglia
Vieste, beautifully situated on a tip of the Gargano Peninsula, surrounded by coves, cliffs and beaches, is a popular resort. The town is dominated by a castle

and a cathedral. There are no saints here, and fewer monuments, but who cares? There is plenty to do. Apart from shops and restaurants, there are all sorts of caves within reach of the town, accessible either on foot or by boat (tours) – just to the south are the Grotta Smeralda (Emerald Cave) and the Grotta dei Marmi (Cave of the Marbles). South of the town are the beaches of Pizzomunno and Castello – both long. From Vieste ferries run to the Tremiti Islands.

i *Corso Lorenzo Fazzini 8*

▶ *Take the coastal road going
north to join the SS89 at
Peschici. Continue along the*

**RECOMMENDED
WALKS**

Surrounding Vieste are extensive beaches, good for long, hard walks after a drowsy lunch. In particular head south from town towards the Grotta Smeralda.

---

coast on the *SS89 to Rodi
Garganico before striking
inland. Follow the main road
to the turning for Apricena
and San Severo.*

❺ San Severo, Puglia
Much of San Severo has a baroque overlay. For example, the town's main landmark, the medieval cathedral, looks anything but ancient, having been revamped in a baroque style. The important Romanesque Church of San Severo did not escape. It retains its rose window, but manages to combine it rather cleverly with some baroque details. Other churches include San Giovanni Battista, also Romanesque but with a baroque belltower and Santa Maria degli Angeli. About 13km (8 miles) from San Severo, you can visit the ruins of Castel Fiorentino, where the Emperor Frederick II died in 1250.

▶ *Take the SS160 to Lucera,
about 22km (14 miles).*

One of the Gargano Peninsula's delightful stretches of beach

6 Lucera, Puglia

The windy hilltop site of Lucera was once the town in which the Emperor Frederick II preferred to live. It contains the remains of the biggest castle he ever built (1233), one of the most magnificent in Puglia. The turreted walls survive, extending for about 900m (½ mile) and dominating the town and the great Tavoliere plain beyond. Charles I of Anjou transformed the castle (1269–83), and today there are only ruins of Frederick II's palace inside the walls. Lucera has a strange history. Cosmopolitan Frederick lured here from Sicily about 20,000 Saracen subjects who transformed Lucera into an Arab city. In 1300 most of these were massacred by Charles II, but there are traces of their existence around the town.

The 14th-century duomo (cathedral), the second largest in southern Italy, is an impressive building and thought to be one of the least altered of its date anywhere. More French Gothic than anything else (people from Provence replaced the Saracens after 1300), its high altar is made from a slab of marble that was once Frederick II's dining table in his Castel Fiorentino (see page 156). In Lucera's Museo Civico (Civic Museum), you can see ceramics from the doomed Saracen period as well as some fine remains from the old Roman settlement of *Luceria Augusta*, in particular, a marble statue of Venus.

▶ *Take the* **SS160** *south for 18km (11 miles) to the turnoff for Troia, a further kilometre (½ mile).*

7 Troia, Puglia

Troia is one of the loveliest towns on this tour. It owes its fame to a splendid Romanesque cathedral, of which the rose window – its most noteworthy adornment – is slightly Arabic-looking and dates from Frederick II's time. There are two bronze doors, that at the front of the building dates from 1119 and the one on the south side from 1127. They show classical and oriental influences. Inside, you should look at the 12th-century carved pulpit as well as the illuminated manuscripts in the cathedral treasury. A museum in the Convent of San Benedetto contains part of the treasure from the cathedral, church paintings and some baroque furnishings.

▶ *Take the* **SS160** *for to the junction with the* **SS90**. *Branch slowly for 7km (4 miles) then turn left on to the* **SS161** *for 1km (½ mile) before taking the winding country road on the right for 9km (5½ miles) to Bovino.*

8 Bovino, Puglia

Bovino was once a Roman settlement called *Vibinum*. Its claim to fame, until about 80 years ago, was that it was an infamous centre of brigandage.

Its ruined 15th-century castle dominates Monte Sant'Angelo

Up on its hill, its remoteness protected its reputation. Bovino is a good centre for excursions into the surrounding countryside. At Giardinetto, about 17km (10½ miles) on the return to Foggia, is a wonderful 11th-century cathedral. Take care to examine its bronze doors. Then, closer to Bovino, is the Castello di Deliceto (about 8km/5 miles).

▶ *Retrace your route to the* **SS90** *which leads to Foggia, 43km (27 miles).*

MOTORING IN ITALY

ACCIDENTS

If you have an accident, place a warning triangle 50m (55 yards) behind the car and call the police (tel: 112 or 113). Do not admit liability or make statements which might later incriminate you. Ask any witness(es) to remain, make a statement to the police and exchange names, addresses, car details and insurance companies' names and addresses with other driver(s) involved. A report must be made to the insurance company. If the accident involves personal injury, medical assistance must be sought for the injured party. On some *autostrada* there are emergency telephones as well as emergency push-button call boxes.

BREAKDOWNS

If your car breaks down, put on hazard warning lights and place a warning triangle not less than 50m (55 yards) to the rear of the vehicle. Call the Automobile Club d'Italia (ACI) 24-hour emergency number (tel: 116) and give the operator your location, car registration and make. Roadside assistance will not be given. The car will be towed to the nearest ACI affiliated garage. The service is free to any visiting motorist driving a foreign registered vehicle.

CARAVANS
Brakes

Check that the caravan braking mechanism is correctly adjusted. If it has a breakaway safety mechanism, the cable between the car and caravan must be firmly anchored so that the trailer brakes act immediately if the two part company.

Caravan and luggage trailers

Take a list of contents, especially if any valuable or unusual equipment is being carried, as this may be required on arrival. A towed vehicle should be readily identifiable by a plate in an accessible position showing the name of the make of the vehicle and the production and serial number.

Lights

Make sure that all the lights are working – rear lights, stop lights, numberplate lights, rear fog guard lamps and flashers (check that the flasher rate is correct: 60–120 times a minute).

Tyres

Both tyres on the caravan should be of the same size and type. Inspect them carefully: if you think they are likely to be more than three-quarters worn before you get back, replace them before you leave. If you notice uneven wear, scuffed treads, or damaged walls, get expert advice on whether the tyres are suitable for further use.

Find out the recommended tyre pressures from the caravan manufacturer.

CAR HIRE AND FLY/DRIVE

Car hire is available in most cities and resorts. Many international firms operate this service. Rates generally include breakdown service, maintenance and oil, but not petrol. Some firms restrict hire to drivers over 21 years of age. Generally you must have had a valid licence for at least one year before applying for car hire. People travelling by air or rail can take advantage of special inclusive arrangements.

CHILDREN

Children under four must not travel in the front or rear seats unless using a suitable restraint system. Children between four and 12 may only travel in the front seat if using such equipment. Note: under no circumstances should a rear-facing restraint be used in a seat with an airbag.

CRASH (SAFETY) HELMETS

Visiting motorcyclists and their passengers must wear crash or safety helmets.

DIMENSIONS AND WEIGHT RESTRICTIONS

Private cars and towed trailers or caravans are restricted to the following dimensions: height – 4m; width – 2.5m; length – 12m.

DOCUMENTS

Visitors bringing their own (foreign registered) car to Italy must be at least 18 years of age (also for motorcycles over 125cc or with a passenger) and carry the vehicle's registration documents (logbook) and a full, valid driving licence (*patente* in Italian).

Third party insurance is compulsory; an international green card, though not compulsory, is recommended. A green UK, red Eire or other foreign licence is acceptable accompanied by a translation, available free from the ACI or the Italian State Tourist Office in the country of origin. The translation is not required for the new, pink EU, UK or Republic of Ireland licence.

DRINKING AND DRIVING

The laws in Europe regarding drinking and driving are strict and the penalties severe. The best advice is, as at home, if you drink don't drive.

DRIVING CONDITIONS

Italian traffic rules follow the
Geneva Convention and Italy
uses international road signs.
Driving is on the right and you
should give way at intersec-
tions to vehicles coming from
your right.

You should keep close to the
nearside kerb, even when the
road is clear.

Vehicles travelling in opposite directions and wishing to
turn left must pass in front of
each other.

Motorcycles under 150cc are
not allowed on motorways.

See also **speed limits.**

FUEL

Petrol (*benzina*) in Italy is some
of the most expensive in
Europe. Diesel (*gasolio*) is
cheaper.

Petrol stations follow normal
shop hours (closed 1–4pm) and
most close all day on Sunday
(except on motorways).

Self-service and 24-hour
pumps which take L10,000
and L50,000 notes are increasingly common.

INSURANCE

Fully comprehensive insurance, which covers you for
some of the expenses incurred
after a breakdown or an accident, is advisable.

LIGHTS

Full-beam headlights can be
used only outside cities and
towns. Dipped headlights are
compulsory when passing
through tunnels, even if well-
lit.

The Italian authorities
recommend that visiting
motorists equip their vehicles
with a spare set of vehicle
bulbs.

MOTORING CLUBS

The Touring Club Italiano
(TCI) has its headquarters at
10 Corso Italia, 20122 Milano.
Tel: (02) 85261. The
Automobile Club d'Italia
(ACI) has its headquarters at
8 Via Marsala, 00185 Roma.
Tel: (06) 44771. The ACI

provides towage from a breakdown to the nearest affiliated
garage. Call from telephone
columns placed along the
motorway.

ROADS

Main and secondary roads are
generally good, and there are
an exceptional number of by-
passes.

Mountain roads are usually
well engineered. Italy has
some 4,000 miles of motorway
(*autostrada*) with tolls payable
on most sections (see also
tolls).

ROUTE DIRECTIONS

Throughout the book the
following abbreviations are
used for Italian roads:

A – Autostrada (motorway)
SS – Strada Statale (state road)
dir, ter, bis, q, qu – suffixes to
state roads (**SS**) relating to
links and extensions of major
roads
minor roads – unnumbered
roads

SPEED LIMITS

The speed limit in built-up
areas is 50kph (31mph);
outside built-up areas – 90kph
(55mph) on ordinary roads,
110kph (68mph) on main
roads and 130kph (80mph) on
motorways. For cars towing a
caravan or trailer the speed
limits are 70kph (43mph)
outside built-up areas and
80kph (49mph) on motorways.

Note: a maximum autho-
rised speed sticker must be
displayed at the rear by all
vehicles, including caravans
and trailers, whose maximum
permitted speed is less than
130kph (80mph). The stickers
are on sale at Italian petrol
stations; fines between
L30,000 and 120,000 are
levied for failure to display.

TOLLS

Tolls are payable on many
motorways in Italy. Visiting
motorists may purchase a
motorway toll card (Via card)
from ACI offices and motorway toll booths.

WARNING TRIANGLE/HAZARD WARNING LIGHTS

The use of a warning triangle
is compulsory in the event of
an accident or breakdown. It
should also be used to give
advance warning of any
stationary vehicle which is
parked on a road in fog, near
a bend or on a hill at night
when the rear lights have
failed. The triangle must be
placed on the road not less
than 50m (55 yards) behind
the vehicle.

Motorists who fail to do this
are liable to an administrative
fine of between L25,000 and
L100,000.

CAMPING AND CARAVANNING SITES
Sites

Most Italian campsites are on
the coast or around lakes. The
International Reservation
Centre in Calenzano (near
Florence) *Federcampeggio*
provides a campsite informa-
tion and reservation service.
Tel: (055) 882391.

The *Assessorati Regionali per
il Turismo* (ART) and the *Ente
Provinciale per il Turismo*
(EPT) have regional and
provincial information offices
and can provide details of
campsites within their locality.
In northern Italy, especially by
the lakes and along the
Adriatic coast, sites tend to
become very crowded and it is
advisable to book in advance
during the season which
extends from May to the end
of August.

If you are camping exten-
sively invest in the widely
available *Campeggi e Villaggi
Turistici*, published by the
Touring Club of Italy (TCI).

Off-site camping

Off-site camping is permitted
provided the landowner's
permission has been obtained,
but it is strictly prohibited in
state forests and national
parks.

In built-up areas, if parking
is allowed, the towing vehicle

must remain connected to the trailer or caravan and the corner steadies must not be used.

SITES

TOUR 1
ASTI, Asti
Umberto Cagni strada Valmanera 152 (tel: 0141 271238)
Open April to September.

CUNEO Cuneo
Turistico Comunale Bisalta San Rocco Castagnaretta (tel: 0171 491334)
Open all year.

TOUR 2
ARONA Novara
At Dormelletto (5km south)
Lago Azzurro via E-Fermi 2 (tel: 0322 497197)
South of Arona off SS Sempione 33.
Open all year.

Lago Maggiore via Leonardo da Vinci 7 (tel: 0322 497193)
Access from SS33, well signposted.
Open April to September.

Lido Holiday Inn via Marco Polo 1 (tel: 0322 497047)
Turn off the SS33 at Km60/VII and the IP petrol station.
Open April to September.

Smeraldo via Cavour 125 (tel: 0322 497031)
Access from SS33.
Open March to October.

ANGERA Varese
Città di Angera via Bruschera 99 (tel: 0331 930736)
Open 2 February to December.

BRESCIA Como
International via Cecilio (031 521435)
Off A9 Como–Milan road.
Open 20 April to 15 October.

DESENZANO DEL GARDA Brescia
Vò via Vò 9 (tel: 030 9121325)

On the banks of Lake Garda 2km from Desenzano, between Padenghe and Sirmione.
Camping card compulsory.
Open April to September.

TOUR 3
BOLOGNA Bologna
Città di Bologna via Romita 12/IVA (tel: 03951 325016)
Located in the northern part of the town.
Open all year.

FERRARA Ferrara
Estense via Gramicia (tel: 0532 752396)
Northeast outskirts of Ferrara.
Open all year.

PARMA Parma
Cittadella (tel: 0521 961434)
Camping card compulsory.
Open April to October.

TOUR 4
GATTEO MARE Forli
Rose via Adriatica 29 (tel: 0547 86213)
Turn off SS16, at Km 186.
Open May to 25 September.

CESENATICO Forli
Cesenatico via Mazzini 182 (tel: 0547 81344)
1.5km north at Km 178, turn off SS16 towards the sea.
Open 29 March to 21 September.

Zadina via Mazzini 184 (tel: 0547 82310)
Open 23 April to 16 September.

CERVIA Ravenna
Adriatico via Pinarella 90 (tel: 0544 71537)
Located shortly before Pinarella di Cervia. Access by via Caduti per le Liberta (SS16) 600m from sea.
Open 9 May to 13 September.

LIDO DI SPINA Ferrara
Spina via del Campeggio 99 (tel: 0533 330179)
Off SS309. Signposted.
Open 18 April to 20 September.

MARINA DI RAVENNA Ravenna
International Piomboni via Lungomare 421 (tel: 0544 530230)
Access is 1km south from town centre off coast road.
Open May to 15 September.

TOUR 5
CHIOGGIA Venezia (off route)
Miramare via A-Barbarigo (tel: 041 490610)
Access from Strada Romeo (SS309) in direction of Chioggia Sottomarina, turn right on reaching beach and continue 500m.
Open May to 20 September.

Villaggio Turistico Isamar via Isamar 9, Isolaverde (tel: 041 498100)
Access via the SS309.
Caravans are advised to approach via Km84/VII near the Brenta village.
Open 9 May to 26 September.

TOUR 6
VERONA Verona
Romeo & Giulietta (tel: 045 8510243)
Access via A22 exit 'Verona Nord' towards Borgo Trento.
Open March to 3 November.

VICENZA Vicenza
Vicenza Strada Pelosa 239 (tel: 0444 582311)
Access via A4 exit 'Vicenza-Est'.
Open 22 March to 3 September.

TOUR 7
SAN REMO Imperia
Villagio dei Fiori via Tiro a Volo 3 (tel: 0184 660635)
1.5km from the town.
Open all year.

TOUR 8
BOGLIASCO Genova
Genova Est via Marconi, Localitá Cassa (tel: 010 3472053)
Exit A12 at Nervi, then 8km east.
Open February to November.

SESTRI LEVANTE Genova
Fossa Lupara via Costa 31
(tel: 0185 43992)
Open all year.

TOUR 9
PISA Pisa
Torre Pendente viale della
Cascine 86 (tel: 050 561704)
Situated on the northern
outskirts of Pisa.
Open April to 15 October.

VIAREGGIO Lucca
Paradiso via dei Tigli (tel:
0584 392005)
2.5km south off via Aurelia at
Km354/V on to via Comparini
towards the sea to site in
600m.
Open May to 15 September.

Pineta via dei Lecci (tel: 0584
383397)
Open May to 20 September.

Viareggio via Comparini/
viale dei Tigli (tel: 0584
391012)
1.5km south of town.
At Km354/V head towards

Vineyard in the Chianti region

the coast.
Open 19 April to 15
September.

SAN GIMIGNANO Siena
Boschetto di Piemma Santa
Lucia (tel: 0577 940352)
April to 15 October.

VOLTERRA Pisa
Balze via di Mandringa 15 (tel:
0588 87880)
Open March to October.

TOUR 10
SIENA Siena
Montagnola Sovicille
(tel: 0577 314473)
From the A1 westbound,
exit at Siena; the campsite
is signposted towards Sovicille.
Open 7 April to September.

Sienna Colleverde strada di
Scacciapensieri 47 (tel: 0577
280044)
The only campsite in Siena
situated just to the north.
Open 21 March to 10
November.

Soline casciano di Murlo (tel:
0577 817410)

Take the left turning at
Fontazzi and ascend hill.
Open all year.

FIRENZE Firenze
At Marcialla.
Toscana Colliverdi via
Marcialla 349, Certaldo
(tel: 0571 669334)
Access via 'Firenze-Cerosa'
exit on Autostrada del Sole or
'Tavarnelle Valpesa' exit on
Autostrada del Palio.
Open 20 March to 10 October.

TOUR 11
ASSISI Perugia
Internationale via San
Giovanni, Campiglione 110
(tel: 075 813710)
West via SS147.
Open Easter to October.

ORVIETO Terni
Orvieto Lago di Corbara (tel:
0744 950240)
Turn off SS448 at Km 3.770.
Open all year.

TOUR 12
CIVITANOVA MARCHE
Macerata
Nuove Giare via Delle Fosse

46 (tel: 0733 70440)
Exit A14 at Civitanova
Marche, signposted.
15 May to 15 September.

PORTO SANT'ELPIDIO
Ascoli Piceno
Risacca via Gabbie 6
(tel: 0734 991423)
Turn off main SS16 north of
village, follow road seawards
under railway (narrow underpass maximum height 3m),
then 1.2km along field paths
to site. Caravan access 400m
further south along SS16 then
under railway and along field
paths to site.
Open 16 May to 15
September.

TOUR 13
SAN MARINO
Centro Turistico San Marino
Strada San Michele 50
(tel: 0549 903964)
Access via 'Rimini Sud' exit on
A14.
Open all year.

SENIGALLIA Ancona
Summerland via Podesti 236
(tel: 071 7926816)
3km on SS16.
Open June to 15 September.

MAROTTA Pesaro and
Urbino
Gabbiano via Faa' di Bruno
95 (tel: 0721 96691)
Exit A14 at Marotta, join SS16
and site is 2.5km in the direc-
tion of Fano.
Open May to September.

FANO Pesaro and Urbino
Mare Blu (tel: 0721 884201)
Exit A14 at Fano and travel
south for 3km.
Open April to September.

PESARO Pesaro and Urbino
Marinella via Adriatica 244
(tel: 0721 55795)
Access through railway
underpass from Km 244 of
SS16.
Open April to 10 October.

TOUR 14
ROMA Roma
Flaminio via Flaminia Nuova

821 (tel: 06 3332604)
From ring road follow via
Flaminia, SS3, for 2.5km
towards city centre.
Open all year.

Happy via Prato della Corte
1915 (tel: 06 33626401)
Exit No 5 'Grande Raccordo
Anulare' (ring road).
Open 15 March to
October.

Roma via Aurelia 831 (tel: 06
6623018)
From ring road follow SS1
for 1.5km towards town
centre turn off to site at
Km8/11.
Open all year.

Seven Hills via Cassia 1216
(tel: 06 30310826)
2.5km northeast of the outer
ring road via exit 3.
Open all year.

Tiber via Tiberina (tel: 06
33612314)
North of city. Signposted from
ring road. Access from north
via Exit 3 or from south follow
signs 'Prima Porta'.
Open March to 10 November.

FORMIA Latina
Gianola via delle Vigne (tel:
0771 720223)
Access via Roma-Napoli road,
from San Croce 800m.
Open April to September.

TERRACINA Latina
Badino Porto Badino
(tel: 0773 764430)
Open April to September.

TOUR 15
ROMA Roma (see sites on
tour 14)

TOUR 16
POZZUOLI Napoli
Vulcano Solfatara via
Solfatara 161 (tel: 081
5267413)
Leave Nuova via Domiziana
(SS&) at KM 60/1 (6km short
of Naples) and turn inland
through stone gate.
Open April to October.

POMPEII Napoli
Spartacus via Plinio (tel: 081
5369519)
Lies near the motorway exit,
Pompeii, and access is from
the main Napoli road, opposite
Scavi di Pompei near an IP
petrol station.
Open all year.

LAURA Salerno
Hera Argiva (tel: 0828
851193)
Signposted from Km88/VII
SS18.
Open April to September.

PAESTUM Salerno
Vilaggio del Pini (tel: 0828
811030/811323
Camping card compulsory.
Turn off via Tirrenia at
Km95/IX and continue for
1km.
Open all year.

ACCIAROLI Salerno
Ondina (tel: 0974 904040)
Turn off towards the sea at
Km35/VII.
Open April to October.

SORRENTO Napoli
Campogaio via Capo 39
(tel: 081 8073579)
2km from town centre and
400m beyond the turning from
the SS145 on road towards
Massa Lubrense and 50m from
sea.
Open April to September.

Giardino delle Esperidi S
Agnello (tel: 081 8783255)
Situated 2km from the centre
of Sorrento and 250m from La
Marinella beach.
Open March to October.

**International Camping
Nube d'Argento** via Capo
21(tel: 081 8781344)
Lies on narrow terraces just off
a steep concrete road between
the beach and the outskirts of
town. Access is rather difficult
for caravans.
Open all year.

Santa Fortunata via Capo
(tel: 081 8073579)
Camping Card compulsory.

SPECIMEN BOOKING LETTER FOR RESERVATIONS

ITALIAN

Egregio Signore
Ho intenzione di remanere presso di voi per .... giorni. Arriverò il .... e partirò il ....
Siamo un gruppo di .... persone in totale, compreso .... adulti e .... bambini (de età ....) e vorremo un posto per .... tenda (tende) e/o spazio per parcheggiare la nostra vetture/cvarovana/roulette.
Desideriamo affittare una tenda/carovana/bungalow.
Vi preghiamo do quotare i prezzi completi quando ci risponderete, e darci informazioni sul deposito richiesto, che vi sarà rimesso senza ritardo.

English translation

Dear Sir
I intend to stay at your site for .... days, arriving on .... (date and month) and departing on .... (date and month)..
We are a party of .... people, including .... adults and .... children (aged ....) and shall require a pitch for .... tent(s), and/or parking space for our car/caravan/caravan trailer.
We should like to hire a tent/caravan/bungalow.
Please quote full charges when replying and advise on the deposit required, which will be forwarded without delay.

1km from town and 50m from sea.
Open April to September.

TOUR 17
POZZUOLI Napoli (off route)
See Tour 16.

TOUR 18
ROSETO DEGLI ABRUZZI
Teramo
Eurocamping-Roseto
(tel: 085 8993179)
Leave the SS16 within the town, then continue for 500m to the site.
Open all year.

Gilda viale Makarska (tel: 085 8941023)
Open June to August.

PINETO Teramo
Heliopolis via Villa Fumosa
Situated near a golden sandy beach.
Open April to September.

International Loc Torre Cerrano (tel: 085 930639 and 9354262)
Turn off SS16 at Km431.2 and continue under railway underpass. Adjoining railway line.
Open May to September.

Pineto Beach (tel: 085 930639)
At Km425 on SS16 'Adriatica'.
Open June to September.

VASTO Chieti
Europa (tel: 0873 801988)
At Km522 of road SS16.
Open May to September.

Grotta del Saraceno via Osca 6, loc Vignola (tel: 0873 310213)
Turn off SS16 at Km512.200.
Open 15 June to 15 September.

Pioppeto (tel: 0873 801466)
Camping card compulsory.
Open May to September.

TOUR 19
L'ÁQUILA L'Áquila
Funivia del Gran Sasso
Fonte Cerreto (tel: 0862 606163)
1,100m above sea level near a medieval town and a National Park.
Open 15 May to 24 September.

BARREA L'Áquila
Grenziana Parco Nazionale d'Abruzzo, Tre Croci (tel: 0864 88101)
In picturesque wooded surroundings on the shore of a lake.
Open all year.

TOUR 20
PALMI Reggio di Calabria
San Fantino via S-Fantino (tel: 0966 479430)
Site on several terraces with lovely views over the bay of Lido di Palmi; 200m to the beach. Turn off road SS18 seawards north of Palmi.
Open all year.

MARINA DI PIZZO
Catanzaro
Pinetamare (tel: 0963 534871)
From the Salerno/Reggio motorway take the Pizzo exit and site is north of town.
Open 2 June to 29 September.

The beach at Viareggio

TOUR 21
CORIGLIANO CÁLABRO
Cosenza
Thurium Contrada Ricota
Grande (tel: 0983 851955)
The site is close to the beach.
Open June to 15 September.

ROSSANO SCALO Cosenza
Marina di Rossano Contrada
Leuca (tel: 0983 516054)
In wooded surroundings close
to the beach. Access via N106.
Open 6 April to 20 October.

CIRO MARINA Catanzaro
Punta Alice (tel: 0962
31160)
2km from town. From SS106
(Strada Ionica) turn off at
Km290 seaward to Cira
Marina. Pass through the
village and follow the beach
road for 1.5km towards the
lighthouse.
Open April to September.

Villagio Torrenova via
Torrenova (tel: 0962 31482)
Directly on sea.
Open May to September.

TOUR 22
LIDO DI METAPONTO
Matera
Camel Camping Club viale
Magna Greca (tel: 0835
741926/7)
Open June to September.

TOUR 23
GIOVINAZZO Bari (off
route)
Campofreddo (tel: 080
8942112)
Turn off the SS16, 20km north
of Bari at Km784,300.
Open May to September.

TOUR 24
OTRANTO Lecce
Mulino d'Acqua via S Stefano
(tel: 0836 802191)
Camping card compulsory.
Close to the beach.
Open 15 June to 15
September.

GALLIPOLI Lecce
Baia di Gallipoli (tel: 0832
315542 or 358957)
Camping card compulsory.
Open May to September.

Vecchia Torre (tel: 0833
209083)

5km north of Gallipoli and
200m south of Hotel Rivabella
at seaward side of coast road.
Open 15 May to
September.

TOUR 25
MATTINATA Foggia
Degli Ulivi (tel: 0884
550118)
Camping card compulsory.
Lies in an old olive grove
facing a picturesque bay. Off
SS89, 0.6km north of turning
to Mattinata.
Open June to September.

**Villaggio Turistico San
Lorenzo** (tel: 0884 4152)
Camping card compulsory.
The site is situated above the
coast road in the direction of
Vieste.
Open all year.

VIESTE Foggia
Baia dei Lambardi Santa
Maria di Merino (tel: 0884
706480)
Open April to September.

Baia Turchese Lungomare
Europa (tel: 0884 708587)
1km north of Vieste on
Strada Panoramica towards
Peschici.
Open May to September.

Capo Vieste (tel: 0884
706326)
By the sea with a large bathing
area. Off coastal road to
Peschici about 7km beyond
Vieste.
Open 15 March to 30
October.

Castello Lungomare E-
Mattei 77 (tel: 0884 707415)
Access to beach.
Open Easter to September.

Umbramare Santa Maria di
Merino (tel: 0884 706174)
On A14 leave at Poggio
Imperiale and take route via
Rodi Garganico and Peschici.
Open all year.

Vieste Marina (tel: 0884
706471)
Adjacent to the coast road in a

UNFAMILIAR ROAD SIGNS

ACCENDERE LE LUCE
Switch on lights

ACCENDERE I FARI
Switch on headlights

BANCHINA NON TRANSITABLE
Keep off hard shoulder

CADUTA MASSI
Falling rocks

CROCEVIA
Crossroads

CURVA PERICOLOSA
Dangerous bend

DISCESA PERICOLOSA
Dangerous downhill

DIVIETO DI ACCESSO
No entry

DIVIETO DI SORPASSO
No overtaking

DIVIETO DI SOSTA
No parking

ENTRATA
Entry

INCROCIO
Crossroads

PARCHEGGIO
Parking

PARCHEGGIO AUTORIZZATO
Parking allowed

PASSAGGIO A LIVELLO
Level crossing

PERICOLO
Danger

RALLENTARE
Slow down

SENSO UNICO
One way

SENSO VIETATO
No entry

SOSTA AUTORIZZATA
Parking permitted

SOSTA VIETATA
No parking

SVOLTA
Bend

USCITA
Exit

VIETATO INGRESSO VEICOLI
No entry for vehicles

VIETATO TRANSITO AUTOCARRI
Closed to commercial vehicles

---

quiet situation. 5km north of Vieste, signposted.
Open June to September.

Village Punte Lunga
(tel: 0884 706031)
A terraced site in wooded surroundings encompassing two sandy bathing beaches and a rocky peninsula. 2km north of Vieste, signposted from coast road.
Open 3 April to 30 September.

PESCHICI Foggia
Centro Turistico San Nicola
Loc San Nicola (tel: 0884 964024)
Terraced site in lovely situation by the sea, in a bay enclosed by rocks. Turn off coast road Peschici–Vieste, follow signs along winding road to site in 1km.
Open April to 15 October.

Internazionale Manacore
(tel: 0884 911020)
Meadowland with a few terraces in attractive bay, surrounded by wooded hills.

Turn off the coastal road (Peschici–Vieste) towards the sea in a wide U-bend.
Open April to 20 October.

Parco degli Ulivi (tel: 0884 963404)
Open 29 May to 25 September.

RODI GARGANICO
Foggia
Ripa via Ripa (tel: 0884 965367)
Attractive site close to the beach.
Open June to September.

Portonovo, on the Adriatic

i   Tourist Information Office
[12] Tour Number

Practical Information

The addresses, telephone numbers and opening times of the attractions mentioned in the tours, including the telephone numbers of the Tourist Information Offices are listed below tour by tour.

TOUR 1

i Via Roma 226, Torino.
Tel: 011/535 901 or 535 181.

i Piazza Alfieri 34, Asti.
Tel: 0141/530 357.

i Via Savona 26, Alessandria.
Tel: 0131/251 021.

i Corso Nizza 17, Cuneo.
Tel: 0171/66 615 or 693 258.

2 Asti
San Pietro in Consavia and Archaeological Museum
Corso Alfieri.
Tel: 0141/877 891.
Open Tue–Sat 9–noon, 3–7, Sun 3–7 (closes 6 between Oct–Mar).

3 Alessandria
Museo del Capello Borsalino
Tel: 0131 202111.
Normally closed, but may allow visitors on request.

4 Acqui Terme
Castello dei Paleologi and Archaeological Museum
Adjacent to Cathedral.
Open Tue–Sat 4–7, Sun and public holidays 10–noon.

TOUR 2

i Via Marconi 1, Milano.
Tel: 02/725 24300.

i Piazza Cavour 17, Como.
Tel: 031/330 0111.

i Via Nazario Sauro 6, Lecco.
Tel: 0341/362 360.

i Via Vittorio Emanuele 20, Bergamo.
Tel: 035/213 185 or 210 204.

i Piazza A Mantegna 6,

Mantova.
Tel: 0376/328 253.

i Piazza del Comune 5, Cremona.
Tel: 0372 217 22 or 412 642.

i Via Fabio Filzi 2, Pavia.
Tel: 0382/27 238 or 27 706.

2 Lago Maggiore
Villa Pallavicino Gardens
Lake Front, Stresa.
Open mid-Mar–mid-Oct, daily 9–6.

Palazzo Borromeo and Gardens
Isola Bella (boat from Stresa).
Tel: 0323/30 556.
Open Apr–Sep/Oct, daily 9–noon, 1.30–6.

Palace and Botanical Garden
Isola Madre (boat from Stresa).
Open late-Mar–Oct.

Navigazione Lago Maggiore
Arona.
Tel: 0322/46 651.
Open daily in summer; reduced service autumn and winter.

3 Como
Museo Civico Via Vittorio Emanuele.
Open all year, Tue–Sun 9–noon, 3–5; mornings only on Sun and public holidays.

Museo Alessandro Volta
Public Gardens, Lake Front.
Open daily 10–noon, 2 or 3–4 or 6.

4 Lago di Como
Villa Carlotta
Tremezzo.
Tel: 0344 40405.
Open mid-Mar and Oct, daily 9.30–12.30, 2–4.30; Apr–Sep, daily 9–6.

Villa Monastero
Varenna.
Open Apr–Oct daily (garden only).

5 Lecco
Villa Manzoni
Via Promessi Sposi.
Tel: 0341/481 447.
Open all year, Tue–Sun 9.30–2.

6 Bellagio
Villa Serbelloni
Behind the Church of San Giacomo.
Tel: 031/950 204.
Open (grounds only) Mar–Oct, Tue–Sun, guided walks 10 and 4, weather permitting.

Villa Melzi d'Eril
On the Loppia road.
Tel: 031/950 318 or 950 132.
Open Mar–Oct, daily 9–6 (grounds only).

Malpaga Castle
South of Bergamo.
Tel: 035/840 003.
Open for guided tours Sun and public holidays 2.30–dusk; other times by appointment.

7 Bergamo
Biblioteca Civica
Piazza Vecchia 15.
Tel: 035/399 430 or 399 431.
Open Mon, Tue, Thu, Fri 8.30–6.30, Wed, Sat 8.30–12.30. Closed Sun, also Sat Jul–Aug.

Natural History Museum (Museo di Scienze Naturali)
Piazza della Citadella 10.
Tel: 035/233 513 or 399 422.
Open Tue–Fri, 9–12.30, 2.30–5.30 (till 7.30 Apr–Oct), and Sun 9–5.30 (till 7.30 Apr–Oct).

Museo Donizettiano
Via Arena 9.
Tel: 035/399 269 or 247 116.
Open Tue–Sat 9.30–noon, 2–5, Sun 10–4 (ring bell for custodian).

Accademia Carrara
Piazza dell'Accademia.
Tel: 035/399 643.
Open all year Fri–Mon 9.30–12.30, 2.30–5.30.

8 Lago di Garda
Vittoriale degli Italiani
Via Vittoriale 12, Gardone.
Tel: 0365/20 130.
Open all year, Tue–Sun 9–12.30, 2 or 2.30–6 or 6.30.

Rocca and Museo Civico
Lake Front, Riva del Garda.
Tel: 0464/554 490.
Open Tue–Sun 9–noon, 2.30–6.

Castello Scaligero
Malcesine.
Tel: 030/916 468.
Open Tue–Sun, summer 9–6; winter 9–1.

Castle
Sirmione.
Open all year, daily 9–6.30 (summer); Tue–Sun 9–1 (winter).

9 Mantova
Palazzo Ducale and Castel di San Giorgio
Piazza Sordello, Mantova.
Tel: 0376/320 283.
Open Mon–Sat 9–5, Sun 9am–10pm.

Casetta dei Nani
Open Mon 9–2, Tue–Sat 9–2, 2.30–6 or 7.

Palazzo del Te
Viale Te.
Tel: 0376/323 266.
Open Mon 1–6, Tue–Sun 9–6.

10 Cremona
Museo Stradivariano
Via Palestro 17, Cremona.
Tel: 0372/461 886.
Open Tue–Sat 8.30–5.45, Sun and public holidays 9.15–12.30, 3–6.

Museo Civico
Palazzo 'Ala Ponzone', Via Ugolani Dati 4, Cremona.
Tel: 0372/461 884.
Open Tue–Sat 8.30–5.45, Sun and public holidays 9.15–12.30, 3–6.

11 Pavia
Museo Civico
Castello Visconteo, Piazza Castello.
Tel: 0382/33 853.
Open Tue–Fri 9–1.30, Sat and Sun 9.30–1 (and occasional weekend afternoons).

Certosa di Pavia
Viale del Monumento, 9km north of Pavia on Milano road.
Tel: 0382/925 613.
Open Tue–Sun and holiday Mon, 9–11.30, 2.30–4.30 (later in summer).

TOUR 3

i Galleria d'Accursio,
Piazza Maggiore 6, Bologna.
Tel: 051/239 660.

i Via Borgoricco 26,
Ferrara.
Tel: 0532/209 370.

i Piazzetta dei Mercanti,
Piacenza.
Tel: 0523/329 324.

i Piazza Duomo 5,
Parma.
Tel: 0521/523 4735.

i Piazza Prampolini 5c,
Reggio nell'Emilia.
Tel: 0522/451 152.

i Piazza Grande 17,
Modena.
Tel: 059/206 660.

1 Ferrara
Castello Estense
Via Ercole I d'Este 16.
Tel: 0532/299 279.
Open Tue–Sun 9–1, 2–6.

Museo Archeologico
Palazzo di Ludovico il
Moro, Via XX Settembre
124.
Tel: 0532/66 299.
*May be closed for renova-
tion.*

Palazzo Schifanoia
Via Scandiana 23.
Tel: 0532/64 178.
Open daily 9–7.

2 Piacenza
Museo Civico
Palazzo Farnese, Piazza
Citadella.
Tel: 0523/328 270.
*Open Tue–Sun 9–12.30,
also Thu, Sat and Sun
3.30–6.*

Teatro Municipale
Via Chipponi.
*Call at Via Verdi 41 for
admission.*

Galleria d'Arte Moderna
Ricci Oddi
Via San Siro 13.
Tel: 0523/20 742.
*Open Tue–Sun 10–noon, 2
or 3– 4, 5 or 6.*

3 Parma
Pinacoteca, Teatro Farnese
and Museo Archaeologico
Nazionale
Piazzale della Pilotta 15.

Tel: 0521/233 309
(museum 233 718).
*Open Tue–Sat 9–2, Sun and
public holidays 9–1.*

Castello di Sanvitale
Fontanellato.
Tel: 0521/822 346.
*Open 9.30–11.30, 3–5
(longer in summer).*

Palazzo di Soragna
Soragna.
*Open Tue–Sun 9.30–11.30,
3–5 (longer in summer).*

4 Reggio nell'Emilia
Museo Civico and Museo
Numismatico
Museo Spallanzani, Via
Secchi 1.
Tel: 0522/437 775.
*Open Tue–Sat 9–noon, Sun
3–5.*

5 Modena
Museo Lapidario del
Duomo
Via Lanfranco 6.
*May be closed for renova-
tion; enquire at Tourist Office.*

Ghirlandina Tower
Duomo (ask for key at the
Commune).
*Open summer, Sun and
public holidays 10–1, 3–7.*

Biblioteca Estense
Palazzo dei Musei.
Tel: 059/222 248.
Open Mon–Sat 9–1.

Galleria Estense
Palazzo dei Musei.
Tel: 059/222 145.
Open Tue–Sat 9–2, Sun 9–1.

Museo d'Arte Medievale e
Moderne e Etnologia.
Palazzo dei Musei, Largo
Porta Sant'Agostino 337.
Tel: 059/223 892.
*Open Tue–Sat 9–noon, 4–7,
Sun and public holidays
10–1, 4–7.*

TOUR 4

i Piazza Malatesta 28,
Rimini.
Tel: 0541/716 371 or 716
380.

i Viale Roma 112,
Cesenatico.
Tel: 0547/674 411.

i Piazza Caduti per la
Liberta 2/4, Ravenna.
Tel: 0544/541 111.

i Corso della Repubblica
23, Forli.
Tel: 0543/712 435.

2 Ravenna
Museo dell'Arcivescovado
Via G Rasponi.
Open daily 9.30–5.30.

Museo Dante
Piazza di San Francesco.
*No fixed opening times; ring
the bell.*

Accademia delle Belle Arti
Tel: 0544/35 625.
*Open Mon–Fri 9–1, also
2.30–5.30 on Tue and Fri,
Sat 9–1, 3–5, Sun and public
holidays 3–5.*

4 Faenza
Museo Internazionale
delle Ceriche
Viale Baccarini 19.
Tel: 0546/21 240.
*Open summer, Mon–Sat
9–7, Sun and public holidays
9.30–1; winter, daily 9–1.30,
also Sat 3–6.*

5 Brisighella
Rocca and Museo del
Lavoro Contadino
*Open mid-Apr–mid-Oct,
Tue–Sun 10–noon,
3.30–5.30; Oct–Apr, Sat
2.30–4.30, Sun 10–noon,
2.30–4.30.*

6 Forli
Pinacoteca Saffi
Corso della Repubblica.
Tel: 0543/27 935.
*Open Tue–Fri 9–2, Sat
9–1.30, Sun and public holi-
days 9–1.*

Museo Archeologico
Corso della Repubblica 72.
Tel: 0543/32 771.
*Open Mon–Fri 9–2, Sun
10–1.*

TOUR 5

i Piazza Trento e Trieste
9, Feltre.
Tel: 0439/2540.

i Piazza Monte di Pieta
8, Treviso.
Tel: 0422/547 632.

i San Marco 71f, Venezia.

Tel: 041/520 8964.

Villa Barbaro
Maser. Tel: 0423/923 004.
*Open Mar–Oct, Tue, Sat, Sun
and public holidays 3–6;
Nov–Feb, Sat, Sun and public
holidays 2.30–5.*

1 Possagno
Canova's House and Art
Gallery
Via Canova.
Tel: 0423/544 323.
*Open Tue–Sun 9–noon, 2 or
3–5 or 6.*

2 Feltre
Museo Civico
Palazzo Villabruna, Via L
Luzzo 23.
Tel: 0439/885 241.
*Open Tue–Sun 10–1, also
Sat and Sun 4–6.*

Museo Rizzarda
Via del Paradiso 8.
Tel: 0439/885 234.
*Open summer Tue–Sun
10–1, 4–6.*

3 Conegliano
Cima da Conegliano's
Birthplace
Via Cima 24.
*Open weekends only, 4 or
5–6 or 7.*

Sala dei Battuti
*Open Thu–Tue 9.30–noon,
3–7.*

Castle and Art Gallery
Tel: 0438/22 871.
*Open Tue–Sun 8 or 9–noon,
2 or 3.30–5.30 or 7.*

4 Treviso
Museo Civico
Borgo Cavour 24.
Tel: 0422/51 337.
*Open Tue–Sat 9–noon, 2–5,
Sun and public holidays
9–noon.*

5 Venezia
Palazzo Ducale
Piazzetta San Marco.
Tel: 041/522 4951.
*Open daily 9–7 (closes at 4
in winter); last admission one
hour before closing.*

Ca' d'Oro
Cannaregio
Tel: 041/523 8790.
Open daily 9–2.

Galleria dell' Accademia
Campo della Carita.

Tel: 041/522 2247.
Open Mon 9–2, Tue and Wed 9am–10pm, Thu and Fri 9am–11.30pm, Sun and public holidays 9–8.

6 Murano
Museo Vetrario
Palazzo Giustinian,
Fondenta Giustinian.
Tel: 041/739 586.
Open Thu–Tue 10–5 (closes at 4 from Oct–Mar).

Modern and
Contemporary Glass
Museum
Fondenta Manin. Annexe of Museo Vetrario (above). For enquiries tel: 041/739 586.

7 Burano
Scuola dei Merletti
Piazza Baldassare Galuppi.
Tel: 041/730 034.
Open Wed–Mon 10–5.

San Francesco del
Deserto
By boat from Burano (20 minutes).
Tel: 041/528 6863
Open daily 9–1, 3–5.

8 Torcello
Museo dell'Estuario
Piazza, opposite Cathedral.
Tel: 041/730 761.
Open Tue–Sun 10–12.30, 2–4.

**9 Castelfranco
Veneto**
Casa del Giorgione
Piazzetta del Duomo.
Tel: 0423/491 240.
Open Tue–Sun.

i Via Leoncino 61,
Verona.
Tel: 045/592 828.

i Piazza Matteotti 12,
Vicenza.
Tel: 0444/320 854.

i Riviera dei Mugnai 8,
Padova.
Tel: 049/875 3087.

**1 Montecchio
Maggiore**
Villa Cordellina-Lombardi
Via Lovara 36.
Tel: 0444/399 111 or 696 085.

Open Apr–Oct, Tue–Fri 9–1, Sat, Sun and public holidays 9–noon, 3–6.

2 Vicenza
Museo Civico –
Pinacoteca Palazzo
Chiericati (Picture
Gallery)
Piazza Matteotti 39.
Tel: 0444/321 348.
Open Tue–Sat 9–12.30, 2.15–5, Sun and public holidays 9.30–noon (also 2–7 Apr–Sep).

Teatro Olimpico
Piazza Matteotti.
Tel: 0444/323 781.
Open Mon–Sat 9–12.30, 2.15–5, Sun and public holidays 9.30–12.30 (also 2–7 Apr–Sep).

3 Marostica
Castello Inferiore
Piazza del Castello 1.
Tel: 0424/72 127, 470 999 or 479 217.
Open daily 9.30–noon, 2.30–6.

4 Padova
Duomo
Piazza Duomo.
Tel: 049/662 814.
Open Tue–Sun 7.30–noon, 3.30–7.30; baptistery winter, Tue–Sun 9.30–1, 3–6; summer, 9.30–1.30, 5–7.

Museo Civico
Piazza Eremitani.
Tel: 049/654 851.
Open Tue–Sun 9–6 or 7.

Palazzo del Bo' and
Anatomical Theatre
Via 8 Febbraio.
Tel: 049/828 311.
Guided tours: Mon, Wed, Fri 3, 4, 5pm; Tue, Thu, Sat 9, 10, 11am.

5 Arqua Petrarca
Francesco Petrarca's
House and Tomb
Via Valleselle 4.
Tel: 0429/718 294.
Open Tue–Sun.

Villa Barbarigo
Valsanzibio.
Tel: 0444/913 0042.
Open Mar– Nov.

6 Monselice
Ca' Marcello
Open Tue, Fri and Sat, guided tours at 9, 10.30, 3.30, 5;

also 3rd Sun of month 3.30 and 5.

Villa Duodo Gardens
Open (grounds only) daily, dawn–dusk.

7 Este
Museo Nazionale Atestino
Palazzo Mocenigo, Este.
Tel: 0429/2085.
Open daily 9–7.

i Largo Nuvolini 1, San
Remo.
Tel: 0184/571 571.

i Via Boselli, Taggia.

i Via Roma 11, Genova.
Tel: 010/576 791.

i Via XX Settembre 33,
Camogli.
Tel: 0185/771 066.

i Via Roma 35,
Portofino.
Tel: 0185/269 024.

i Via Diaz 9, Rapallo.
Tel: 0185/230 346.

1 Camogli
Museo Archeologico and
Biblioteca Civica
Via Gio Bono Ferrari 41.
Tel: 0185/729 048 or 771 570.
Open Tue–Thu and Sat 8.45–1.45. Closed Mon, Fri and Sun.

Museo Marinaro
Via Gio Bono Ferrari 41.
Tel: 0185/729 049.
Open Mon, Thu and Fri 9–noon; Wed, Sat and Sun 9–11.45, 3–5. Closed Tue.

Acquario
Castello della Dragonara,
Piazza Colombo.
Tel: 0185/773 375.
Open Tue–Thu 10–noon, Fri–Sun 10–noon, 2–6 (until 7 in summer). Closed Mon.

2 Portofino
Castello di San Georgio
The Harbour. Tel: 0185/26 907.
Open Tue–Sun 10–7. Closed Jan.

Abbey of San Fruttuoso

San Fruttuoso di Camogli
(also called San Fruttuoso di Capodimonte), near Portofino (accessible only by boat or on foot, about 2 hours' walk). Tel: 0185/772 703.
Open May–Sep, daily 10–4; Mar, Apr and Oct, Tue–Sun 10–3.30; Dec–Feb weekends and holidays only. Closed Nov.

3 Rapallo
Museo Civico
Castello, The Harbour.
Open Tue, Wed and Sat 3–6, Thu 10–11.30.

6 Portovenere
Ruined Fortress
Above the village.
Open summer, daily 10–noon, 2–6; winter, daily 3–5.

i Piazza Duomo, Pisa.
Tel: 050/560 464.

i Viale G Carducci 1,
Viareggio.
Tel: 0584/962 233.

i Piazza Guidiccioni 2,
Lucca.
Tel: 0583/401 205.

i Piazza Duomo 4,
Pistoia.
Tel: 0573/21 622.

i Piazza Duomo 1, San
Gimignano.
Tel: 0577/940 008.

i Piazza dei Priori 20,
Volterra.
Tel: 0588/87 257 or 87 580.

Puccini's House
Piazzale Belvedere Puccini,
Torre del Lago Puccini.
Tel: 0584/341 445.
Open daily.

2 Lucca
Pinacoteca Nazionale
Palazzo Mansi, Via Galli Tassi 43.
Tel: 0583/55 570.
Open Tue–Sat 9–7, Sun and public holidays 9–2.

Museo Nazionale di Villa
Guinigi
Villa Guinigi, Via della Quarquonia.

Tel: 0583/46 033.
*Open May–Sep, Tue–Sat
9–7, Sun and public holidays
9–2; Oct–Apr Tue–Sun 9–2.*

Museo della Cattedrale
Via Arcivescovado.
Tel: 0583/490 530.
*Open Mar and Oct, Tue–Sun
10–6; May–Sep, Tue–Fri
10–6, Sat, Sun and public
holidays 10–7; Nov–Feb,
Tue–Fri 10–4, Sat, Sun and
public holidays 10–5.*

3 Pistoia
Palazzo del Comune
Piazza del Duomo.
Tel: 0572/371 278.
*Open Tue–Sat 9–6, Sun and
public holidays 9–1.*

4 Prato
Castello dell'Imperatore
Piazza Santa Maria delle
Carceri.
*Open Wed–Mon
9.30–11.30, 3.30–7
(3–5.30 in winter); mornings
only on Sun.*

Galleria Comunale
Palazzo Pretorio, Piazza del
Comune.
Tel: 0574/30 224.
*Open Sun, Mon and
Wed–Fri 9.30–12.30,
3–6.30, Sat 9.30–12.30.*

**Museo dell'Opera del
Duomo**
Piazza del Duomo.
Tel: 0574/29 339.
*Open Wed–Mon
9.30–12.30, 3–6.30, Sun
and public holidays mornings
only.*

Museo Pittura Murale
Chiesa di San Domenico.
Open Mon–Sat 9–noon.

5 Poggio a Caiano
Villa and Gardens
Piazza Medici.
Tel: 055/877 012.
Open Tue–Sun.

6 Artimino
Villa di Artimino
Viale Pap Giovanni 23.
Tel: 055/879 2040 (villa);
055/871 8124 (museum).
*Open – villa Tue mornings by
appointment; museum daily,
except Wed mornings.*

7 Empoli
Museo Collegiata
Piazza Farinata degli
Uberti.
Open Tue–Sun 10–noon.

8 Certaldo
Palazzo Pretorio
Tel: 0571/661 219.
Open summer, daily

*10–12.30, 4.30–7.30;
winter, 10–noon, 3–6.*

Casa del Boccaccio
Tel: 0571/666 590.
*Open daily 10–12.30,
3–6.30.*

9 San Gimignano
Collegiata museums
Piazza del Duomo 1.
Tel: 0577/940 316.
*Open daily 9.30–12.30, 3–6
(5.30 Oct–Mar), except
when mass is in progress.*

**Museo Civico and
Pinacoteca**
Palazzo del Popolo, Piazza
del Duomo.
Tel: 0577/940 340.
*Open Mar–Oct, daily
9.30–7.30; Nov–Feb,
Tue–Sun 9.30–1.30,
2.30–4.30.*

10 Volterra
Museo Etrusco Guarnacci
Via Don Minzoni 15.
Tel: 0588/86 347.
*Open Apr–Oct, daily 9–1,
3–6.30; Nov–Mar, daily 9–2.*

**Pinacoteca Comunale and
Museo Civico**
Palazzo Minucci-Solaini, Via
dei Sarti 1.
Tel: 0588/87 580.

***Soriano, to the east of
Bagnaia, is dominated
by Castello Orsini***

*Open summer, daily 9.30–6;
winter, daily 9–1, 3–6.30.*

**Castle and Leonardo da
Vinci Museum**
Castello dei Conti Guidi.
Tel: 0571/56 055.
Open daily.

TOUR 10

i Via Manzoni 16,
Firenze.
Tel: 055/23 320.

i Via Campana 18. Colle
di Val d'Elsa.
Tel: 0577/920 015
(summer only).

i Via di Citta 43, Siena.
Tel: 0577/42 209.

i Costa del Municipio 8,
off Piazza del Popolo,
Montalcino.
Tel: 0577/849 331.

i Via Nazionale 42,
Cortona.
Tel: 0575/630 352.

i Piazza Risorgimento
116, Arezzo.

Tel: 0575/23 952.

i Piazza Amerighi, Poppi.

1 Colle di Val d'Elsa
Civic Museum
Palazzo dei Priori, Via del
Castello.
*Open Apr–Sep, Tue–Fri 5–7,
Sat 10–noon, 5–7, Sun and
public holidays 10–noon,
4–7; Oct–Mar, Tue–Fri
3.30–5.30, Sat, Sun and
public holidays 10–noon,
3.30–6.30.*

Museum of Religious Art
Palazzo Vescovil.
Tel: 0577/920 180.

2 Siena
Palazzo Pubblico
Piazza del Campo 1.
Tel: 0557/292 226 or 292
232.
*Open mid-Mar–mid-Nov,
9.30–7.30 (closes 1.30 Sun
and public holidays); winter,
Mon–Sat, except public holi-
days, 9.30–1.30.*

**Museo dell'Opera del
Duomo**
Piazza del Duomo 8.
Tel: 0577/283 048.
*Open mid-Mar–Sep, daily
9–7.30; closes 6 in Oct;
closes 1.30 from Nov–mid
Mar.*

Pinacoteca Nazionale
Palazzo Buonsignori, Via
San Pietro 29.
Tel: 0577/286 143 or 281
161.
*Open summer, Tue–Sat 9–7,
Sun 8–1; winter, Tue–Sat
8.30–1.30, 2.30–4 or 5.30,
Sun 8–6.*

Casa di Santa Caterina
Via Camporegio, Siena.
Tel: 0577/44 177.
Open daily.

Abbey
Monte Oliveto Maggiore
(about 27km south of
Siena on the SS2).
Tel: 0577/70 716.
*Open daily 9.15–noon,
3.15–5.45 (5 in winter).*

3 Montalcino
Rocca
Entrance through Enoteca
(Wine Shop), Piazzale della
Fortezza, Montalcino.
Tel: 0577/849 211.
Open summer, daily 9–1,

*2.30–8; winter, Tue–Sun 9–1,
2–6.*

**Museo Civico and Museo
Diocesano**
Palazzo Vescorile, Via
Spagni 4.
Tel: 0577/848 135.
*Open May–Sep, Tue–Sun
9.30–1, 3.30–5; Oct–Apr,
10–1, 3–5.*

4 Cortona
Museo Diocesano
Chiesa del Gesu, Piazza del
Duomo 1.
Tel: 0575/62 830.
*Open Tue–Sun 9–1, 3–6.30
(closes 5 Oct–Apr).*

**Museo dell'Accademia
Etrusca**
Palazzo Casali, Piazza
Signorelli 19.
Tel: 0575/637 235 or 630
415.
*Open May–Sep, Tue–Sun
10–1, 4–7; Oct–Apr, 9–1,
3–5.*

5 Arezzo
Casa del Vasari
Via XX Settembre 55.
Tel: 0575/300 301.
*Open daily 9–7 (ring door
bell for admission).*

Museo Archeologico
Via Margaritone 10.
Tel: 0575/20 882.
*Open daily (except 1st and
3rd Mon of month) 9–2
(closes 1.30 on Sun and
public holidays).*

8 Caprese
Michelangelo
Michelangelo's Birthplace
Casa di Michelangelo.
Tel: 0575/793 912.
Open 9–noon, 3–5.

9 Poppi
Palazzo Pretorio
Castello.
Tel: 0575/529 964.
*Open summer, daily
9.30–12.30, 3.30–7; winter,
9.30–12.30, 2.30–5.30.*

Abbey
Camaldoli (8km north).
*Open weekdays 8.30–
11.15, 3–6; Sun and public
holidays 8.30–10.45, 3–6.*

i Via Mazzini 21, Perugia.

Tel: 075/572 5341.

i Piazza Oderisi 56,
Gubbio.
Tel: 075/922 0693 or 922
0790.

i Piazza del Comune 12,
Assisi.
Tel: 075/812 534.

i Piazza della Libertà 7,
Spoleto.
Tel: 0743/220 311.

i Piazza Umberto 16,
Todi.
Tel: 075/894 3395 or 894
2686.

i Piazza del Duomo 24,
Orvieto.
Tel: 0763/341 772.

1 Gubbio
Museum and Art Gallery
Palazzo dei Consoli, Piazza
Grande.
Tel: 075/927 4298.
*Open summer, daily 10–1,
3–6; winter, 10–1, 2–5.*

Palazzo Ducale
Via Federico Da
Montefeltro.
Tel: 075/927 5872.
*Open daily 9–1, 2.30–7,
mornings only on Sun.*

2 Assisi
Basilica di San Francesco
Piazza San Francesco.
Tel: 075/813 337.
*Open Apr–Oct, daily
dawn–sunset; Nov–Mar,
daily 7–noon, 2–sunset.*

Duomo Museum & Crypt
Chiesa di San Rufino,
Piazza San Rufino.
Tel: 075/812 283.
*Open Museum daily
10–noon, 3–6. Crypt, daily
10–noon, 2–5 (till 6
Mar–early Nov).*

Pinacoteca Comunale
Piazza del Comune.
Tel: 075/812 579.
*May be closed for restora-
tion.*

4 Trevi
Pinacoteca Comunale
Largo Don Bosco – ex
Convento di San Francesco.
Tel: 0742/381 628.
*Open Apr, May and Sep,
Tue–Sun 10.30–1, 2.30–6;
Jun and Jul, Tue–Sun
10.30–1, 3.30–7; Aug,*

*Tue–Sun 10.30–1, 3–7.30;
Oct–Mar, Fri–Sun 10.30–1,
2.30–5.*

5 Montefalco
**Museo Civico di San
Francesco**
Via Ringhiera Umbra.
Tel: 0742/379 598.
*Open Mar–May, Sep and
Oct, daily 10.30–1–6; Jun
and Jul, daily 10.30–1, 3–7;
Aug, daily 10.30–1, 3–7.30;
Nov–Feb, Tue–Sun 10.30–1,
2.30–5.*

6 Spoleto
Rocca
Piazza Campello, Spoleto.
*May be closed for renova-
tion.*

**Museo Archeologico and
Teatro Romano**
Via 5 Agata.
Tel: 0743/223 277.
*Open daily 9–1.30, 2.30–7,
holidays 9–1.*

7 Narni
Art Gallery
Palazzo del Podesta.
Open Mon–Sat 8–2.

9 Orvieto
**Museo dell'Opera del
Duomo**
Palazzo Soliano, Piazza del
Duomo.
Tel: 0763/342 477.
*May be closed for restora-
tion.*

Pozzo di San Patrizio
Viale Sangallo.
Tel: 0763/343 768.
*Open Mar–Sep, daily
9.30–7; Oct–Feb, daily
10–6.*

i Via Thaon de Revel 4,
Ancona.
Tel: 071/33 249 or 34 938.

i Via G Solari 3, Loreto.
Tel: 071/970 276 or 977
139.

i Via Garibaldi 87,
Macerata.
Tel: 0733/231 547.

i Piazza del Popolo 5,
Fermo.
Tel: 0734/228 738.

i Piazza del Popolo 1,
Ascoli Piceno. Tel:

[i] Tourist Information Office

[12] Tour Number

0736/257 288.

[i] Via Luigi Ferri 17, Cingoli.
Tel: 0733/602 444.

3 Loreto
Santa Casa and Santuario della Santa Casa
Piazza Santuario.
Tel: 071/970 108.
Open daily 6–noon, 4–7.

4 Macerata
Art Gallery
Piazza Vittorio Veneto.
Open Tue–Sat 9–1, 5–7.30, Sun 9–1.

6 Ascoli Piceno
Art Gallery
Palazzo Comunale, Piazza Arringo.
Tel: 0736/298 213.
Open Tue–Sun 9–1 (also afternoons in summer).

7 Tolentino
Museum, Basilica di San Nicola da Tolentino
Tel: 0733/969 996.
Open daily 9–noon, 3.30–6.30.

TOUR 13

[i] Piazza Rinascimento 1, Urbino.
Tel: 0722/2613.

[i] Viale Trieste 164, Pesaro.
Tel: 0721/69 341.

[i] Via C Battisti 10, Fano.
Tel: 0721/803 534.

[i] Piazza Manin II, Fabriano.
Tel: 0732/629 690.

1 San Leo
Rocca
Via Leopardi.
Tel: 0541/916 231.
Open daily.

3 Pesaro
Casa Rossini
Via Rossini 34.
Tel: 0721/387 357.
Open Tue–Sun 8.30–1.30.

Conservatorio
Piazza Olivieri 5.
Tel: 0721/33 670.
Open Mon–Sat mornings.

Museo Archeologico Oliveriano
Via Mazza 97.

Tel: 0721/33 344.
Open Mon–Sat mornings.

Museo Civico, Museo delle Ceriche and Pinacoteca
Piazza Mosca 29.
Tel: 0721/31 213.
Open Tue–Sun 8.30–1.30.

4 Fano
Museo Civico and Pinacoteca
Corte Malatestiano, Piazza XX Settembre.
Tel: 0721/828 362.
Open Tue–Sun (mornings only in winter).

6 Jesi
Pinacoteca and Museo Civico
Palazzo Pianetti, Via XX Settembre.
Tel: 0731/538 342.
Open Tue–Sun.

7 Fabriano
Museum of Papermaking
Convent of San Domenico.
Open Tue–Sat 9–noon, 3–6, Sun 9–12.30.

Art Gallery
Palazzo Vescovile, Piazza Umberto di Savoia.
Open Tue–Sat 10–12.30, 4–7, Sun 10–12.30.

9 Urbania
Palazzo Ducale
Tel: 0722/319 985.
Open Apr–Sep, Tue–Sun; Oct–Mar, ask at library to gain admission.

TOUR 14

[i] Via N Fabrizi 171, Pescara.
Tel: 085/421 1707.

[i] c/o Centro Polifunzionale, Via G Mazzini, Pineto.
Tel: 085/949 1745.

[i] Via del Castello 10, Teramo.
Tel: 0861/244 222.

[i] Via B Spaventa 29, Chieti.
Tel: 0871/636 409.

2 Teramo
Museo Archeologico
Villa Delfico 30.
Open daily 10–noon, 5–7

(midnight in summer).

5 Loreto Aprutino
Galleria Acerbo delle Antiche Ceramiche Abruzzesi
Palazzo Acerbo.
Tel: 085/829 0484.
Open daily.

9 Chieti
Museo Nazionale Archeologico
Villa Comunale.
Tel: 0871/331 668.
Open daily 9–6.30.

TOUR 15

[i] Piazza Santa Maria di Paganica 5, L'Aquila.
Tel: 0862/410 808.

[i] Via Piave, Pescasseroli.
Tel: 0863/910 461.

[i] Piazza Umberto 1, Pescocostanzo.
Tel: 0864/691 440.

[i] Via Roma 21, Sulmona.
Tel: 0864/53 276.

5 Sulmona
Museo Civico
Palazzo Santa Maria dell'Annunziata, Corso Ovidio.
Tel: 0864/210 216.
Open Mon–Fri 9–1, Sat–Sun 10–1, 4–7.

TOUR 16

[i] Via Parigi 5, Roma.
Tel: 06/4889 9200.

[i] Largo Garibaldi, Tivoli.
Tel: 0774/334 522 or 21 249.

[i] Piazza Traniello, Gaeta.

[i] Piazza Liberta 5, Castel Gandolfo.
Tel: 06/936 0340.

[i] Piazza G Marconi 1, Frascati.
Tel: 06/942 0331.

1 Tivoli
Villa Adriana
Via di Villa Adriana.
Tel: 0774/530 203.
Open daily 9–5 (till 6 Feb and Oct; 6.30 Mar and Sep; 7 Apr; 7.30 May–Aug) – tickets sold until one hour before closing.

Villa d'Este
Piazza Trento.
Tel: 0774/312 070.
Open daily 9–one hour before sunset.

Villa Gregoriana
Largo S Angelo.
Tel: 0774/334 522.
Open daily, Apr 9.30–6, May–Aug 10–7.30, Oct–Mar 9.30–4.30.

3 Subiaco
Monastery of Santa Scolastica
3km east of Subiaco.
Tel: 0774/85 525.
Open daily.

5 Sperlonga
Zona Archeologica, including Grotta di Tiberio, Roman Villa and Museo Archeologico Nazionale di Sperlonga
Via Flacca.
Tel: 0771/54 028.
Open daily.

7 Frascati
Villa Aldobrandini
Tel: 06/942 0331.
Open Mon–Fri 9–1.

8 Ostia
Ostia Antica and Museo Ostiense
Via Ostrense.
Tel: 06/565 0022.
Open daily 9–6 (till 5 Oct–Mar); museum 9–2.

TOUR 17

[i] Via Parigi 5, Roma.
Tel: 06/4889 9200.

[i] Piazza Cavour 1, Tarquinia.
Tel: 0766/856 384.

[i] Piazza S Carluccio, Viterbo.
Tel: 0761/304 795.

1 Cerveteri
Etruscan Remains: Banditaccia Necropolis
Via delle Necropoli, 3km west of town centre.
Tel: 06/994 0001.
Open Tue–Sun 9–one hour before sunset.

3 Tarquinia
Museo Nazionale Tarquiniese
Palazzo Vitelleschi, Piazza Cavour.

Practical Information

[i] Tourist Information Office
[12] Tour Number

Tel: 0766/856 036.
Open Tue–Sun 9–7.

Necropolis
2km southeast of Tarquinia.
*Open Tue–Sun 9–one hour
before sunset.*

5 Caprarola
Villa Farnese
Piazza Farnese.
Tel: 0761/646 052.
*Open daily 9–5 (till 4
Oct–Mar).*

6 Viterbo
Palazzo dei Papi
Piazza San Lorenzo.
*If not open, enquire at the
curia.*

7 Bagnaia
Villa Lante

Tel: 0761/288 008.
*Open (parkland only) 9–one
hour before sunset.*

9 Bomarzo
Parco dei Mostri
Tel: 0761/924 029.
*Open daily 8.30–7 (till 5
Oct–Mar).*

TOUR 18

[i] Piazza dei Martiri 58,
Napoli.
Tel: 081/405 311.

[i] Via Campi Flegrei 3,
Pozzuoli.
Tel: 081/526 1481 or 526
2419.

[i] Via Sacra 1, Pompeii.

Tel: 081/850 7255.

[i] Piazza Cerio 11, Capri.
Tel: 081/837 0424 or 837
5308.

[i] Via del Saracino 4,
Positano.
Tel: 089/875 067.

[i] Corso delle
Repubbliche Marinare 19-
21, Amalfi.
Tel: 089/871 107.

[i] Piazza Duomo 10,
Ravello.
Tel: 089/857 096.

[i] Via Velia 15, Salerno.
Tel: 089/224 322.

[i] Via Magna Grecia 151,
Paestum.

Tel: 0828/811 016.

Cumae
About 5km from Pozzuoli.
Tel: 081/854 3060.
*Open daily 9–5 (closes
earlier in winter).*

Baia
About 4km from Pozzuoli.
*Glass-bottomed boat trips to
submerged ruins Apr–Sep
weekends.*

1 Pozzuoli
**Archaeological Park,
including Amfiteatro Flavio**
Via Rossini.
*Open daily 9–one hour
before sunset.*

2 Ercolano
Herculaneum Roman Site
Corso Ercolano.
Tel: 081/861 1051 or 739
0963.
*Open daily 9–one hour
before sunset (closes earlier
in winter).*

3 Pompeii
Ruins
Piazza Esedra 5.
Tel: 081/861 1051.
*Open daily 9–one hour
before sunset; last admission
one hour before closing.*

**Napoli Museum (for finds
from Pompeii)**
Piazza Museo Mazionale
19.
Tel: 081/440 166.
*Open Jun–Sep, daily 9–7;
Oct–May, daily 9–2 (closes
at 1 on Sun); last admission
one hour before closing.*

4 Capri
Villa Jovis
Via Tiberio.
Tel: 081/837 0381.
*Open daily 9–one hour
before sunset.*

Villa San Michele
Anacapri.
Tel: 081/837 1401.
*Open summer, daily 9–6;
winter 10.30–3.30.*

Grotta Azzurra
Boats from Marina
Grande.
*Tours from 9, except when
sea is too rough.*

*The Church of San
Michele, in the little
town of Lucca*

6 Positano
Grotta dello Smeraldo
Southeast on SS163 coast road.
Open Apr–Oct, daily 9.30–5; Nov–Mar, daily 10–6.

7 Ravello
Villa Cimbrone Gardens
Tel: 089/857 138.
Open 9–one hour before sunset.

Villa Rufolo
Tel: 089/224 322.
Open daily 9.30–1, 3–7.

Cathedral Museum
Open daily 9–1, 3–7.

8 Salerno
Museo del Duomo
Piazza Alfano, Salerno.
Open daily 9–1, 4–7.

Provincial Museum
Via San Benedetto 28.
Tel: 089/231 135.
Open 9–1. Closed 1st and 3rd Mon in month.

9 Paestum
Temple Remains and Museum
Zona Archeologica, Via Aquilia.
Tel: 0828/811 016.
Open daily 9–two hours before sunset. Closed 1st and 3rd Mon in month.

TOUR 19

i Piazza dei Martiri 58, Napoli.
Tel: 081/405 311.

i Palazzo Reale, Piazza Dante 35, Caserta.
Tel: 0823/321 137.

i Piazza Roma, Benevento.
Tel: 0824/25 424.

i Via Due Principanti 5, Avellino.
Tel: 0825/74 695.

2 Capua
Santa Maria di Capua Vetere Roman Remains
Piazza Adriano.
Tel: 0823/798 864.
Open daily.

Museo Campano
Via Roma.
Tel: 0823/961 402.
Open Tue–Sun mornings.

3 Caserta
Palazzo Reale
Viale Douhet.
Tel: 0823/321 400.
Open daily 9–1; gardens 9–4.

4 Benevento
Roman Remains
Piazza Gaio Ponzio Telesino.
Open Tue–Sun.

TOUR 20

i Galleria Mancuso, Via Spasari 3, Catanzaro.
Tel: 0961/743 901.

i Via D Tripepi 72, Reggio di Calabria.
Tel: 0965/898 512.

1 Stilo
La Cattolica
2km from Stilo on Via Cattolica.
Tel: 0965/898 496.
Open daily.

Ancient Remains and Antiquarium
Southwest of Locri.
Tel: 0964/390 023.
Open daily.

5 Reggio di Calabria
Museo Nazionale della Magna Grecia
Piazza de Nava 26.
Tel: 0965/812 255.
Open Tue–Sun 9am–10pm. Closed public holidays.

TOUR 21

i Corso Mazzini 92, Cosenza.
Tel: 0984/27 821.

4 Rossano
Museo Diocesano
Palazzo Arcivescorile.
Tel: 0983/520 282.
Open daily 10–noon, 5–7, mornings only on Sun.

Museum
Via Risorgimento, Crotone.
Tel: 0962/23 082.
Open Tue–Sun 9–7.

TOUR 22

i Via De Viti De Marco 9, Matera.
Tel: 0835/333 541.

i Piazza del Gesu, Maratea.
Tel: 0973/876 908.

1 Metaponto
Old City Ruins and Antiquarium – Museo Archeologico Nazionale
Via Laveran, Metaponto Borgo.
Tel: 0835/745 327.
Open daily 9–7.

Remains of *Siris-Heradeia* and Museo Nazionale della Siritide
Via Colombo 8, Policoro.
Tel: 0835/972 154.
Open daily 9–7.

5 Melfi
Castle and Museum of Antiquities
Via Castello.
Tel: 0972/238 726.
Open daily 9–7.

6 Venosa
Castle and Museo Archeologico Nazionale
Piazza Umberto 1.
Tel: 0972/36 095.
Open daily 9–7.

Roman Remains (Parco Archeologico)
Via Vittorio Emanuele.

TOUR 23

i Piazzo Moro 32a, Bari.
Tel: 080/524 2244.

i Via Cavour 140, Trani.
Tel: 0883/588 830.

i c/o Comando Vigili Polizia Urbana, Barletta. Tel: 0883/331 331 or 531 555.

4 Barletta
Museo Civico
Corso Garibaldi.
Open Tue–Sun 9–1.

5 Canosa di Puglia
Roman Remains
Open all year 9.30–1.

Museo Civico
Open Tue–Sun 8–2.

7 Castel del Monte
Near Ruvo di Puglia.
Open Mon–Sat 8.30–7 (till 2 Oct–Mar), Sun 9–1.

8 Ruvo di Puglia
Museo Archeologico Nazionale Jatta

Palazzo Jatta, Piazza Bovio 35.
Tel: 081/812 848.
Open daily.

TOUR 24

i Via C Colombo 88, Brindisi.
Tel: 0831/562 126.

i Via Continelli 47, Ostuni.
Tel: 0831/303 775.

i Via Monte San Michele 20, Lecce.
Tel: 0832/314 117.

i Lungomare Kennedy, Otranto.

5 Lecce
Roman Amphitheatre
Piazza Sant'Oronzo.
Open daily 8.30–4 (closes at 2 on Sun)

6 Otranto
Castle
Beside the port, Otranto.
Undergoing restoration, enquire at Tourist Office for current situation regarding opening times.

TOUR 25

i Via Senatore E Perrone 17, Foggia.
Tel: 0881/723 141.

i Corso Manfredi 26, Manfredonia.
Tel: 0884/21 998.

i Piazza Europa 104, San Giovanni Rotondo.
Tel: 0882/456 240.

i Corso Lorenzo Fazzini 8, Vieste.
Tel: 0884/708 806.

1 Manfredonia
Museo Archeologico del Gargano
Open Tue–Sun 9–1, 5–7.

4 Vieste
Boat Tours to Caves
Enquire at the port.

6 Lucera
Castle
Open daily until dusk.

Museo Civico
Via de Nicastri 44.
Tel: 0881/547 041.
Open Tue–Sun.

INDEX

Index and Acknowledgements

The Automobile Association

wishes to thank the following libraries and photographers for their assistance in the preparation of this book.
ROBERT HARDING PICTURE LIBRARY back cover (a); EDMUND NÄGELE, F.R.P.S. front cover main picture; PICTURES COLOUR LIBRARY LTD inside flap, 121; SPECTRUM COLOUR LIBRARY 7, 20, 27, 29, 39, 51, 106a, 122, 150, 152, 153b; ZEFA PICTURES LTD front cover inset.

The remaining photographs are held in the Association's own library (AA PHOTO LIBRARY) with contributions from:

J EDMUNSON 55, 62; J HOLMES 90, 143, 168; D MITIDIERI back cover (b), 120; R NEWTON 130; K PATERSON 43a, 56, 58/9, 60, 70, 76, 161, 172; C SAWYER 4, 6, 8, 14, 16/7, 19, 21, 22, 25, 32, 33, 34, 35, 36, 37, 38, 40, 41, 42, 50, 57, 63, 64, 67, 71, 77, 80, 83, 89, 96, 100, 101, 103, 113, 114, 115, 116/7, 117, 126, 127, 137, 144, 154, 155, 156; B SMITH 43b; A SOUTER 2, 9, 10, 11, 12/3, 15, 18, 23, 24, 26, 28, 30/1, 31, 44, 45, 46, 47, 48/9, 52, 54, 66, 68, 69, 73, 74, 75, 78/9, 81, 82, 84, 85, 86, 87, 91, 92, 93, 94, 95, 97, 98, 99, 102, 104/5, 106b, 107, 108, 109, 110, 111a, 111b, 112, 118, 119, 124, 125, 128, 131, 132/3, 133, 134, 135, 136a, 136b, 138/9, 140, 141, 142, 145, 146, 147, 148, 149, 151, 153a, 157, 164; T SOUTER 165; P WILSON back cover (c), 88.

Contributors

Copy editor: Audrey Horne   **Indexer:** Marie Lorimer
Thanks to **Paul Duncan** for his updating work.